EAST GERMANY:
CONTINUITY AND CHANGE

GERMAN MONITOR No. 46
General Editor: Ian Wallace

EAST GERMANY: CONTINUITY AND CHANGE

Edited by

Paul Cooke and
Jonathan Grix

Rodopi

Amsterdam - Atlanta, GA 2000

ISBN: 90-420-0579-3 (bound)
©Editions Rodopi B.V., Amsterdam - Atlanta, GA 2000
Printed in The Netherlands

Table of Contents

Preface

The rapid demise of the GDR in 1989/90 gave rise to a widespread expectation that GDR studies as a field of research would suffer a similar fate. In fact, the very opposite has happened. A combination of factors - including ready access to previously unexplored archives, a flood of memoirs from and interviews with some of the principal actors in the GDR's forty-year history, the undeniable persistence of an East German identity ("die Mauer im Kopf") as political and economic unification refused to translate easily into the kind of cultural unity which would have allowed the memory of the East-West division to fade or even disappear - such factors have ensured that research into the GDR and into post-1990 Eastern Germany has continued to flourish.

The papers collected in the present volume demonstrate the continuing fascination of the GDR/Eastern Germany for researchers and, more specifically, for *younger* researchers. Each contribution was first presented at a colloquium for postgraduate students which took place at the Institute for German Studies at the University of Birmingham in 1998. Taken together, they reflect the striking number and variety of GDR-linked projects which a new generation of researchers are pursuing at British universities. Making full use of resources which had not been available to earlier research, they draw attention to new data, challenge some established perceptions, and offer fresh insights.

German Monitor takes particular pleasure in devoting this volume to the valuable work being produced by new colleagues in the field. Special thanks are due to Paul Cooke and Jonathan Grix for organising the original conference and then seeing the project through to its successful completion.

Ian Wallace
Bath, September 1999

SECTION ONE

THE ROLE OF THE EAST GERMAN WRITER

Martin Kane

INTRODUCTION

The following four essays on Wolfgang Hilbig, Christoph Hein and Helga Königsdorf not only highlight the complex relationship between writers and the state in the former GDR, and give a valuable account of the adjustments of position brought about by the *Wende*, they also remind us of the necessity of avoiding the *Pauschalurteil* in our evaluation of individual east German authors. The essays are an invitation to differentiating judgement, they are a reminder of the need – as Christa Wolf once put it in a related context – 'von Fall zu Fall [zu] *erzählen*'.[1] Wolfgang Hilbig, it would seem, had very little to rethink as a result of the *Wende*; not only was his verdict on the GDR fixed and solid long before he left the GDR, but the self-confessedly obsessional preoccupation with both the historical and personal dimension of his roots there – the 'visceral link', as Paul Cooke puts it – would continue unbroken after unification. Christoph Hein's adopted role as a dispassionate chronicler concerned with literature rather than message enables him to carry on much as before – his writing, as both Simon Bevan and David Clarke demonstrate so persuasively, is an affirmation of business as usual rather than radical new directions. As clearly emerges from Diana Alberghini's piece on the other hand, Helga Königsdorf has experienced a considerable disruption of position and perspective. For her, as a believer in the *Ersatzfunktion* of literature (something of which Hein and Hilbig have always been deeply suspicious), the media freedoms brought about by the *Wende* seem to have rendered superfluous her erstwhile role as spokesperson, mediator between State and people, and purveyor, in her short stories and novels, of that brand of observation and comment which, in the GDR, only literature could deliver. All three writers would undoubtedly subscribe to a view of art encapsulated in the title of the Christoph Hein essay, 'Worüber man nicht reden kann, davon kann die Kunst ein Lied singen', cited by David Clarke, but only Königsdorf interpreted it in such a wholeheartedly messianic fashion. The consequence has been that while for Hein and Hilbig, 'continuity' rather than any dramatic change of course has characterised their writing since the *Wende*, Königsdorf, due to the opening up of new sources of information and comment, has had to confront and re-assess her identity and role as an east German writer. While the *Kassandra*-function of her essays and fiction is still in evidence, the onerous obligations of spokesperson and 'moral authority' have been, with some sense of relief, abandoned.

In conclusion, one might note that what these essays demonstrate above all is that while the GDR may have been consigned to the dustbin of history, its leading writers are as vibrant and productive as ever they were.

---

[1] Christa Wolf, in Ernest Wichner and Herbert Wiesener, *Zensur in der DDR* (Berlin, 1991), p. 85 and 87 [Wolf's emphasis].

Paul Cooke

CONTINUITY AND TABOO: SEXUAL REPRESSION AND *VERGANGENHEITSBEWÄLTIGUNG* IN WOLFGANG HILBIG'S *DIE WEIBER*

The following examines the interrelation of sexual repression and and the question of Vergangenheitsbewältigung *in Wolfgang Hilbig's* Die Weiber, *the first major prose text he wrote after leaving the GDR in 1985. The piece explores the apparent prudishness of the state's official discourse, which treated all open discussion of sex and sexuality as a taboo subject, and the destructive effect of this taboo on the psyche of the text's central protagonist. It then goes on to discuss how this examination of sexual repression becomes a metaphorical springboard for Hilbig's exploration of the destructive results of the state's refusal to address the consequences of its National Socialist prehistory.*

Unlike many writers of the former GDR, Wolfgang Hilbig did not feel that the East German state was in any way necessarily *das bessere Deutschland.* Growing up to be a manual worker in this so called *Arbeiter-und-Bauern-Staat*, Hilbig understood better than many GDR artists the true nature of *real existierenden Sozialismus.* Whilst other writers, even those who were to become critical of the state, maintained a fundamental belief in the value of the project of socialism, Hilbig's connection to the state was never ideological, but rather profoundly visceral in nature. It was his *de facto Heimat.* It is then perhaps no surprise that at a time when many writers of the GDR are still attempting to find a new direction for their work, there is a strong sense of thematic continuity in Hilbig's writing. As he suggested in an interview with Haro Zimmermann: 'Ich glaube, ich bin einer von den Schriftstellern, die ewig an einem Thema hängen und nie glauben, das Thema bewältigen zu können. Die DDR und die Landschaft um Meuselwitz werden für mich unausrottbar vorhanden sein.'[1] Hilbig's work continues to explore the period of German history which formed him.

One of the clearest expressions of this sense of a visceral link to the GDR is to be found in *Die Weiber*, the first extended prose piece he wrote after leaving the East in 1985.[2] In this story, Hilbig explores the potentially destructive psychological effects on the individual of the GDR's interpretation of Marxist-Leninist ideology. Specifically, he questions what he sees as the treatment of all open discussion of sex and sexuality as taboo by the state's official discourse. *Die Weiber* describes the decline of a man who, forbidden by the state from exploring and expressing his sexuality, develops a sexual neurosis. The reader then follows the narrator on a journey of psychological decay as he searches for 'die Weiber', an almost mythological 'race' of non-repressed women who have not been worn down by the machinations of the SED dictatorship, and who have apparently disappeared from the world he inhabits (W 16). We are presented with a frustrated love story, in which the narrator desperately searches for a union with these idealised women, through which he hopes to be able to overcome the limitations of the state and finally give expression to his sexual self.

The initial reception of *Die Weiber* was somewhat mixed, with many critics seeing Hilbig's at times graphic descriptions of sexual acts as rather self-indulgent.[3] In this article I hope to counter such criticism, showing how Hilbig's disturbing exploration of sexual neurosis is to be read within the broader social context of a critique of the GDR. The state of the narrator's consciousness becomes a metaphor for the state of the GDR as a whole. This reading of the text is then underlined by the metaphorical use of the taboo of sex in *Die Weiber*. I go on to suggest that Hilbig's discussion of sexual repression becomes a vehicle for his exploration of a similarly profound sense of *historical* repression within the official discourse, an aspect of the text which has been largely ignored by other commentators.[4] The central protagonist's need to rediscover his sexual identity becomes a provocation to the state and people to embark upon a process of *Vergangenheitsbewältigung*, in order to explore continuities in the relationship between the GDR and the National Socialist period of German history, the discussion of which was similarly seen as a taboo topic. In the tradition of works such as Christa Wolf's *Kindheitsmuster*, the narrator of *Die Weiber* also seems to pose the question, 'Wie sind wir so geworden, wie wir heute sind?'[5] His search for 'die Weiber' becomes a search for an understanding of Germany's National Socialist past, the memory of which remains locked within the ground upon which this new, self-affirmed antifascist, state was built.

Sex as a taboo in the GDR

In his article on sex and politics in the GDR, J.H. Reid writes of the state's 'small-minded repressiveness,' which he suggests could be seen as resulting from the need to 'combat the early accusations levelled against Marx and his friends that they were propagating free love and wife-sharing'.[6] However, the root of this prudishness may in fact also be traced, at least in part, to the opposite impulse in the writing of Marx and Engels. In the *Manifest der Kommunistischen Partei* they describe institutionalised sexual relations under capitalism (that is, the institution of marriage and the family) as being based on oppression. The family exists solely for the benefit of the bourgeoisie and, even then, is designed for the exploitation of its female and juvenile members.[7] Intimacy between a man and a woman under capitalism is always a form of prostitution. Women are 'bloß[e] Produktionsinstrumente', a commodity to be exploited like any other.[8]

For Marx and Engels, and then later Lenin, the end of capitalism was to bring the end of the family and with it the end of female exploitation.[9] Furthermore, the energy expended by individuals on their private life could then be harnessed for the public good and the promotion of socialism. Roberto Cazzola confirms this impulse to suppress the private life within Marxist-Leninist ideology in his discussion of *Die Weiber*. He notes: 'Es ist ein Erbe der Zweiten und Dritten Internationale, die Sexualität und ihre Befreiung als kleinbürgerliche und dekadente Fragen anzusehen, denn der klassenbewußte Proletarier macht nicht Liebe, er macht Revolution.'[10] As Cazzola goes on to note, Hilbig's narrator is acutely aware of this official view of the need for the worker to be a non-sexual being: 'Schon Lenin hatte, wie von Clara Zetkin berichtet, das *Herumwühlen im Sexuellen* als eine *Liebhaberei der Intellektuellen* bezeichnet, wofür beim *klassenbewußten* Proletariat kein Platz sei' [Hilbig's emphasis] (W 39f.).

However, far from overcoming the need for the bourgeois institutions of the family and marriage, the net effect of this denial of the private sphere was merely to outlaw the explicit discussion of sex and sexuality. Ulbricht, in his infamous attack on writers at the Eleventh Plenum of the Central Committee of the SED in 1965, condemns the apparent proliferation of literature in the early 1960s which discussed issues of sex, setting out a direct link between such 'Nihilismus, Halbanarchismus,' and 'Pornographie', as he terms it, and the Eastern Bloc's capitalist enemies. Writers were ignoring the educational, or social, function of literature, he argues, in aping what he sees as 'amerikanisch[e] Lebensweisen'.[11] Rather than attempting to lead society forward to socialism, such writers are wallowing in humanity's base urges and thereby aiding the forces of reaction. In an interview with Manfred Treib, Hilbig himself has spoken of his personal experience of this impulse in the official rhetoric. Here he suggests that, particularly in his youth, sex was seen 'als die unmoralische und auch anarchische Komponente der geschlechtlichen Partnerbeziehung' which had no place within socialism. Sex was 'dem unmoralischen Westen zugeschoben', apparently leaving the citizens of the GDR free to realise an unsullied sense of 'wahre Liebe' in their relationships with other members of society.[12] The narrator of *Die Weiber* also makes a direct link between discussions of sex and the capitalist West: 'Ich wuchs unter der Herrschaft von Psychopathologen auf, die den Geschlechtstrieb für abnorm erklärten ... und den *Sex* für kapitalistisch, schon das Wort, da es zu amerikanisch klang, war beinahe verboten' [Hilbig's emphasis](W 50). In the GDR, the very word 'Sex' is practically taboo.[13]

Public discussion of sex was forbidden by the authorities. However, as is clear from Ulbricht's statement, the state's construction of sex as a taboo has as much to do with its fear of the potentially corrupting influence of the West on the minds of its citizens, as it does with any abstract moral agenda. The suppression of all discussion of sexuality was a means of controlling its citizens. As Hilbig claims in the interview with Treib, sex is the 'anarchische Komponente' of human relations, which was feared by the state, and it is the exploration of this 'anarchistische Komponente' which is a central concern of the narrator of *Die Weiber*: 'Dunkel ahnte man das Unheil, das von den Schwänzen meiner Generation ausging, [...] der Untergang des Staates stand bevor, wenn man die Schwänze nicht unten halten konnte' (W 50). The state dreaded the unleashed sexuality of its citizens, which it feared would divert the masses from working for the public good and would ultimately lead to the destruction of society.

In *Die Weiber*, fearing this destruction, the state attempts to separate individuals from their sexual identity. This separation process manifests itself primarily through the language of its official rhetoric. Everything connected with sex is constructed linguistically as *filthy*. The filth of sexual expression is then juxtaposed with the GDR itself, which is, conversely, constructed as clean, the embodiment of Enlightenment rationalism and purity. The narrator recollects his sex education as a child: 'Man begann also, es war eine sehr aufgeklärte Methode, mich vom Bewußtsein meines Schwanzes zu trennen, dieses Bewußtsein nahm die Aufklärung selbst in die Hand, denn die Sauberkeit meiner Empfindungen mußte gewahrt bleiben' (W 50f.). Libidinal urges are denied to such an extent that the narrator perceives his sex education as a process of castration. This castration process is then seen as paradigmatic of all levels of his socialisation. As an adult, he claims that when one talks of socialisation one must 'von Kastration [...] reden, von einer Verstümmelung meiner Innenwelt durch Kastration. Man operierte mich nicht, man ließ alles an mir hängen, aber man verfinsterte die Zellen, die es steuerten, meine Zellen, bestimmte davon wurden sterilisiert und kastriert' (W 49). Indeed, he goes so far as to claim that the perfect socialist is to be like Lenin, a man, he sarcastically suggests, 'der keinen Schwanz besaß' (W 54).

The narrator is the product of this 'reinen Staat' (W 108), which shuns the apparent impurity of sex. He even imagines himself being born from a quasi immaculate conception between his mother and the 'Vater Staat' (W 67). His mother is seen as typical of the women of the *Aufbau* generation in the GDR in that she eschews all discussion of sex. Indeed, all the women with whom the narrator ever has any real contact are described as having completely lost their sexuality, which is again seen in terms of a process of castration. The narrator laments that, whilst 'die Unterkörper der Weiber' have been cut away and shipped off to the West, 'ach, ich erkannte, daß die Oberkörper der Weiber ebenfalls hierblieben, es waren hochgeschlossene, grau oder blau gekleidete Oberkörper, mit muskulösen Armen, die danach verlangten, den Aufbau zu umarmen' (W 52f.).

Castration acts within *Die Weiber* as a metaphor for the limitations placed upon the individual under the SED dictatorship. In order to survive the state's oppressive machinations one must become an *Anpasser*, and in so doing, must give up crucial aspects of one's identity. In an earlier story by Hilbig, 'Der Brief', the narrator uses the metaphor of schizophrenia to express a similar sense of limitation. In the GDR, he suggests, one must have multiple personalities, which must be able to change according to the situation one is in. This idea is, to an extent, now received wisdom in GDR studies. One thinks of Günter Gaus's notion of the GDR as a 'Nischengesellschaft', in which individuals would publicly pay lip service to the official rhetoric, whilst privately, within certain *Nischen*, such as their family, or church group, they would express hostility towards the state.[14] In 'Der Brief', the narrator cannot accept the need for a distinction between one's public and one's private identity. He laments, 'Ich bin nicht schizophren... viel eher noch wollte ich, ich wäre es'.[15] The narrator cannot accept the level of ontological destruction he sees within those who accept the authority of the state unquestioningly.

Hilbig's metaphor of castration is, however, even more apposite than that of schizophrenia in that it also highlights the acutely *self*-destructive nature of the state. The women the narrator encounters in the East have had their sexuality removed. In the narrator's eyes this is equivalent to becoming men. Curiously, the narrator's 'castration-complex' turns 'complete' women, into 'incomplete' men, a reversal of Freud's view (from whom Hilbig would appear to have taken the motif), which sees woman as 'incomplete', having been castrated by birth and are consequently 'doomed' forever to 'envy' the male member.[16] The narrator suggests, for example, in an imagined encounter with a 'Staatsanwältin' who works at the 'Arbeitsgericht'(W 43): 'Sie sind kein Weib, Frau Staatsanwalt, Sie sind mein Vater' (W 57). As Norbert Schachtsiek-Freitag has noted, 'Frauen in staatlichen Funktionen sind für ihn keine Weiber, sie sind Teil der autoritären Männergesellschaft.'[17] The GDR is seen as an authoritarian 'Männergesellschaft', in which all the 'real' women have been removed. Consequently it is seen as a sterile society which is condemned to extinction. It can only hang on to life as a stagnant 'Gerontokratie', as Hans-Jürgen Schmitt terms it, desperately attempting to avoid its inevitable end.[18]

The narrator's sexuality has been forbidden by the state. As a result of this, he begins to develop a profound sense of sexual neurosis, the expression of which is found in his sexual fantasies and incessant self-abuse, which in turn only helps to increase the narrator's sense of crisis and feelings of self-loathing. The goal of the narrator's search is a union with the mythical 'Weiber', which exist beyond the confines of the GDR's sterility. 'Die Weiber' are, on one level, an image of the erotic. They are the women who have not allowed themselves to become non-sexual beings and have consequently been excluded from the state. Through these 'Weiber' he wishes to reverse the process of castration he has undergone and to become a complete individual. At the beginning of the text, the narrator claims to have found 'die Weiber' whilst he is working in a so-called 'Frauenbetrieb'. All his life he had been looking for these women (W 57). Now, having found them, he spends his time in onanistic fantasy. He spies on the women, fetishising their bodies and eroticising their activity, as he imagines them pulling at the 'phallusartigen Hebelarm' of their machinery (W 11). However, although the narrator is able to give some expression to his sexual feelings, such expression is far from satisfactory. Indeed, his proximity to the women merely highlights his inability to form a relationship with then. The narrator is a depraved voyeur. His obsession with masturbation communicates his sense of isolation and despair.

At the end of the text, the narrator seems to have overcome his crisis and there appears to be a rare moment of hope in Hilbig's work. The narrator begins to recover. He leaves his home and travels to Berlin. In Berlin he finds a job in a 'Wäscherei' next to a women's prison (W 105). As he climbs up on the roof of his work-place and looks into the exercise yard of the prison, he believes, once again, that he has found 'die Weiber': 'hier sah ich sie wirklich, hier fand ich sie' (W 107). These are the women that the state has excluded, those women who have not been castrated by complicity with the authorities. He screams 'ich liebe dich' indiscriminately at the women, in the hope that one of them will look up, thereby giving him a feeling of community with them and, in so doing, allowing him to overcome his sense of isolation. They do not look. They do, however, give him a sign: 'Sie machten mir ein Zeichen, ein paar von ihnen hatten den Daumen zwischen Zeigefinger und Mittelfinger hindurchgeschoben und die Hand vorsichtig bis in Brusthöhe angehoben' (W 107). The narrator realises that in this gesture, 'sie machten mir ein schmutziges Zeichen, das schmutzigste, das möglich war, sie hatten sich mit mir verbündet, es war ein Zeichen gegen den reinen Staat. Und es bedeutete auch: warte auf uns' (W 107f.). In these women the narrator does find a potential sense of community. However, this sense of community is never realised. The women remain in prison. Both he and the women are still confined within the state's discourse. Consequently, they can only communicate *negatively*, that is, they are only able to communicate a sense of defiance by appropriating that which is considered obscene. He does not ultimately escape the state's rhetoric to find a sense of union with these women. There is no final moment of resolution in the text. Nevertheless, having found the women, the narrator is given new hope, and commits himself to wait for them. The text ends with his defiant declaration: 'ich konnte auf sie warten' (W 109). He will not resign himself to the limitations of the state. He will wait for the time when the 'Weiber' will be released.

Sexual *Verdrängung* and the taboo of *Vergangenheitsbewältigung*

The narrator wishes to reappropriate the 'anarchische Komponente' of his sexuality which has been neutralised by the authorities and without which he feels he will never be able to develop as an individual. The taboo of sex then, in turn, becomes a vehicle for Hilbig's exploration of another fundamental taboo subject within the official discourse of the GDR, namely the state's relationship to the National Socialist period of German history. Unlike the West, the GDR authorities claimed they had no need for rhetorical devices such as the 'Stunde Null', or the 'Kahlschlag' to give the impression that 8 May 1945 had brought with it a *de facto* new dawn for Germany.[19] The GDR declared its population the 'Sieger der Geschichte', constructing itself self-consciously as an antifascist state. Its designated citizens, the 'workers and peasants' of Germany, were told they had been the victims of rampant late capitalism, and that they had been failed by their leaders, who had not provided a unified front against fascism. Now, with the creation of the *Sozialistische Einheitspartei Deutschlands*, this unified front had been achieved. As a result, the GDR set itself apart from the perpetrators of atrocities during fascism, and consequently insisted that there was no need for its citizens to dwell on questions of guilt for past deeds. They were to be 'der Zukunft zugewandt', as its national anthem informed the people and, as such, were to look forward to socialism, and not backwards to the past.[20] However, the net result of this policy was a process of *Vergangenheitsverdrängung* which lasted well into the 1970s and which outlawed public discussion of individual responsibility for this period of history.

In *Die Weiber*, just as the narrator is condemned to the isolation of a life of sexual depravity since his sexual nature is repressed, the GDR cannot develop as a state because it will not acknowledge from where it has come. Unable to discuss the National Socialist period of history openly, the narrator becomes obsessively fixated upon it and it becomes a central element of his sexual fantasies. As a result, his journey in search of the 'Weiber' is also a journey of *Vergangenheitsbewältigung*, that is, it is also an articulation of his wish to gain a comprehension of the past from which he feels he has been excluded. As we have already seen above, he imagines himself as being born after the creation of the state. However, it is clear that the narrator was in fact born during the war, since he also describes himself as 'dieses wahnsinnig kreischende Bündel, das ich in den letzten Kriegsjahren war', which his mother carried to the shelters during air-raids (W 67). The child was not the physical product of socialism, but rather of National Socialism. Within the state's official rhetoric, this earlier period of his life is denied. Consequently, he feels cut off from the historical period of his actual birth.

The narrator's sexual neurosis has at its root a neurosis of history. The term 'die Weiber' comes from the narrator's childhood. His playground for the first twelve years of his life was the empty barracks of a concentration camp on the outskirts of M. (W 34). 'Die Weiber' were the inmates of the camp (W 96). This normally derogatory term for women therefore becomes an 'Ehrenname' (W 96), since these were the women who were the prisoners of the fascists, and therefore are to be honoured, particularly, of course, in this so-called antifascist state. However, their existence is not even mentioned officially. Indeed, as already discussed, the narrator suggests that 'die Weiber' continue to be imprisoned in the GDR (W 107), implying a degree of continuity with the past in the repressive policies of the present, a notion which is completely denied by the state.

As a child he imagines that he is the only person to know the secret 'höllischen Zweck' of the ruin where he played (W 34). He knows that discussion of the ruin's history is forbidden. Nevertheless, he is drawn to it. He imagines the blood-spattered walls, and the corpses hanging on hooks. His 'verbrecherische Vorstellungskraft' is obsessed with the 'Grauen über die vormalige Beschaffenheit des Lagers'(W 34). The narrator goes on to explain that his fascination with this forbidden history brought with it his first sexual desires. The horror of the *KZ* is bound up 'mit den ersten kindlichen Gelüsten' (W 34). Since he is unable to discuss the past openly, the fragments of information he hears become the inspiration for exotic sexual fantasies. He hears stories of the women being shaved from head to foot (W 34f.). He then begins to fetishise this image, becoming obsessed with the women's hair. This obsession with the women from the concentration camp subsequently leads the narrator to become fixated upon the women in his 'Frauenbetrieb.' The factory where they work used to be a 'Munitionsfabrik', in which prisoners from a similar concentration camp would work (W 8). They are, to a degree at least, the successors of the 'Weiber' from the past.

This 'Frauenbetrieb' is a gateway to the past. History is seen as locked away, hidden beneath the ground of the state he now lives in, which can only be accessed in irrational moments of sexual fantasy. It is a forbidden, private discourse, which cannot be discussed publicly. In his delirium, he dreams that he is back in the cellar of his 'alten Frauenbetrieb' (W 81). The narrator searches for a safe place to masturbate, going 'tiefer und tiefer in die höllischen Stockwerke der Katakomben [...], in das Labyrinth, über dem sich die ehemalige Munitionsfabrik aufbaute.' Deep beneath the factory he finds the remains of the war period, such as rusted signs on which he can just make out the message: '*Achtung Feind hört mit*' [Hilbig's emphasis] (W 82). He imagines the activity of the women above, as they make grenades. His dream then degenerates into a whirl of images, through which the narrator's mind passes in his attempt to reach climax:

> Hoch über mir hörte ich den nervenzerrüttenden Lärm, mit dem die Granaten gedreht wurden. Granaten, Granaten, eine Unzahl von Granaten, säuberlich in handlichen Kisten aufgereiht, Granaten, die allesamt das Aussehen rötlich gelber, praller Eicheln hatten, auf steifen Männerschwänzen, Granaten, (W 82)

The narrative circles around the word 'Granaten', as, in his mind, the past joins with the present in a frenzy of sexual imagery. However, rather than this allowing the narrator any sense of *Bewältigung*, he feels destroyed by the weight of the past. The imagined noise of the grenade production is described as a 'Lärm [...] der [seinen] Geist pulverisierte' (W 82). As with his sexual nature, the past consumes him obsessively. It exists within his consciousness. It is part of him. However, it cannot be understood by him.

The pornographer as 'historian'
The narrator is unable to form a union with the 'Weiber' in the physical world. That is, he can neither overcome his sexual neurosis, nor can he come to an understanding of the past. As a result, he resorts to the private world of writing in order to achieve his aim of overcoming the limitations of the state and finding a more complete sense of identity:

> Wenn es mir gelang, den Besitz einer Identität zu verspüren, wenn ich irgendeine schleierhafte Wertvorstellung von meinem Ich je zu entwickeln imstande war, so stets nur dadurch, daß ich mich schreibend als ein Subjekt erfuhr (W 27f.)

As in many of Hilbig's stories, his protagonist is only able to achieve any sense of identity through the written word. In his texts he attempts to objectify his experience and thereby come to a better understanding of himself. Specifically, in *Die Weiber* the narrator is a writer of pornography. His writing is, of course, an extension of his voyeuristic activity.

However, through writing he hopes to be able finally to leave the world of the peeping-Tom, and find a more satisfactory expression of his sexuality.

Metaphorically, the narrator's need to give expression to, and eventually overcome, his sexual neurosis through writing becomes symbolic of his society's need to give expression to its depraved past. The pornographic stories the narrator writes correspond to his society's 'forbidden' history. Once dismissed from the 'Frauenbetrieb', he becomes obsessed with the rediscovery of a pornographic text he wrote years before, the memory of which he finds repulsive: 'Es war ein Manuskript, dessen Existenz mir ungeheuer peinlich war, und ich hatte es versteckt, verlegt, verdrängt, vergessen' (W 29). Now the story returns to his mind and will not be suppressed: 'es ließ sich nicht mehr leugnen' (W 30f.). Although the narrator is disgusted by the story he wrote, nevertheless, he realises that he must attempt to find it, since the story is a document of his sexuality (W 85), and thus is part of his psyche. If he is to overcome his sense of psychological decay, this text must be faced.

The connection between the pornographic text and his nation's history soon becomes overt as it is revealed that the details of this story are inextricably interwoven with the details of Germany's sordid past. His story is merely one of the many 'verdrängten Beschreibungen' which cause the 'Unterboden dieses Landes' to ache (W 90). Specifically, the text in question is a description of himself and a girlfriend having intercourse on a mound of hair, and as such, draws directly on the narrator's fascination with the shaved bodies of the inmates of the concentration camp (W 33f.). Indeed, he perceives of writing as the only reliable means of preserving the memory of these women. It is

> als sei Haar gelagert, vergessenes, verlorenes Haar hinter alle Hügel
> dieses Landes. Haar, das nicht zu retten war, wenn ich es nicht aufnahm
> in meine Sprache [...], krank von Schamgerüchen, und in der kranken
> Farbe des Königs David gelb unter dem Himmel fliegend. (W 35)

In an image which calls to mind the threnodic mood of the 'Knochenberg' sequence of Günter Grass's *Hundejahre*, the memory of the hair becomes a metonym for Germany's shameful past, which he cannot allow to be forgotten.[21]

The search for the narrator's old story brings him to the outskirts of the city and to its refuse area. It is here that he hopes to be able to face his text, thereby overcoming his 'unhealthy' past and, as a result, find a sense of union with the 'Weiber': 'Dennoch hielt ich mich lange und häufig in der Nähe dieser Tonnen auf; in einer solchen Stadt, meinte ich, ist es möglich, daß eine Frau gerade, der schaumgeborenen Aphrodite gleich, aus dem Innern eines derartigen Gefäßes auftaucht und ans Licht steigt' (W 18). Amidst the filthy detritus of the city he hopes to find the goddess of love and overcome his personal sense of crisis.

The need for the writer to search the rubbish of the city, in order to rediscover the past is taken up by Hilbig again in *Die Kunde von den Bäumen*.[22] In this text, Waller, like the narrator of *Die Weiber*, realises that he is confined by his nation's history. He realises 'daß ich voll war von all jenen Mitteilungen an die Luft, die von diesem historischen Boden ausgingen. Es war wie ein Erz, das mich plötzlich auszufüllen begann' (K 28). Yet, although he is filled with the past, he cannot articulate it. It remains 'unbeschreiblich' within him (K 28). In order to gain access to history, he is drawn to the ever increasing 'Müllanlagen' on the edge of the town. The past is buried in the city's rubbish. He declares: 'Niemand, sagte ich, könne mehr wissen von der Vergangenheit, niemand könne gründlicher Bescheid wissen als die Müllarbeiter' (K 71). Those who work at the rubbish tip are the keepers of history. Hilbig's protagonist, identifying himself with these 'Müllarbeiter', goes on to explain this connection between the city's refuse and history:

> in dem altmodischen Kulturgut; zwischen defekten Kaffeemühlen, Radios und Klodeckeln, [...] in den tausend und abertausend Tonnen Vergangenheit ... darin ist etwas, das noch nicht gelernt hat zu schweigen. Und wir sind welche, die ebensowenig gelernt haben zu schweigen. (K 101)

Waller's writing is a refusal to be silent, even when society refuses to listen to his voice. Society ignores the 'Müllarbeiter'. They 'wurden nicht gefragt, denn sie waren diejenigen, die nach der Meinung der Welt die geringste Stimme hatten' (K 71). Nevertheless, the 'Müllarbeiter', cannot forget, since it is their job constantly to work through the refuse of the past (K 101). In *Die Weiber*, the narrator similarly works through society's rubbish in an attempt to overcome the state's self-destructive drive to forget history. This is the 'riesig[e] Ansammlung von Abfällen, die meine Stadt geboren hatte' (W 97). The town is 'born' of the refuse of history, a metaphor which once again suggests his awareness of a sense of continuity between the past and present which he feels is being denied.

The narrator fails to find his lost text and so is forced to attempt to recreate the 'Weiber' from what he can find in the city's refuse. This search through the refuse becomes symbolic of his attempts to create the 'Weiber' in his writing:

> die Weiber, da ich sie nicht mehr finden konnte, mußten neu beschrieben werden. Ja, sie mußten neu zusammengesetzt werden, aus den Materialien, die mir zur Verfügung standen. Was ich sehen konnte, waren Beschreibungen von Frauen, aus der Literatur, aus Zeitungen ... es gab unzählige, es gab ganze Insektenschwärme von schwarzen Typen, die Frauen beschrieben, war ich nicht völlig eingehüllt davon, Scharen von Fliegen, riesige Alphabete von Mücken, schwarze Moskitos, Heuschrecken. (W 93)

However, in searching the rubbish of the town the narrator fails to find the 'Weiber'. Rather, he finds the rotting remains of that which the state itself has created: its limited, corrupted language and its banal self-image, which can be found in its newspapers and literature. He then goes on to suggest that in order to find these mythical women he must look to that which is 'absent' from the rubbish: 'Aber mir war, als müsse ich auf das schon Vorhandene verzichten, denn diese Beschreibungen waren von Männern gemacht' (W 93).[23] Curiously, here Hilbig's text, which might be seen as an extreme example of 'male' writing, with its fetishised descriptions of women, seems to adopt an overtly feminist world-view. By looking to the dirt of the town he is still forced to use old, patriarchal means of describing the 'Weiber', since everything there has been created by his *Männergesellschaft*: 'Ich würde mir wieder nur eins der alten Vorbilder erwählen' (W 94). To describe the women accurately, he suggests that he must cut himself off from this world and find a 'weiblichen Blick', which has not been corrupted by the state (W 94). However, it is clear that Hilbig's notion of a 'weiblichen Blick' has very little to do with any specifically feminist agenda. The image of 'die Weiber' clearly operates within the text on the level of 'phantasmic space', that is, it is a function of the narrator's psyche and has very little to do with the specific role of women within his society.

Ultimately, the narrator cannot adopt a 'weiblichen Blick'. He can never step outside the state's rhetoric and gain an understanding of history. He continues rather to be condemned to a position of opposition which is still defined by the official discourse. Thus, he remains confined by the state's definition of morality, able only to work through the scraps of the past to which he has access. Towards the end of the text, he returns again to the city's rubbish and attempts to call to the 'Weiber' directly (W 98). In so doing, the narrator seems to re-enter the onanistic delirium one finds in his dream of the 'Frauenbetrieb' (W 81f.). Once again, the narrative begins to take on a threnodic quality, as the central themes of sexual and historical repression return. He calls to his state: 'An den schönen Kern deiner Seele, an die Gosse deiner Fäkalien. An die krepierte Bombe in deinem Fleisch' (W 101). His city remains a 'Verdammte Stadt' which is destroying itself through its 'mörderische Reinheit' (W 101), and its denial of the past. At this point in the text, the narrator seems to recall the words of Rimbaud, a central influence on Hilbig, in his wish to become a *voyant*, 'Um sehen zu lernen, um mich zu erkennen in euch' (W 100).[24] However, he can never come to an understanding of history. Consequently, he is condemned, rather, to remain the voyeur, the peeping Tom of the opening of the story. 'Die Weiber' remain absent, unable to answer him: 'Keine Antwort. Ich wußte, mir war es nicht gelungen, die Weiber zu beschreiben; sie blieben abwesend, abwesend in dieser Stadt, abwesend in meiner Beschreibung' (W 103).

Yet, in the narrator's final lament, there is still a sense of fragile hope. Although he cannot stand outside the oppressive patriarchy of the state, he will not allow himself to be subsumed within it. He refuses to give up 'und mich in meinen Vater verwandeln' (W 98). There is no final sense of *Vergangenheitsbewältigung*. The text remains unresolved. Yet, whilst he cannot overcome the past, it has also not been forgotten. Hilbig's narrator refuses silent capitulation. He still does not understand the National Socialist period of history. Nevertheless, he will not give up the search for understanding. He remains defiant. Whilst he has not found a union with the 'Weiber', he knows 'ich konnte auf sie warten' (W 109).

Three years after the publication of *Die Weiber* the GDR finally self-destructed. In the wake of this self-destruction came, of course, the need for a *Bewältigung* of the 'Second German Dictatorship'. However, it would appear that the 'First Dictatorship' remains a major thematic preoccupation of Hilbig's work, as can be seen, for example, in the story *Alte Abdeckerei* (1991), where he returns to the legacy of National Socialism within the GDR. Furthermore, the notion of the writer as an explorer of society's 'rubbish' also continues to be a central impulse within his work. In his *Frankfurter Vorlesungen* of 1995 he recalls Heinrich Böll's *Frankfurter Vorlesungen* of 1963, similarly maintaining that the purpose of writing is to work though society's *Abfall* in order to reveal its flaws. Hilbig uses the image of writers as the rats and bluebottles of society: 'Ratten und Schmeißfliegen sind sehr notwendige Geschöpfe, sie weisen auf verborgene Fäulnisstellen eines Gemeinwesens hin'.[25] Today in Germany, the problems of *Vergangenheits-bewältigung* are perhaps more complex than ever before in recent history. Hilbig's texts do not offer any simple solutions to these problems. Nevertheless they do, at least, continue to articulate them, thereby refusing to allow the past simply to disappear into silence.

NOTES

[1] Haro Zimmermann, 'Sprache war für mich zwingende Suchbewegung: Ein Gespräch mit dem ehemaligen DDR-Schriftsteller Wolfgang Hilbig', *Frankfurter Rundschau*, 20 June 1990.

[2] Wolfgang Hilbig, *Die Weiber* (Frankfurt/Main, 1987), hereafter referred to as (W).

[3] Karl Corino suggest, for example 'Es gibt eine Reihe von Passagen in Hilbigs Text, die meines Erachtens an einem Zuviel an Grauem und Ekelhaftem leiden'. See Karl Corino, 'Wo die Neurosen blühn: Wolfgang Hilbigs DDR Prosa „Die Weiber"' , *Stuttgarter Zeitung*, 6 October 1987. Similarly, Uwe Wittstock argues 'Was immer durch diese freudianische Selbsterkundung aus dem Unbewußten in den Text gespült wird – es ist gewiß für den Autor interessant, nicht immer aber für den Leser.' Uwe Wittstock, 'Kellerreden von Jack the Ripper: Wolfgang Hilbigs Prosaband „Die Weiber"', *Frankfurter Allgemeine Zeitung*, 28 November 1987, reprinted as '„Schmutzige Zeichen" Wolfgang Hilbig und sein Prosaband „Die Weiber"', in Uwe Wittstock, *Von der Stalinallee zum Prenzlauer Berg: Wege der DDR-Literatur 1949-1989* (Munich, 1989), pp. 203-207.

[4] Whilst the theme of history is mentioned by some critics, there has been no detailed study of this aspect, with critics preferring to examine the story in terms of the narrator's sexual neurosis. Gabriele Eckart, for example, in her book, the first full-length study of Hilbig's work, examines the text using Lacanian psychoanalysis, and only mentions National Socialism in as far as it relates to the narrator's own childhood. See Gabriele Eckart, *Sprachtraumata in den Texten des ehemaligen DDR "Arbeiterschriftstellers" Wolfgang Hilbig* (New York, 1996), pp.86-90. The only other detailed examination of the text similarly mentions National Socialism only briefly. See Roberto Cazzola, 'Verseucht sind das Land, die Menschen, die Sprache: Zu der Erzählung *Die Weiber*' in *Wolfgang Hilbig: Materialien zu Leben und Werk*, ed. by Uwe Wittstock (Frankfurt/Main, 1994), pp. 153-173 (p. 170).

[5] Christa Wolf, *Kindheitsmuster* (Frankfurt/Main, 1979), p. 284.

[6] J.H. Reid, 'Sex and Politics: The Case of the GDR', in *Taboos in German Literature*, ed. by David Jackson (Providence, 1996), pp. 183–202 (p. 185).

[7] See Karl Marx and Friedrich Engels, *Manifest der kommunistischen Partei* (Berlin, 1945), p. 64.

[8] ibid., p. 65.

[9] The *Bericht der Enquete-Kommission, Aufarbeitung von Geschichte und Folgen der SED-Diktatur in Deutschland* (Baden-Baden, 1995, p. 291) notes how Lenin, following Marx and Engels, called for house work to be 'industrialisiert' and the bringing up of children to be 'vergemeinschaftet', in order for women to be able to come out of the home. This was never completely achieved in any Eastern Bloc state and the family was actually enshrined within the *Familiengesetzbuch der DDR* of 1964 as the 'kleinste Zelle der Gesellschaft'. Nevertheless, such a formulation implies that the energies of a married couple and the family were to be used primarily for the benefit of society.

[10] Cazzola, p. 161.

[11] Walter Ulbricht 'Probleme des Perspektivplans bis 1970: Referat auf dem 11. Plenum des ZK der SED, 16 bis 18. Dezember 1965', in *Dokumente zur Kunst-, Literatur- und Kulturpolitik der SED*, ed. by Elimar Schubbe (Stuttgart, 1972), pp. 1081-1088 (p. 1087).

[12] Manfred Treib, 'Sex im deutsch-deutschen Vergleich: Interview mit Wolfgang Hilbig', *Voyeur* July/August 1988, cited here from Cazzola, p. 161.

[13] This image of the unspeakability of the word 'Sex' is further humorously echoed in Thomas Brussig's post-*Wende* novel, *Helden wie wir*. The mother of Karl, the central protagonist, who would be approximately the same age as Hilbig's narrator, is also troubled by the word. Karl tells the American journalist to whom he is dictating his story: 'Sie sprach 'Sex' nur mit stimmhaftem S: Sechs. 6idol, homo6uell, 6film.' Thomas Brussig, *Helden wie wir* (Berlin, 1996), p. 58.

[14] Günter Gaus, *Wo Deutschland liegt* (Hamburg, 1983), pp. 156-227.

[15] Wolfgang Hilbig, 'Der Brief' in *Der Brief* (Frankfurt/Main, 1985), pp. 77-167 (p. 83).

[16] See Sigmund Freud, 'Neue Folge der Vorlesungen zur Einführung in die Psychoanalyse', in *Gesammelte Werke* XV (Frankfurt/Main, 1944), pp. 132-139.

[17] Norbert Schachtsiek-Freitag, 'Realistisch, phantastisch, utopisch: Die DDR als erzählter Ort', *Deutschland Archiv* ,10 (1988), 1116-1119 (p. 118).

[18] Hans-Jürgen Schmitt, 'Ich jage allein im Wahnsinn meiner Träume: Wolfgang Hilbigs Prosa *Die Weiber* – eine Kellerrede in „kranker" Sprache gegen den „sauberen" Staat', *Suddeutsche Zeitung*, 7 October 1987.

[19] See Alexander Stephan '"How did we become as we are?" The treatment of fascism in GDR literature', *GDR Monitor* 3 (1980), 5 – 16; Ingrid Dinter *Unvollendete Trauerarbeit in der DDR-Literatur: Ein Studium der Vergangenheits-Bewältigung* (New York, 1994), pp.1-30.

[20] Johannes R. Becher, 'Nationalhymne der Deutschen Demokratischen Republik', in *Gesammelte Werke* 6, ed. by Johannes R. Becher Archiv der Akademie der Kunst der Deutschen Demokratischen Republik (Berlin, 1972), p. 61.

[21] Günter Grass, *Hundejahre* (Neuwied/Rhein, 1963), pp. 357-427.

[22] Wolfgang Hilbig, *Die Kunde von den Bäumen* (Frankfurt/Main, 1994), hereafter referred to as (K).

[23] The notion of looking to that which is absent from the official discourse in order to find a more satisfactory expression of one's identity is a constant motif in Hilbig's work. Indeed, the title of his first collection of poetry published is entitled *abwesenheit*. See Wolfgang Hilbig, *abwesenheit* (Frankfurt/Main, 1979)

[24] For Rimbaud, the role of the poet is to be a seer, a *voyant*, the holder of a transcendental vision, which separates him from the rest of society. See Arthur Rimbaud, 'Lettre à Paul Demeny', in *Poesie* ed. by Daniel Leuwers (Paris, 1984), pp. 200-205.

[25] Wolfgang Hilbig, *Abriß der Kritik* (Frankfurt/Main, 1995), p. 93. Here Hilbig would also seem ironically to echo the attacks of the CDU/CSU on writers such as Grass and Böll in the 1960s and 1970s, both of whom were considered *Nestbeschmutzer* of the FRG by these parties.

Simon Bevan

CHANGE AND CONTINUITY IN THE WORK OF CHRISTOPH HEIN: A COMPARISON OF *HORNS ENDE* (1985) AND *VON ALLEM ANFANG AN* (1997)

This article provides a comparative analysis of Christoph Hein's Horns Ende *and* Von allem Anfang an *as examples of his prose writing before and after the* Wende, *both texts which illuminate the interplay between continuity and change in his writing. Despite similarities in historical setting and characterisation, there are significant changes in emphasis and narrative approach between the two works. In addition to providing a revealing perspective from which to study Hein's personal development as a writer, these elements of continuity and change give a good indication of his response to the demise of the GDR and of his determination to prevent the GDR years being seen as another closed era in German history.*

Christoph Hein has repeatedly described himself as a 'Chronist'[1] whose role is to chart the development of his society, but without giving simplified explanations of the problems it faces. Aware of the dangers of restricting his perspective too narrowly to the present, Hein, in his approach to this task, has characteristically set contemporary issues against a wider historical background, and the questions and dilemmas he has raised have also found resonance outside the German-speaking world. His career has been marked by significant changes of creative focus, the most notable being the enforced move away from drama towards prose-writing around 1980. In keeping with his understanding of the constant need for artists to face new creative challenges (distinguishing them from craftsmen who use an acquired skill[2]), there have been considerable variations within this prose work. He has produced both short stories and longer pieces that are narrated from a range of perspectives.

There are, however, important dimensions of continuity in Hein's work. Historical events and characters have been a productive source of material for him and his approach has often been to highlight elements of continuity across different historical eras. During the GDR's existence, he successfully challenged its official self-image as an autonomous entity within German history by exposing fundamental aspects of its *unbewältigte Vergangenheit* in relation to the Nazi past. Since its collapse, Hein, unlike many former GDR writers, has responded positively to the new opportunities created by the *Wende*. Whilst maintaining his socialist principles, he believes that political change should be embraced by its artists as a liberating stimulus for their work, an attitude neatly encapsulated in his comment: 'Die alten Themen habe ich noch, jetzt kommen noch neue dazu. Auf diese Chance sollten gerade Künstler und Intellektuelle mit Risikobereitschaft und nicht mit Depressionen und Ängsten reagieren.'[3] When asked what his new themes would be, Hein has replied that, just as he wrote about the victims of Stalinism in the GDR, he will now write about the victims of de-Stalinisation in reunified Germany.[4]

Hein has also maintained the vigorous public role that underpins his understanding of the chronicler's responsibilities. Examples of this are his work on the committee which investigated Stasi violence during the peaceful demonstrations of October and November in 1989 and his position on the editorial board of the weekly newspaper *Freitag* which he has used, for example, as a platform to support Günter Grass's stand on asylum seekers' rights in Germany.[5] This continuing commitment to public life has been recognised in the most impressive way through his election as the first president of the all-German PEN association in October 1998.

This paper will deal with two works which exemplify the interplay of continuity and change in Hein's writing. The first of these, *Horns Ende*[6], was published in 1985 after a long battle with the state censor and provoked a great deal of controversy by challenging the image of the 1950s as a 'golden age' for socialism in the GDR. It consists of five characters recalling events from the time of the museum curator Horn's suicide, which occurred in 1957 in the fictional provincial town Bad Guldenburg. It highlights the problems associated with memory, most notably in the case of Thomas who was a twelve year-old boy at the time. Each chapter is introduced by a dialogue between Thomas and Horn's ghost who urges him to remember. The differences in detail and emphasis between the various first-person accounts reveal the subjective nature of memory and the problems this causes in accurately recording the past.

At the time of the publication of *Horns Ende*, a commentator in *Neue Deutsche Literatur* argued that Thomas' story could have been continued.[7] At first sight, *Von allem Anfang an*[8], Hein's most recent piece of prose, appears to have done just that. Published in the autumn of 1997, it enjoyed almost unanimous praise from the critics. Amongst others, *Der Spiegel* welcomed the return (after the very mixed reception of *Das Napoleon-Spiel*) of Hein's old strengths of focusing on the details of everyday life. In Britain, Peter Graves applauded 'this richly understated text' and Martin Kane thought it was 'related with rich and vivid precision of detail.'[9] Like *Horns Ende*, it is narrated by an adolescent boy, Daniel (the sole narrator in this case), who is just one year older than Thomas. A further element of continuity with *Horns Ende* is that, despite its post-reunification origins, Hein deliberately returns to the same historical setting of the middle 1950s: Daniel recounts events in his life from Christmas 1955 to autumn 1956. These initial similarities invite a comparison of the texts as a means of studying Hein's understanding of his society's development, and his own progression as a writer. On the other hand, Hein's comment in 1994 that he could no longer write stories such as *Horns Ende* because the present-day context of the narrative had changed so fundamentally[10] suggests that there is more to *Von allem Anfang an* than simply being a continuation of *Horns Ende*. I will, therefore, also focus on the changes of emphasis between the two books.

Thematic continuity

Horns Ende was heavily criticised by GDR 'Kulturpolitiker' for the emphasis it laid on the continued survival in the 1950s of authoritarian attitudes fostered in the Third Reich.[11] Although the story takes place in a period of great political and technological change (there is a reference to the arrival of the first television in the town), the unbroken links with the Nazi past are unmistakable. Unnerving reactions to the Nazi era can be found among the locals, such as the civil servant Bachofen, who argues 'jedenfalls war da noch Ordnung'(HE 190). A more widespread, and politically dangerous, desire to forget the past is highlighted by reactions to the arrival of gypsies in the town from people who themselves were 'Umsiedler' only a few years previously. Whilst some seek to disassociate themselves entirely from 'Die Nazis' (e.g. Gertrude Fischlinger, one of the five narrators) as if they had been some kind of occupying force in Germany, the local Doctor, Spodeck, tells us 'Die Denunzianten und Mörder kamen nicht von irgendwo [...]. Sie sind aus unseren Wohnungen hervorgekrochen, unter unserer Haut' (HE 163). The fact that this kind of recognition is not very widespread, however, shows how many GDR citizens seized on the idea of a fresh start or 'Stunde Null' in 1945 as a convenient way of drawing a line under their Nazi past. Although this term is primarily used to describe the attempt in the FRG to suppress uncomfortable memories of Nazism, Hein believes that it is equally pertinent to the GDR which claimed it was the only German state to make a clean ideological break with the Hitler era.[12] Any tendencies he might have had to overplay the negative elements of continuity in his society were, in his view, entirely justified due to the overplaying of the positive elements of change elsewhere in GDR propaganda.[13]

Von allem Anfang an also reveals the problems associated with the notion of a 'Zero Hour', albeit in a more personal way. Daniel attempts to reconstruct the beginnings of his intellectual and moral development in a time when, like Thomas, he could have had no real understanding of the legacy of the Third Reich. He was still at an age where it was difficult to imagine a world before he was born. The cyclical structure of the story confirms the problem of identifying a starting point for this personal development. At the end of the book, we are taken right back to the beginning ('Von allem Anfang an') as the first chapter is the last in chronological terms. The book appears to be suggesting that there is no real starting point and that everything is a consequence of a consequence, but also that the GDR was fundamentally flawed right from the beginning. In Von allem Anfang an, Hein continues to confront subjects which were taboo during the GDR era, a significant approach in terms of its contribution in encouraging a balanced and honest recording of the GDR's past in the post-Wende era. He picks up the theme from Horns Ende of challenging the official state view that the GDR was a 'sozialistische Menschengemeinschaft' by showing it to be rife with prejudice and spite. Whereas Thomas receives preferential treatment in school for being the son of a chemist (a bourgeois profession compatible with the needs of the new state), Daniel is discriminated against for being the son of a pastor, which stands in direct contradiction to state ideology. Hein points to reasons for failure and inefficiency in the realm of agriculture (a recurrent theme in his prose) where Party membership was more important than practical competence – Daniel's grandfather being replaced by an incompetent Party official for refusing to join the SED.

Given the importance Hein attaches to recognising the thread which ties together elements of the past, present and future, it is no surprise that he focuses his attention in both books on a character who is on the cusp of puberty. This is the time, after all, when the conflict of these elements, in personal development, is probably most intense. Hein has also explained that the ages of these boys served a more symbolic function in reflecting some of the wider social and technological changes in GDR society I briefly mentioned earlier in this section: 'Ich wollte einen Text schreiben über einen Wechsel, der in der deutschen Gesellschaft Mitte der 50er Jahre stattfand. Der Wechsel von den agrarischen Lebensformen zu den moderneren, industriellen. Dafür fand ich dann eine sehr geeignete

Entsprechung mit einem pubertierenden Kind, wo auch ein kleiner Wechsel stattfindet, der vom Kind zum Halbwüchsigen oder Erwachsenen.'[14] Thomas and Daniel share many similar experiences and make similar discoveries. They both feel confusion at the lack of logic in the adult world, which they are on the verge of entering. We witness their early bitter-sweet experiences with girls and both of them take great pride in their friendships with older children. Yet Thomas' delight in referring to another boy who was 'über zwei Jahre älter als ich und trotzdem mit mir befreundet' (HE 230) is countered by the despair and frustration at later being excluded by him. Daniel has a similar sense of exclusion when he finds himself playing gooseberry to a young couple (VA 83-103).

Although Thomas and Daniel are trying to recall moments from their past, Hein resists the temptation to add retrospective comments from a more authoritative perspective to fill in the gaps in the memory process. In *Von allem Anfang an* we listen to the adult Daniel confront a long-held desire to talk about his family, something which has always failed until this point. His childhood is not, however, suddenly put into perspective or given a definitive interpretation by the adult self. Whilst Michael Opitz in *Freitag* saw this as a missed opportunity by Hein ('Das Alter des Protagonisten bedingt eine gewisse Naivität in der Weltsicht, die [...] dem Autor [...] die Chance verbaut, ihn bewegende Fragestellungen von Anfang an aus einer intellektuellen Draufsicht zu entwickeln'[15]), I would argue that he has misinterpreted the direction of the relationship between author and protagonist in terms of who is asking questions of whom. Daniel is shown to be searching painstakingly for his roots with the help of incidences which happened before his very eyes and which he still does not understand. Similarly, in *Horns Ende*, the ghost of Horn does not provide the missing details, despite being in the best position to do so. He steers Thomas away from using other peoples' subsequent accounts as an 'aide-mémoire', insisting on his responsibility to use his own memory. His insistence to Thomas that 'du bist es, der darüber reden muß' (HE 233) suggests that it is the younger generation which must make a special effort to maintain the link to the past and to make sense of it.

Changes of perspective

There are, however, significant differences between the two works in terms of narrative approach, characterisation and emphasis. The most obvious ones result from limiting the narration to one person in *Von allem Anfang an* as opposed to the multi-perspective narration of *Horns Ende*. Although Thomas is the main character in *Horns Ende*,[16] his account only forms part of a fragmented portrayal of small-town society. In *Von allem Anfang an*, in contrast, we focus in depth on one single family. Bad Guldenburg is too small for the characters to avoid each other and the connections between them are mentioned on a number of occasions (e.g. Thomas is the friend of Gertrude Fischlinger's son), but the main principle of *Horns Ende* is to look at the same event from various perspectives, and the links are somehow never complete. This is not a priority in the later work which gives more emphasis to the interaction between characters, highlighted by the increase in dialogue. If we compare the endings of the two books, for instance, *Von allem Anfang an* has dialogue right into the last page whereas *Horns Ende* leaves us with the image of lonely or bitter individuals not communicating with each other.

Whilst acknowledging the continuity from the character of Thomas to Daniel, Hein identifies the 'warmer temperature' at which Daniel is portrayed as being the most important difference between them.[17] Naturally the restriction of the narration to him alone allows us to get to know him better, but there does also seem to be less distance between him and the author than in the case of Thomas. We learn more about the members of his family as individuals even though they appear at first sight to be just as dominated and stifled by an authoritarian father figure as Thomas' family is. This warmer, more relaxed 'temperature' led one commentator to ask whether *Von allem Anfang an* represented 'a breather' for Hein from heavy, political subject-matter and whether his next book would revert to type.[18] Hein's answer was that 'Je älter ich werde, desto weniger denke ich in den Kategorien von Stoff oder Thema. Das Handwerkliche, Artistische schiebt sich immer in den Vordergrund. Aber komisch soll es wieder sein.' It is perhaps on the basis of this comment, which suggests an even greater move away from overtly political aims in his writing, that we are to understand Hein's view that he could not write stories like *Horns Ende* in post-*Wende* Germany.

The mood is also more relaxed in *Von allem Anfang an* with regard to the urgency of rediscovering the 'truth' of the past through memory. In the earlier book, Horn makes many statements, in real life and from beyond the grave, about the importance of this exercise to mankind, such as 'Löschen Sie das Gedächtnis eines Menschen, und Sie löschen die Menschheit' (HE 281) and 'wenn du mich vergißt, erst dann sterbe ich wirklich' (HE 71). For Horn, there is a clear division between truth and falsehood and he sees it as his responsibility to draw the line explicitly between the two. When Thomas comes to help him in the museum, Horn tells him: 'Es ist nur ein kleines Museum, das wir haben, und doch schreiben auch wir die Geschichte. Wir sind es, die dafür einzustehen haben, ob die Wahrheit oder die Lüge berichtet wird' (HE 81). He totally dismisses Spodeck's view, similar to Claudia's from Hein's first long piece of prose, *Der fremde Freund*, that we should ignore memories if they are painful to us.

We should, admittedly, guard against wholly accepting Horn's message to Thomas for a number of reasons. Firstly, Horn himself did not apply such rigour in his own lifetime to talking about the past as a safeguard against forgetting it.[19] Furthermore, Kruschkatz, mayor of Bad Guldenburg, complains of the sleepless night a very vivid memory can cause, and Hein himself has admitted that he too has been tempted to suppress unpleasant memories, a confession which shows at least a degree of understanding for Spodeck's view. Even as early as his first collection of short stories, Hein produced a modern version of Kleist's *Michael Kohlhaas* story which, less heroically than the original, appeared to ridicule an individual's dogmatic battle to establish the truth, highlighting the damage this can cause.[20] Hein sees the attitude that 'die Gerechtigkeit möge siegen, mag auch die Welt darüber zugrunde gehen' as being a typically Prussian-German one.[21]

There is, nevertheless, a significant change of emphasis in the later work. *Von allem Anfang an* challenges Horn's insistence that a definite truth about past events exists and that it is merely a question of accessing this through memory. Daniel shows that searching the past will never produce a full answer and the sense of urgency in *Horns Ende* to learn lessons from the human misery of the 1950s before it is too late gives way to a painstaking process of subjective re-evaluation in *Von allem Anfang an*. In a newspaper interview shortly after the publication of *Von allem Anfang an*, Hein stressed the importance of personal memories in this subjective approach: 'Sie sind das einzige, was wir wirklich haben. Sie sind für uns das Allerverläßlichste, auch da, wo sie falsch sind [...]. Für mich, wie für jedes Individuum, sind die Erinnerungen die absolute Wahrheit.'[22]

This defence of the validity of personal memories provides the link to a central question surrounding the publication of *Von allem Anfang an*, namely, whether Hein, by returning to the same historical context and writing about the past rather than the present, had taken the easy option of avoiding current issues. Peter Jakobs hinted at this in *Die Welt* when he accused Hein of fleeing to the 1950s in a defiant attempt to prove his earlier claim that the *Wende* had not altered his writing.[23] Yet, reflecting his views on the importance of keeping memories alive in order to salvage something of the past, Hein is actually revealing his determination to be the sole interpreter of his own experiences, a feeling he made abundantly clear in 1994: 'Das alte Gebilde DDR ist vorbei, nicht aber mein Leben [...]. Die bisher gelebten 50 Jahre [...] völlig aus dem Blickfeld zu verlieren, wird mir nicht gelingen. Ja, ich werde den Teufel tun und auf all diese Erfahrungen verzichten – sie sind der Reichtum, mit dem ich arbeiten kann'.[24] For post-*Wende* Germany, this is a significant statement on the need, and indeed right, of former GDR citizens not to abandon their past.

It is important to point out here that both Thomas and Daniel are broadly autobiographical creations by Hein. The ages, setting and family background have striking similarities not only with each other but also with the author's. These similarities are more developed in *Von allem Anfang an*. Both Hein and Daniel have fathers who are pastors (a fact which made it necessary for both of them to leave the GDR for West Berlin in order to continue their schooling), and, for the first time, the three spheres of influence on Hein's childhood are all presented in one of his novels. The town where Daniel lives with his parents is similar in size to the one where Hein grew up (Bad Düben near Leipzig), Daniel spends some of the holiday at his grandparents' house in the country and, by the end of the story, he is preparing to leave for the big city of Berlin, which is ever present in the text as an alternative to his small and boring, yet reassuring, home town.

Hein has resisted any interpretations of these works as being purely autobiographical, arguing that these are fictitious characters. A strictly autobiographical project would have been too sterile, requiring him to undertake a painstaking search through his own memory which would leave many more gaps than his deliberately fragmented fictions do. Writing, he claims, is no fun without the masks of fiction. Reviewers of the book also warned against reading it as a purely autobiographical piece: Lothar Baier, for example, recognised that this was almost irresistible, but claimed that the reader would miss the literary text if (s)he did.[25] In a post-*Wende* context, it is significant that Hein maintains a degree of artistic licence in line with his insistence that GDR writers free themselves from the burdens of supplying 'information' in an easily digestible form. He has explained that he needs to know his subject matter well before he can write about it and personal experience is therefore the primary source of material for him. In his view, the first eighteen years in a person's life are especially influential and character-forming, and he claims that these artistic forays into childhood and youth, based on his own experience, have been a feature of all his previous works.[26] All in all, though, the reduction in distance from Thomas to Daniel in relation to Hein suggests that in the 1980s Hein was more cautious about the validity of his personal experience than he is today.

Conclusions: the post-*Wende* context

Although he has embraced the new creative opportunities provided by reunification, Hein has decided in *Von allem Anfang an* to use personal material from the GDR era rather than offering a hurried view of post-*Wende* Germany. The fact that he has chosen to return to this short, but important, period in his early life instead of focusing on more contemporary material suggests that he still sees unresolved issues rooted in the GDR past which its citizens have to deal with in order to avoid the temptations of viewing 1989 as another 'Stunde Null'. Perhaps an early indication of Hein's appreciation of the need for a thorough re-evaluation of the past can be found in a comment he made in 1992. As Stasi revelations became public knowledge, he grimly confessed: 'Wir lebten in einem Land, das wir erst jetzt kennenlernen.'[27]

In *Von allem Anfang an* he has chosen to use a narrow temporal framework (one year) as a necessarily modest start to *Vergangenheitsbewältigung* after the upheaval of the *Wende*. Just as the element of self-confidence in his refusal to abandon his life in the GDR as a source of inspiration for his work should not be under-estimated, nor should his decision to maintain a fictive element in his work. Writers such as Günter de Bruyn have attempted to provide a more comprehensive view of the GDR era in conventional autobiographical form, an approach which has provoked criticism from some commentators on the grounds of its superficial coverage of a longer time-span.[28] Fritz Raddatz highlighted the strength of Hein's approach in *Von allem Anfang an* when he wrote: 'Sie ist so atmosphärisch genau, daß man das Grollen des nahenden Gewitters zu hören meint'.[29]

Despite the changes of emphasis and narrative technique between the two books discussed here, there is also a great deal of thematic continuity. In *Horns Ende*, Hein refused to accept the creation of the GDR as a 'Stunde Null'. *Von allem Anfang an* insists on a similar appreciation of continuity from the perspective of post-unification Germany. Unlike many of his fellow GDR authors Hein has not suffered a confidence-crisis since 1989 and, in many respects, his perception of his role has not changed very much. This is partly due to the sense of detachment he had always felt towards the GDR, a feeling very much apparent in his claim that 'I was an enemy of the state as a baby – that sharpens one's focus'.[30] No doubt this detachment helped to save him from experiencing overwhelming feelings of loss at its demise. He recognises that there is a continued need for critical voices in reunified Germany, just as there was in the GDR, an attitude that some Western commentators who would prefer a more dismissive view of the GDR experience in its entirety might find difficult to accept. In *Von allem Anfang an,* Hein has undertaken a process of reassessment by presenting personal experience in a fictive form as a means of initiating a more complex debate about why the GDR failed. Such a return to the past is not a way of avoiding current issues, but surely a necessary first step for reunified Germany if it wishes to come to a proper understanding of the effects of forty years of division.

NOTES

[1] See, for example, 'Ich bin ein Schreiber von Chroniken', in Christoph Hein, *Als Kind habe ich Stalin gesehen* (Berlin and Weimar, 1990), pp. 201-207.

[2] Christoph Hein, 'Lorbeerwald und Kartoffelacker. Vorlesung über einen Satz Heinrich Heines', in *Öffentlich arbeiten* (Berlin and Weimar, 1989), pp. 5-28 (p. 20).

[3] In Lothar Baier (ed.), *Christoph Hein: Texte, Daten, Bilder* (Frankfurt am Main, 1990), p. 39.

[4] Interview with *Junge Welt*, 27 February 1990.

[5] Christoph Hein, 'Ein Landfriedenspreis für Günter Grass', *Freitag*, 24 October 1997, p. 2.

[6] The edition I refer to is Christoph Hein, *Horns Ende* (Berlin, 1995) in the Aufbau Taschenbuch series. All subsequent page references will be indicated by the letters HE and the relevant page number.

[7] Gabriele Lindner, 'Ein geistiger Widergänger: Christoph Heins „Horns Ende"', in *Neue Deutsche Literatur*, 10/1986, 155-161 (p. 161).

[8] The edition I refer to is Chistoph Hein, *Von allem Anfang an* (Berlin, 1997). All subsequent page references will be indicated by the letters VA and the relevant page number.

[9] 'Leuchtschrift am Kudamm', *Der Spiegel*, 25 August 1997, p. 178; Peter Graves, 'A boy's Soviet Zone story', *Times Literary Supplement*, 17 October 1997; Martin Kane *PEN International*, 1/1998, p. 23.

[10] See 'Absurditäten der deutschen Gegenwart', *Neues Deutschland*, 5 April 1994.

[11] See, for example, a letter from Ursula Ragwitz of the department for culture in the SED Central Committee to Kurt Hager, Politbüro member with special responsibility for culture, on 8 November 1985, especially the accompanying document 'Information zu Christoph Heins Roman Horns Ende' dated 23 October 1985. This can be found in file DY30/42322/2 at the 'Bundesarchiv' in Berlin. One of the most pertinent criticisms of the book was: '... von den erregenden Vorgängen des Aufbaus einer gänzlich neuen Gesellschaft scheinen die Einwohner Guldenburgs kaum berührt. Sie nutzen die große Chance eines geistig moralischen Neubeginns nicht. Und darin liegt das Problematische des Buches, das durchaus zu falschen Schlüssen führen kann.' For a sample of the state's reception of *Horns Ende* see Ernest Wichner and Herbert Wiesner (eds.), *Zensur in der DDR: Geschichte, Praxis und 'Ästhetik' der Behinderung der Literatur* (Berlin, 1991), pp. 102-104.

[12] Christoph Hein, 'Weder das Verbot noch die Genehmigung als Geschenk', *Als Kind habe ich Stalin gesehen*, pp. 178-183 (p. 179).

[13] Lothar Baier (ed.), *Christoph Hein: Texte, Daten, Bilder*, p. 60.

[14] 'Der Kürbis, die Mauer und ein Gärtner in Berlin', *Mitteldeutsche Zeitung*, 7 October 1997.

[15] Michael Opitz, 'Formen des Beginnens', *Freitag*, 10 October 1997.

[16] Heinz Dörfler has calculated that Thomas has ten per-cent more lines than any of the other narrators in *Horns Ende*. See Heinz Dörfler, 'Das Integrationsmodell zur Erschließung von Christoph Heins Roman „Horns Ende"', *Moderne Romane im Unterricht* (Frankfurt am Main, 1988), pp. 79-106 (p. 86).

[17] This phrase was used by Hein in a conversation with me at Swansea University in March 1998.

[18] 'Im Gespräch – Christoph Hein', *Der Tagesspiegel*, 9 September 1997, p. 24. This echoes a criticism in *Freitag* that *Von allem Anfang an* suffered from a lack of conflict between biographical and political elements, something which had never previously been the case in a text by Hein. See *Freitag*, 10 October 1997.

[19] The details surrounding his clash with the authorities which led to him losing his doctor title, for example, are virtually taboo for him.

[20] 'Der neue (glücklichere) Kohlhaas. Bericht über einen Rechtshandel aus den Jahren 1972/73' in Christoph Hein, *Einladung zum Lever Bourgeois* (Berlin and Weimar, 1980). In the second edition (1986) the page references for this story are 73-92.

[21] 'Ich bin ein Schreiber von Chroniken', *Neues Deutschland*, 2/3 December 1989.

[22] *Mitteldeutsche Zeitung*, 7 October 1997.

[23] Peter Jakobs, 'Von der Bindungslosigkeit der Artistentruppe', *Die Welt*, 2 September 1997.

[24] 'Die Weisheit der Regierenden', *Thüringer Allgemeine*, 8 April 1994.

[25] 'Blick zurück in Zärtlichkeit', *Die Wochenzeitung*, 31 October 1997.

[26] 'Ich bin der entschiedenste Kritiker meiner Texte', *Leipziger Volkszeitung*, 15 October 1997.

[27] Christoph Hein, *Als Kind habe ich Stalin gesehen*, p. 198.

[28] See, for example, Michael Opitz, 'Ohne zu stören', *Freitag*, 20 December 1996.

[29] Fritz J. Raddatz, 'Besonnte Vergangenheit', *Die Zeit*, 19 September 1997.

[30] Transcript of an interview with Hein by Holly Aylett for a programme on culture in the GDR, entitled 'A Footnote in History?', shown on *The South Bank Show*, ITV, October 1990.

David Clarke

'MIT KUNST DER WELT BEIKOMMEN': CHRISTOPH HEIN ON LITERATURE, IDEOLOGY AND THE POSSIBILITY OF CHANGE IN THE GDR

This paper examines the role which Christoph Hein, in his essays of the 1980s, assigns to literature in the promotion of change on an individual and social level. It asks to what extent Hein's approach to this problem may be conditioned by the context in which these ideas were formulated, and sees the function that Hein attributes to literature in terms of his understanding of the workings of ideology. In an analysis of Hein's story 'Die Vergewaltigung', the paper goes on to show how Hein's fiction explores the relationship between a resistance to change on the part of the individual and on the part of the GDR regime.

Perhaps the most interesting issue raised by a consideration of 'continuity and change' in East Germany is the 'Paradox von Stabilität und Revolution'[1] evident in GDR history. In other words, how did it come about that the GDR was relatively stable for so long, and how did citizens who played their part in that stability suddenly become able to overturn the SED regime? In the following I will consider Christoph Hein's prose as a literary exploration of how the workings of human nature can intersect with the demands of the socialist state, offering the reader an insight into the apparent continuity of acquiescence to state power and the sudden ability to bring about change displayed by East Germans during the *Wende*.

Best known for his fiction and drama, Christoph Hein has also produced three volumes of essays containing texts which reveal the author's interest in the workings of ideology. Whilst the term 'ideology' itself is never specifically employed, it would seem the most appropriate definition for what Hein variously calls a 'Weltbild', a set of 'Ewigkeitswerte',[2] or 'eine nützliche zweite Haut' which protects us from coming to terms with the world as it really is (Öa, 50). The term ideology itself is the object of an array of theoretical discourses,[3] yet for my purposes I will define it broadly as consisting of the ways in which men and women represent their world and their place in it to themselves, representations which are inadequate to the true nature of that world.[4] Whatever the origins of these representations, be they the products of the individual's material existence, as Marx argued,[5] or the result of ignorance and superstition, as in the thought of the Enlightenment, the critic of ideology seeks to challenge these false representations and reveal the reality of a given situation, ultimately allowing for the transformation of that situation by those whom this insight empowers.

In his 1985 essay 'Sprache und Rhythmus' (Öa, 39-42), Hein describes an Eden in which language, as the means by which human beings come to terms with the world and their place in it, still provided a precisely adequate representation of that world:

> In dieser ersten Haltung der Welt gegenüber besaßen die Worte und
> Sätze den Klang, die Farbe und erhellende Bedeutung der Poesie, war

> Sprache fähig, direkt die Welt zu bilden, um sie zu erschaffen, das heißt
> das Gesehene wiederzuerkennen und eingreifend zu verändern. (Öa, 39)

So, because human beings were able to describe their world in a way which was congruent
with its true nature, they could (somehow) control and change it. Yet, at some undefined
point, a kind of linguistic Fall occurred: '[eine Kluft] öffnete sich [zwischen] den Dingen
und ihren Namen' (Öa, 39). Language was no longer a tool which could represent the
world as it is, but human beings still needed a sense of being at home in a world; so with
the language which remained to them, divorced from its original function, they created a
number of means of re-imposing this lost sense of order and control upon their
surroundings. The three methods for achieving this are identified as follows: firstly, the
creation of dogma (i.e. a 'Welterklärung' which supports a claim to power); secondly, the
sciences, which attempt to create an 'Apparat der Begriffe' to describe the world; thirdly,
and finally, the arts:

> Die Künste [...] setzten neue Wirklichkeiten. Sie erfanden neue
> Sprachen und künstliche Welten, nicht um der Welt zu entgehen oder sie
> zu fliehen, sondern um ihrer habhaft zu werden. [...] Die erfundene
> Wirklichkeit der Kunst wirkt auf die tatsächliche zurück, erläutert und
> kommentiert sie, erklärt sie beruhigend und beunruhigend. Sie hebt die
> alltägliche und darum unsichtbare Wirklichkeit in unser Blickfeld. Sie
> erhellt (oder verdunkelt und verschönt) eine uns verwirrende Welt. (Öa,
> 40)

In all three cases, Hein sees language being used to bridge the gap between the world and
human understanding, creating an artificial order which can be imposed on a
disconcertingly chaotic reality. The difference between the first two cases and the third is
that art's model realities do not make the same kind of claim to truth evident in the case of
the sciences and dogma. Both of these are basically ideological forms of understanding in
that they are (in their different ways) mis-representations of the world, whilst claiming for
themselves the status of simple representations. Art too can function as an explanation of
the world, and can be comforting to the reader/viewer in this respect. However, as Hein's
other essays make clear, this is not the author's creative ideal.

For Hein, literature is a form of autobiography (see e.g. Öa, 34), yet not in the
narrow sense of a narrative based on the life of the author. Whilst experience is a
precondition for the creation of literature, literature is not the mere retelling of facts or
events, not an 'Ersatz von Publizistik' (AK, 101), but a process by which the author
attempts to bring the 'Welt auf den poetischen Begriff' (Öa, 12) or 'mit Kunst der Welt
beizukommen' (Öa, 99). The work of literature is therefore necessarily an ordering of the
world, but one which is personal to the author.

Hein frequently uses the term 'Makulatur' to denote literature which represents the
world to the reader in such a way that his or her already established means of making
sense of that world (i.e. his or her *ideological* understanding) is either left unchallenged or
has its validity reinforced (e.g. Öa, 13-14). This is attractive to the reader, Hein claims, in
that such literature caters to the human need to feel that one's values and one's means of
making sense of the world are indeed valid and stable ('das Bedürfnis nach sicheren
Werten' [Öa, 22]). Here, art and ideology meet, the former standing in the service of the
latter.

Hein provides one stark example from GDR schoolbooks, which introduce young readers to Mörike and Goethe, but not to contemporary authors describing contemporary experience: 'immer wieder läßt der Frühling sein blaues Band flattern, wenn auch die Lüfte inzwischen stark umweltbeschädigt sind' (Öa, 25). Hein's point here is more than the obvious one that eighteenth- and nineteenth-century poetry deals with the world of the eighteenth and nineteenth centuries. He is, rather, highlighting the use to which art can be put in providing an escape from possibly disturbing contemporary experience, falling back on more comforting, established representations of the world. As Hein writes in an essay on Walter Benjamin from 1986: 'immer, wenn gesellschaftliche, politische, technische oder künstlerische Entwicklungen uns verunsichern, ein Unbehagen in uns erregen, retten wir uns in eine Identität überkommener Werte, das heißt ausgenommener und respektierter, also fraglos gewordener Werte' (Öa, 167).

In this same essay, Hein considers the general inability of human beings to come to terms with the world of their experience. In order to describe this phenomenon, he distinguishes between reason and what, borrowing a phrase from Pascal, he refers to as the 'Vernunft des Herzens' (Öa, 168): the former is associated with 'Erkenntnis' (Öa, 168), whilst the latter is '[ein] beruhigend[er], beschönend[er] und verfälschend[er] Schleier über dem Erkannten', which we need in order to live with our experience (Öa, 171). Within the terms of my discussion, the 'Vernunft des Herzens' may sensibly be described as playing the role of ideology, in that it provides a framework within which the world can be readily understood, but one which also obscures the true nature of that world from us. Art and literature can either become engaged in merely reinforcing the ordering 'Vernunft des Herzens' (become 'Makulatur', as described above) or take on their proper role of breaking through this stable ideological understanding of the world.

Above all, 'Makulatur'-literature fails to fulfil the function of true literature in that it cannot be a catalyst for change. As already shown, the production of true literature is, for Hein, autobiography in the sense that it is born from the author's personal experience of the world, an experience regarded as incompatible with those received means of understanding that world (i.e. ideology) encapsulated in the phrase 'Vernunft des Herzens'. Yet, equally, the consumption of literary texts (whether 'Makulatur' or not) is also a matter of autobiography, in that the reader finds in the text a reflection of his or her own circumstances: 'Ich werde berührt, weil ich mich sehe, weil ich mich erkenne. [...] Das Kunstwerk, das ich betrachte, ist ein anderes als jenes, das der Künstler aus der Hand gab. Er sprach von sich, ich aber sehe mich' (AK, 51). The difference which Hein identifies is between works of literature which reflect the world back to the reader as he or she sees it already, reaffirming the 'Vernunft des Herzens' ('Makulatur'), and those which confront the reader with a representation which threatens the stability of this ideological understanding.

In 'Worüber man nicht reden kann, davon kann die Kunst ein Lied singen' (1985) (Öa, 43-56), this latter potential of literature is a particular concern. Here Hein proposes that it is not so much the experience of men and women which leads them to act, as the representations of that experience at their disposal:

> Ich bemerkte, daß [...] nicht notwendig das Ereignis, der Fakt, das Geschehen selbst als schön oder schrecklich, gut oder schlecht, schädlich oder hilfreich empfunden und bewertet wurde, sondern vielmehr der Bericht darüber. Eine mögliche, vorschnelle Erklärung

wäre: Durch diesen Bericht wurde das zu Berichtende öffentlich und konnte daher erst mit dem Erscheinen des Berichts wahrgenommen werden. Meine Erfahrung kann sich damit nicht zufrieden geben, da ich [...] bemerken mußte, daß wiederholt nicht das berichtete Ereignis, der genannte Zustand es war, sondern der Bericht selbst, die Chronik, die Beschreibung, die zu Aufsehen, zu Erregung, zu Maßnahmen führte. [...] Mehr noch: Die Lage, der Zustand, das Geschehen konnte allgemein bekannt sein und scheinbar hingenommen werden, das Benennen jedoch [...] führte zu einem Aufschrei der Freude oder des Schreckens und zu eingreifenden Maßnahmen. (Öa, 48)[6]

It is this very process which Hein claims to observe in the reception of his 1982 novella *Der fremde Freund* amongst the reading public. In the letters he receives, Hein registers a 'Betroffensein, so was bei sich selbst zu finden' and a 'heftiges Sichwehren, so zu werden, da hineinzurutschen' (Öa, 162-163). This is, for Hein, the one way in which literature can possess a 'pädagogischen Wert' (Öa, 162), in the sense that it forces the reader to see more clearly a situation which he or she too is experiencing (hence 'Betroffensein') and thereby to take action to change that situation, action manifested in the 'Sichwehren' Hein describes. Here, Hein is not claiming that the individual cannot see his or the true situation; rather, he observes how a state of affairs can be excluded from representation when it is incompatible with the individual's tried and tested means of describing the world. Thus 'Erkenntnis' loses its potential to change the way the individual understands the world and, in turn, change that world.

To return briefly to Hein's example of eighteenth- and nineteenth-century lyric poetry in twentieth-century schoolbooks, the point in this case would be that, even though the readers may be well aware that their environment is polluted, the fact that they are confronted only with representations of nature which do not touch upon this contemporary reality means that they are not forced to address the more disturbing aspects of the world in which they find themselves, a confrontation which, Hein suggests, would produce action for change. Thus Hein's version of ideology is perhaps best conceived of as a 'double consciousness'. Not to be confused with an Orwellian 'doublethink', in which the individual's senses perceive the world as he or she is told to perceive it,[7] Hein conceives of a form of ideology in which the world is experienced in one fashion, but described in another; it is the refusal to abandon or even adapt that description in the face of an incongruent reality which functions as an obstacle to change.

Christiane Lemke has spoken of a 'Doppelkultur' in the GDR, that is to say of an ever-widening gap between the ideology of the SED regime and the reality experienced by its citizens.[8] However, the SED had a fundamental need to maintain the dominance of its representations of the society it had created, a need bound up with the claim to power of Marxist-Leninist parties in the Eastern bloc in general. The legitimacy of the Marxist-Leninist party lay in its allegedly superior collective insight into the nature of society at any given stage in the class struggle.[9] As the 'vanguard party', the SED and others like it claimed the right to rule on the basis of this superior insight, so that any divergence of the real world from the world described in party ideology was tantamount to an undermining of that legitimacy.[10] The alternative, of course, when reality could not be made to live up to party ideology, was to maintain ideology's consistency by excluding aspects of reality from representation. Unfortunately, as Rudolf Bahro observes in *Die Alternative* (1977), this failure to face reality makes a mockery of the original function of the party as a 'soziales Erkenntnisorgan'.[11]

Similar points are taken up by another critic of 'real existing socialism', the Czech writer and dissident (and later President) Václav Havel. In his essay 'The Power of the Powerless' (1978), Havel paints a picture of a society ruled by state ideology, but in which not even the leaders believe in its validity; they are perfectly aware of realities which do not tally with their own description of the world, but their insistence that everyone behave *as if* state ideology were still a valid structure through which to describe reality is bound up with their claim to legitimate power. As Havel says, 'the centre of power is identical with the centre of truth'.[12] Because such regimes are forced to maintain the appearance of a total interpretation of the world in the face of a contradictory reality they are driven to implement repressive measures and falsify the past, the present and the future, becoming 'captive to [their] own lies'.[13] Here, as Havel states: 'The significance of phenomena no longer derives from the phenomena themselves, but from their locus as concepts in the ideological context'.[14]

Whilst Hein's essayistic texts emphasize how and why ideology must be challenged on a personal level, insisting that literature can help individuals to see their world more truly and, in doing so, help them to change it, Hein's fictional texts describing GDR society, such as *Der fremde Freund* or *Der Tangospieler* (1989), show how the desire of the individual to cling to a comforting yet erroneous representation of the world can exist alongside, and sometimes intersect with the state's need to defend an ideology which is equally divorced from the true state of affairs. Although the individual world view and the ideology of the state are seldom identical, the state's potential violence towards those who try to challenge its ideology is another obstacle to the individual's revision of his or her own 'Weltbild'.

One example of the interaction of state ideology and personal world view can be found in Hein's 'Die Vergewaltigung' (EK, 131-138), a short text originally written in 1988, but not published until December 1989.[15] Here, Hein tells the story of Ilona R., who, in the last days of the Second World War, is hidden by her grandmother as Russian soldiers enter their village. Her grandmother is raped, but the soldiers responsible are not brought to book. Ilona leaves her village the next year to begin a career in the civil service, moving to Berlin and eventually attaining a high-ranking post in one of the ministries. She is happy with her successful life until she is invited to be a guest speaker at a 'Jugendweihe' ceremony:

> Vor den festlich gekleideten Jugendlichen [...] stand Ilona [...] und sprach über den Tag der Befreiung vom Hitlerfaschismus und über die schweren Anfangsjahre der Republik. Sie berichtete, wie sie als Halbwüchsige die Niederlage der deutschen Wehrmacht erlebt hatte, vom Einmarsch der Sowjetsoldaten in ihrem Dorf und von der Erleichterung der Bauern, daß die Jahre der Nazibarbarei endlich vorbei waren. (EK, 135)

Ilona's version of events here is plainly far from being a true representation of her experience of the events of August 1945. Yet, when her husband (who knows the true story from Ilona herself) questions the version she gave in her speech, she insists 'es war alles die Wahrheit, was ich erzählte' (EK, 137). Nevertheless, when her husband continues to challenge her, she breaks down and, after calling him a 'fascist', has to be sedated. It is obvious to the reader that Ilona has not managed to come to terms with her grandmother's rape and the sense of guilt she must feel that the old woman sacrificed her own dignity for the sake of her. On the other hand, from the point of view of the GDR state, of which Ilona has become a functionary, it is taboo to talk publicly about any brutality by Russian soldiers towards the German population at the end of the war.

In order to avoid coming to terms with a painful personal experience, Ilona has adopted an ideology which represents the world in such a way that this experience need not be faced. However, the state-sponsored version of events which she subscribes to in order to achieve this is underwritten by the threat that those who challenge it will fall onto the wrong side of the friend/foe divide which, as Rolf Henrich points out, the SED regime was fond of cultivating.[16] The charge of being a 'fascist' which Ilona levels at her husband is simultaneously part of her attempt to maintain her own reassuring 'Vernunft des Herzens', which allows her to avoid the pain of dealing with her grandmother's rape, and also the state's threat of violence towards the dissenter who challenges its ideological representation of the past, a threat which Ilona may well feel herself. In this 'double consciousness', Ilona's childhood experience has not in any sense been erased; she is after all capable of telling her husband about it. Nevertheless, she maintains, as it were, an 'official' representation of her past when presenting her biography to others, much in the same way as the state maintains an official history which excludes certain events from representation. The motivations of the state and of Ilona are different, the former being concerned with its maintenance of power, and the latter attempting to avoid confronting painful personal experience, yet the techniques employed by both are comparable. Interestingly, it is the insistence of another on bringing the repressed back into representation (i.e. her husband's comments) which may allow Ilona to grieve. Thus it seems that she will be forced to reintegrate this experience into her 'Weltbild', a process which, within the terms of Hein's conception of ideology, may lead her to take action to change her situation. Will she be able, the reader asks, to remain a functionary of the state, given that any revision of her view of the past must also call into question the official account of history, and thus the authority of the SED regime? The husband in 'Die Vergewaltigung' can be said to play the role which Hein proposes for the author. He is the figure who insists on giving representation to experiences which other world-views ignore, thereby challenging their claim to describe the world.

As Gert Joachim Glaeßner has observed, state repression was the necessary condition of the GDR regime's maintenance of its own 'Festhalten an überholten Vorstellungen'.[17] Once it was unwilling or unable to use violence against its population, for whom the gap between the state ideology's description of their society and their experience of that society was all too clear, change could take place.[18] In 'Die Vergewaltigung' and elsewhere, Christoph Hein addresses the consequences of . this situation for individuals whose ideas about themselves and their situation are inadequate, but whose ability to revise those ideas and thus, possibly, change their circumstances involves them in a process which, if universalized, would represent a major challenge to the SED regime. Therefore, I would suggest, if Hein can help us to understand the GDR's 'Paradox von Stabilität und Revolution', then we must read his work as an exploration of the effect of state repression on the capacity of GDR citizens to come to terms with the world as individuals and as members of society.

NOTES

[1] Sigrid Meuschel, *Legitimation und Parteiherrschaft: Zum Paradox von Stabilität und Revolution in der DDR 1945-1989* (Frankfurt/M., 1992).

[2] Christoph Hein, *Öffentlich arbeiten* (Berlin, 1987), 13. I will refer to works by Christoph Hein using the following abbreviations and the relevant page number(s) in parentheses:

> *Öffentlich arbeiten* = Öa
> *Als Kind habe ich Stalin gesehen* (Berlin, 1992) = AK
> *Exekution eines Kalbes* (Berlin, 1996) = EK

[3] For an overview of the various different definitions of the term, see Jorge A. Larrain, *The Concept of Ideology* (Aldershot, 1992) and Terry Eagleton, *Ideology: An Introduction* (London, 1991).

[4] This conception of ideology describes 'a form of false consciousness or necessary deception which somehow distorts men's understanding of social reality: the cognitive value of ideas affected by ideology is called into question.' Larrain, *The Concept of Ideology*, p. 13f: [See note 3 above].

[5] 'Das Bewußtsein kann nie etwas anderes sein als das bewußte Sein, und das Sein der Menschen ist ihr wirklicher Lebensprozeß'. Karl Marx and Friedrich Engels, *Die deutsche Ideologie*, in *Werke* (Berlin, 1983), III, pp. 9-530 (p. 26).

[6] See also Hein's comments in Janice Murray and Mary-Elizabeth O'Brien, 'Interview mit Christoph Hein', *New German Review*, 3 (1987), 53-66 (p. 63): 'Erst wenn Unerträgliches benannt wird, wird es wahrhaft unerträglich. Es ist eine Erfahrung, die wir alle haben machen müssen, daß eben nicht der schreckliche, der tödliche Vorgang das Fürchterliche ist, sondern sein Benennen.'

[7] George Orwell, *Nineteen Eighty-Four* (Harmondsworth, 1989), p. 270.

[8] Christiane Lemke, *Die Ursachen des Umbruchs: Politische Sozialisation in der ehemaligen DDR* (Opladen, 1991).

[9] The idea of the privileged insight of communists can be traced as far back as Marx and Engels's *Manifest der Kommunistischen Partei* of 1848: 'Die Kommunisten sind [...] praktisch der entschiedenste, immer weiter treibende Teil der Arbeiterparteien aller Länder; sie haben theoretisch vor der übrigen Masse des Proletariats die Einsicht in die Bindungen, den Gang und die allgemeinen Resultate der proletarischen Bewegung voraus'. Marx and Engels, *Manifest der Kommunistischen Partei*, in *Werke*, IV, pp. 459-93 (p. 474) [see note 5 above]. For Lenin, in *What Is To Be Done?*, the party claims a theoretical understanding of the condition of the working class superior to that of the workers themselves: 'Class political consciousness can be brought to the workers *only from without*, that is, only from outside the economic struggle, from outside the sphere of relations between workers and employers.' V.I. Lenin, *What Is To Be Done?*, 3rd edn. (Moscow, 1964), p. 75.

[10] As Sigrid Meuschel observes, for example, 'eine marxistisch-leninistische Partei kann ihren Führungsanspruch auf Dauer nur plausibel machen und legitimatorisch absichern, wenn sie sich in der Lage zeigt, die selbstgesetzten Ziele und Aufgaben effektiv zu verfolgen.' *Legitimation und Parteiherrschaft*, p. 200 [See note 1 above].

[11] Rudolf Bahro, *Die Alternative: Zur Kritik des real existierenden Sozialismus* (Cologne, 1977), p. 292.

[12] Václav Havel, 'The Power of the Powerless', in *Open Letters: Selected Prose 1965-1990*, ed. by Paul Wilson (London, 1991), pp. 125-214 (p. 130).

[13] Ibid., p. 137.

[14] Ibid., p. 138.

[15] See William J. Niven, '"Das Geld ist nicht der Gral": Christoph Hein and the *Wende*', *Modern Language Review* 90, 1995 [3]: 688-706 (p. 691).

[16] Rolf Henrich, *Der vormundschaftliche Staat: Vom Versagen des real existierenden Sozialismus* (Hamburg, 1989), p. 193f.

[17] Gert-Joachim Glaeßner, 'Am Ende des Staatssozialismus – Zu den Ursachen des Umbruchs in der DDR', in *Zusammenbruch der DDR: Soziologische Analysen*, ed. by Hans Joas and Martin Kohli (Frankfurt/M., 1993), pp. 70-92 (p. 77).

[18] Ibid., p. 84.

Diana Alberghini

RE-DEFINING THE ROLE OF THE INTELLECTUAL AND THE FUNCTION OF LITERATURE. THE EXAMPLE OF HELGA KÖNIGSDORF

This article examines the reaction of Helga Königsdorf to transformations in the public sphere brought about by the Wende. *The analysis focuses on Königsdorf's re-definition both of her role as an intellectual and of the function of literature, exploring elements of continuity between her pre- and post-*Wende *literary production. In so doing, the article shows Königsdorf's incredible ability to regenerate herself and to grasp the new opportunities offered by the changed political framework. It is precisely the balance that she reaches between her pre- and post-*Wende *literary identity which makes her one of the most interesting case studies of this turbulent period of German history.*

'Was andere nicht lösten, sprachen die Autoren aus.'[1] Such a statement well summarises the role of the intellectuals in the public sphere during the GDR era. The Revolution of 1989 and the subsequent transformation of public discourse put an end to the function of the writer as mediator between the Party and the people. The SED was consigned to history and the openness generated by the *Wende* provided writers with new forums through which they could express themselves. One of the authors who made the best use of these opportunities is Helga Königsdorf. Her prolific production of articles, essays and speeches in the aftermath of the autumn 1989, collected in the two works *1989 oder Ein Moment Schönheit* and *Aus dem Dilemma eine Chance machen*,[2] is evidence of the author's desire to participate constructively in this unprecedented period of transition and to continue the struggle to bring the socialist dream closer to realisation, even when the majority of the GDR population began to see unification as the only valid alternative.

In my examination of this period, misleadingly described by Wolf Lepenies as marking 'das Desaster der interpretierenden Klasse',[3] I will firstly concentrate on the phase of self-questioning which Königsdorf underwent when the GDR system started to crumble. As the crisis unfolded, she felt the need to re-assess separately the many layers of her complex identity – as citizen, Party member, writer and scientist. After exploring her intimate self in such depth, she gains the courage to accept her feelings and to formulate her thoughts on the changing situation with great lucidity. I will focus on how the new awareness achieved by Königsdorf impacted on her understanding of her role as an intellectual as well as of the function of literature, which she now sees as fulfilling the dual purpose of warning and encouraging its readers, the *Kassandra-Funktion*, which she first defined in 1987. Then, after describing the process of adaptation which Königsdorf goes through, I will try to assess the extent to which she managed to retain an element of continuity between her pre- and post-*Wende* literary production. This discussion of the dimension of continuity in her works will enable me to retrace her literary development through the turbulent waters of the *Wende*.

The role of the intellectuals in the GDR

Prior to the Revolution of 1989, many writers in the GDR operated within a very ambiguous space between state censorship, their commitment to the socialist cause and their determination to expose the failings of state socialism as practised in the GDR. If on the one hand they let literature be exploited as a *Leitmedium* which had to fulfil a very important political educational task, on the other hand they were one of the only groups in society who had the possibility, however limited this was, to articulate constructive opposition. In a country where basic freedoms such as that of the press existed only on paper,[4] one of the main privileges enjoyed by the intellectuals was what Königsdorf called their 'Narrenfreiheit', which arose from literature being ascribed the *Ersatzfunktion* of replacing journalism.[5]

Apart from having been doubly privileged in the GDR as a highly regarded mathematician and as a published writer, Helga Königsdorf does not represent in any way an exception to this general image of East German intellectuals. She was, in fact, one of those concerned voices who through her works repeatedly challenged the establishment in the attempt to promote critical thinking among her readers. In her pre-*Wende* collections of short stories,[6] she does not hesitate to draw attention to the lack of creativity and solidarity, to the excessive bureaucracy and the general stagnation characterising GDR society in the Honecker era. To cite an example, the protagonist of 'Sachschaden'[7] is the only one who offers some human warmth to the young boy who, in an accident with his scooter, has damaged a car. In a society supposedly based on solidarity, everyone else seems to be uniquely concerned about the cost the car owner will have to bear. Alternatively, if we look at 'Eine Idee und ich',[8] one story amongst the many located within the GDR's scientific community – so very familiar to the author –, we see how the obsession with planning can lead to stagnation. At the same time, Königsdorf was a firm believer in the socialist model, as demonstrated by the support she continued to offer the SED by remaining a member until it was dissolved in January 1990.

As a consequence of the fact that literature assumed the task of replacing journalism by throwing light on the real problems of the country and on the shortcomings of socialism as practised by the SED, the status of the intellectuals was elevated to that as moral authorities in the eyes of the readers, who had only limited access to sources of critical information within the GDR. At the same time, the importance the intellectuals came to assume became one of the driving forces behind their motivation to commit themselves with ever growing dedication to their job. In this framework, the relationship between readers and writers became one of mutual dependency, in which the two parts felt united by a very special bond of trust. Königsdorf, for example, affirms that writing means for her 'gemeinsam mit dem Leser "Ich" sagen. Und "Ich" sogar wieder in Frage stellen' (E 9).

However, despite her desire to get close to her readership and to engage in a productive dialogue with them, Königsdorf also points to a general failure of the same readers to see the human side of the intellectuals: 'Man fühlt sich ausgeliefert, machtlos wie er [the reader], und braucht, genauso wie er, Trost' (E 8). Even if Königsdorf does admit having enjoyed the very reassuring feeling of 'gebraucht werden' (by the readers), she also stresses the less positive implication of such a role. The high level of expectations placed on the intellectuals by the public was often experienced by writers like her as a very oppressive burden:

> Mißbraucht wurden wir von den Lesern, die uns als Vorhut in die
> Schlacht schickten, die unsere Geschichten nicht als Geschichten,
> sondern als Offenbarungen lasen. Die vorgaben, es wären
> Offenbarungen, um sich selbst nicht offenbaren zu müssen (A 81).

The end of an era: how Helga Königsdorf has re-defined her role as an intellectual
With the fall of the Wall in 1989 and the subsequent emergence of new forums in which
the public could finally voice its opinion after forty years of enforced silence, the general
conditions which had shaped the specific role played by GDR intellectuals ceased to
apply. One of the results of the transformation of the public sphere was the collapse of the
relationship of dependency between readers and writers who also saw their status of moral
authorities seriously challenged by the preference now shown by the readers for
newspapers rather than books. Furthermore, the fact that during the Revolution of 1989
most of the intellectuals spoke in favour of seizing the opportunity to create a truly
socialist society, on the basis of their faith in the reformability of the system, contributed
massively to enlarging the gulf between creative writers and citizens. In the light of this
new situation, the intellectuals could not have but felt disorientated.

Disorientation is also the word one could use to describe Königsdorf's first
reaction to the events of 1989. It was not long, however, before the author realised that the
loss of the intellectuals' established position of power was outweighed by the
opportunities it gave them to define new roles for themselves. Moreover, the fact that the
newspapers had ceased to be an instrument in the hands of the SED also meant that the
writers themselves now had a new forum in which they could freely contribute to debate.
As demonstrated by Königsdorf's copious production of articles and essays around the
time of the *Wende* in the two volumes already mentioned, she did not take long to exploit
these new open spaces to express her ideas. My analysis shows that her non-fictional
writings of this period testify to her capability to adapt and regenerate herself, without
necessarily renouncing her past ideas, above all with regard to the function of literature.
Indeed, she manages to create a distinctive space for herself in which her past positions
blend in with the changed situation and prove capable of further development. In this
sense, therefore, we can talk of a change as far as the manner in which she approaches the
public is concerned, but it is one which co-exists with the continuity of her literary
identity. In the following paragraphs I will concentrate on the devices employed by
Königsdorf in re-defining her role in the public sphere.

Before being able to make the most of these changes, she urgently needed to
reassess her past role. What triggered off a process of profound self-questioning in the case
of Königsdorf is a public debate she went to hear in the Erlöser-Kirche on 28 October
1989 in Berlin entitled 'Gegen den Schlaf der Vernunft'. After this experience, in an
article bearing the title 'Der Schlaf der Vernunft' published on 17 November 1989 in the
Wochenpost, she attempts to come to terms with the fact that she has allowed the regime,
at least to a certain extent, to walk over her sense of dignity as a human being. Her
rationality, her capacity to criticise and judge independently, and above all to act as a
thinking subject seems to have been brought back to life by the Revolution, after a long
period of lethargy. When reflecting on her creative writing she makes the bitter discovery:
'Trotzdem blieb es eine Kunstwelt, in der zwar jede Figur etwas von mir hatte, aber doch
niemals ich war, sondern bereits ein repariertes Ich' (E 58). After this realisation, she has
the courage to drop the mask behind which her subjectivity had been confined all these

years, and to reveal her real self. One thing which has helped her to gain this new sense of self-confidence is the example given by the GDR's people who, in successfully carrying out the Revolution, had individually shown their determination to act for themselves. Looking around she proudly observes: 'Die Menschen in unserem Land sind schöner geworden. Sie tragen den Kopf anders, mit einem neuen Selbstbewußtsein' (E 98).

Therefore, in the light of this new sense of *Selbstbewußtsein* felt by the people, the first step taken by Königsdorf is to renounce her role as a spokesperson. Given the previous interdependency of readers and writers to which I have already referred, this decision to give up her task as a mediator between the Party and the citizen could not have been made without experiencing pain, resulting from the recognition that this role has become redundant. Despite this sense of loss, Königsdorf realises the importance of talking on her own behalf. Her determination in wanting to speak exclusively for herself is particularly evident in her political speeches. Here, with statements such as 'Ich spreche hier zu euch nicht im Namen, im Auftrag, . . . Nein, ich spreche hier in meinem Namen' (E 83), she leaves no doubt that she has now dropped the role which she had assumed during the GDR era. By speaking in the first person, she can keep expressing her personal opinions and it is also thanks to this stratagem that she will become one of the most active intellectuals during the *Wende*.

Furthermore, it is also important to observe that the painful process of self-analysis she undergoes allows her to present a regenerated image of herself to the public. She achieves this through a process in which all her many different and often conflicting identities – the writer, the scientist, the Party member and the private citizen – have been profoundly examined in isolation and then brought together again. In this manner, she reaches a full awareness of the complexity of her personality, in which her different identities can continue to co-exist. In her writings of the *Wende* period, she confronts her multi-voiced subjectivity and provides a full insight into the dialogue that she has been conducting among her various identities.

This is, for instance, the case in *1989 oder Ein Moment Schönheit*, in which the readership is presented with the network of connections between the private and the public, the political and the personal self. This collage of articles, personal and open letters, political speeches and poems offers evidence of the author's desire to reveal herself in a completely authentic way as well as to leave a document to posterity, in which not only the facts but also the feelings that accompanied the *Wende* can be sampled. By ordering official and personal documents chronologically, with a precision befitting her scientific background, Königsdorf manages to present us with a unique account of the *Wende*, in which her ideas on politics, literature and science are humanised by their interconnection with her most intimate feelings. Thus, among her political reflections, one finds poems such as the following one:

> Weit entfernt von mir
> Muß ich mich finden
> Wie kam ich nur
> In dieses fremde Kleid
> Ich bin das Blatt
> In allen Winden
> Niemand hält mich
> Keiner schreit

Von dem Augenblick
Dem schönen
Blieb mir nur
Der falsche Schein
Und der Mut
Zu stolzen Tönen
Wird mir bald
Verkommen sein
Bin das Blatt
In allen Winden
Längst vergessen
Wer ich war
Nur die Schellenklänge
Künden
Was ich bin
Ich bin ein Narr (E 144).

Königsdorf's understanding of literature before and after the *Wende*

Having renounced her role as a spokesperson and having acknowledged the changed
relationship between readers and writers, Königsdorf also feels compelled to re-assess her
conception of literature. Moving away from the initial sadness provoked by the idea of not
being needed any longer, she understands that if in what remains of the GDR they are to
build a society qualitatively superior to its predecessor, there will still be the necessity for
public figures to provide an intellectual stimulus: 'Wir werden gebraucht.
Gebrauchtwerden deutet immer auf ein Defizit. Sagen wir also: Wir werden wieder
gebraucht werden. Leider' (A 11). In this sense, she remains attached to the notion of
committed literature, but one in which the focus of the commitment has now changed
significantly. If during the SED regime, critical literature had to contribute to the
realisation of a truly socialist society, now, in a period of transition such as the *Wende*, it
should foster, according to Königsdorf, the promotion of a framework of values aimed at
ensuring respect for human dignity, which should serve as the foundation of the new
democratic society replacing the GDR. She defines the new role of the writers in the
following words:

> Ein Neuanfang muß auch ein moralischer Neuanfang sein [...] Hier
> haben wir [the intellectuals] eine große Aufgabe. Die Aufgabe, den
> Menschen mit seiner Würde wieder in seine Rechte einzusetzen. Wir
> haben mitzuwirken, daß aus der gewonnenen „Leichtigkeit" in unserem
> Land keine ‚unerträgliche Leichtigkeit'[9] wird. (E 99)

The mistake would be, however, in Königsdorf's view, to ascribe tasks to literature
which it is not designed to fulfil. Literature can at last cast off the *Ersatzfunktion* it had
been forced to take on in the GDR. In her opinion, while journalism should be ideally
devoted to providing information for its readership in a fully transparent manner (E 740),
literature is seen as one of the key elements in the development of a critical culture. To
quote Königsdorf again:

> Sie [die Literatur] kann mit Möglichkeiten spielen und Modelle für das
> Beurteilen von Wirklichkeit anbieten. Mit ihrer Sensibilität für
> Erscheinungen kann sie auf alle Probleme der Welt sehr schnell

reagieren. Sie kann also vorpreschen und unbequem sein. Wird sie aber
als Vorhut allein gelassen, wird ihr gar alles mögliche angetragen, was
ihre Sache nicht ist, gerät sie leicht in zwielichtige Situationen. (E 78f.)

Another important aspect of creative writing on which Königsdorf focuses is what
the author defines as the *Kassandra-Funktion* of literature. This concept is explained by
the author as follows: [Literature should be] 'Eine Kassandra, die nichts beschönigt und
die trotzdem ermutigt, sich gegen das Unheil zu wehren' (E 8). An example illustrating the
manner in which she put such a concept into practice after the *Wende* is provided by a
letter written on 3 November 1989 in which, with extraordinary lucidity, she predicts the
end of the GDR's era and the intellectuals' loss of their specific role:

Ich habe immer gewarnt, daß wir Schriftsteller mit unserer Forderung
nach Glasnost uns selbst das Wasser abgraben. Was soll denn aus uns
werden, wenn unsere Narrenfreiheit plötzlich für alle gilt? Und wenn die
Leute schon mit dem Lesen von Zeitungen hinreichend zu tun haben.
Aber es wollte niemand auf mich hören (E 79).

In this regard, it is crucial to underline the fact that Königsdorf evolved her view of
the *Kassandra-Funktion* of literature before the events of 1989. The essay in which she
first formulates this concept is, in fact, dated 1987. This is therefore an important element
of continuity linking Königsdorf's works written prior to the 1989 Revolution with those
published after the *Wende*. Such a continuity across a time in which East Germany
witnessed a profound political change was made possible precisely by Königsdorf's notion
of the need for literature to be committed. Starting from the assumption that in every type
of society there is room for improvement, Königsdorf's idea of literature as a means of
fostering critical culture becomes one which does not owe its validity to a specific political
or cultural framework, and therefore can be sustained even after the earthquake which
provoked the collapse of the GDR. In the next paragraphs, I will concentrate on
Königsdorf's publications after the *Wende* in order to show how she managed to maintain
her literary identity.

Examples of continuity
To begin with, it can be argued that all the articles and essays written by Königsdorf
during and after the *Wende* have this *Kassandra-Funktion* in mind. To cite an example, if
we take into consideration the articles she published on the subject of unification, we can
see how Königsdorf points to the possible dangers – such as the rise of intolerance towards
everything which does not conform to the norm – contained in such a process, which takes
too little account of the needs and the feelings of human beings as individuals. At the same
time, her conclusion is always very encouraging as she tirelessly urges both East and West
Germans to make an effort in order to tear down all the barriers created by a forty-year
long separation: 'Jetzt kommt die Flut. Bauen wir also gemeinsam Dämme, damit aus der
Welle keine Sintflut wird' (A 90).

Another instance of this *Kassandra-Funktion* is the way in which she tackles
scientific issues in relation to contemporary society. In *Über die unverzügliche Rettung der
Welt*[10] she analyses how global problems resulting from the destruction of the natural
environment could once and for all mean the end of our existence. In this case, her specific
purpose in listing all the dangers faced by the planet Earth is to provoke fear, so that her
readers might start to assume their responsibilities and mobilise themselves to improve

today's conditions. After having stimulated her readers by means of provocation to become aware of the gravity of the present situation, she reassures and encourages them at the end by expressing her optimistic view on the possibility of bringing about radical change. In the above-mentioned collection of articles, for instance, her last line, after a plethora of warnings, reads more reassuringly: 'Die Welt ist rettbar'.[11]

This technique based on the provocation of fear in order to stimulate action is familiar to Königsdorf's readers. She first used it in her prosework *Respektloser Umgang* published in 1986 in which she describes 'Angst aus Wissen' as the stimulus for the 'Mobilisierung der Humanität'.[12] The element of continuity in this specific case is all the more noticeable as in her articles published both in *1989 oder Ein Moment Schönheit* and several years later in *Über die unverzügliche Rettung der Welt*, she articulates the same concepts in approximately the same words as in *Respektloser Umgang*: 'Denn es ist vielleicht der gefährlichste Mythos dieses wissenschaftlichen Jahrhunderts, wir könnten mit der Hilfe der Wissenschaft jede Suppe auslöffeln, die wir uns einbrocken' (E 13).[13]

However, this aspect of continuity does not only involve concepts and ideas. Even some of the character types in her short stories written before the 1989 Revolution are to be found again in her post-*Wende* literary production. *Der Alte*, for example – who first appeared as the main character in 'Autodidakten',[14] published in 1982 and then in *Im Schatten des Regenbogens* which came out only in 1993 – is the same type of person in both works, as demonstrated by the fact that both characters have the same educational background and profession, and belong to the same generation. While in his first incarnation he had been introduced by Königsdorf in order to criticise the science establishment in the GDR, in her second work we find him struggling to adapt himself to the changes brought about by unification. The themes of this more recent work are more specific to the time of transition which the country is going through – for instance the loss of identity, the search for *Heimat*, the disempowerment of women etc. – but presented through the eyes of a character whom we have already encountered before the *Wende*. This stratagem has the effect of giving readers, especially if they have not directly experienced the *Wende*, a comprehensive idea of the impact of the events of 1989/90 on the daily life of individual East German citizens.

Conclusion

Through her instinctive understanding of the significance of the transformation of the public sphere, Helga Königsdorf is amongst those intellectuals who reacted most promptly to the new opportunities offered by the *Wende*. After having re-assessed her past, Königsdorf finds the courage to reveal the full complexity of her sense of subjectivity. Thus, we are confronted with a human being who is trying to re-establish contact with her own feelings in a period of great historical turmoil. The result is, as demonstrated by her non-fictional writings, her regeneration through the dialogue she engages in with her various conflicting identities, in which she involves her readers. By dropping her function of spokesperson, Königsdorf manages to re-define her role as an intellectual.

For Königsdorf, the *Wende* was a time which offered an extraordinary chance to build a new democratic society, and represented a moment of great inspiration for the author. Not only did it finally give her the opportunity to abandon that 'repariertes Ich', which now she recognises as having been derogatory towards herself and her readers; it also allowed her to contribute to the debate on the shape which this new society should take. In spite of the enthusiasm she felt as a witness of each stage in the *sanfte Revolution*, she does not lose her lucidity in the frenzy of this period of radical change. By sustaining her understanding of the *Kassandra-Funktion* of literature, she shows her continuing awareness of the potential dangers which could once again lead to the loss of respect for human dignity within society. Her critical attitude is therefore a feature of her past as well as her present literary identity. The fact that she had the courage to face up to her feelings and to invite us to share her dilemmas should be admired. Indeed, the importance of this openness is perhaps best expressed by the statement which became Königsdorf's motto during the *Wende*: 'Nur wer nicht handelt, macht keine Fehler' (E 82).

NOTES

[1] Christel Berger, 'Konsequenzen in der Zukunft', *Berliner Zeitung*, 1 November 1989, p. 7, cited by Jean E. Conacher, 'Pressing for Change: The Case of Helga Königsdorf', in Elizabeth Boa and Janet Wharton (eds.), *Women and the Wende* (Amsterdam, 1994), p. 165

[2] Helga Königsdorf, *1989 oder Ein Moment Schönheit*, Berlin and Weimar, 1990 and Helga Königsdorf, *Aus dem Dilemma eine Chance machen*, Hamburg and Zurich, 1991. I will refer in the text to these two works using respectively the abbreviations 'E' and 'A'.

[3] See Wolfgang Emmerich, *Kleine Literaturgeschichte der DDR* (Leipzig, 1996), p. 458

[4] See Article 27 of the GDR Constitution, *Verfassung der Deutschen Demokratischen Republik von 7. Oktober 1974*, Berlin, 1974, as quoted by Jean E. Conacher, see footnote 1.

[5] The media in the GDR were under the strict control of the Central Committee (ZK) of the SED. To have an idea of the pressure exercised by the state control on the media, see for example Monika Maron, *Flugasche* (Frankfurt am Main, 1981).

[6] The collections of short stories I refer to here are *Meine ungehörigen Träume* (Berlin and Weimar, 1990) (first published in 1978), *Der Lauf der Dinge* (Berlin and Weimar, 1996) (first published in 1982) and *Lichtverhältnisse* (Berlin and Weimar, 1988).

[7] Included in *Lichtverhältnisse*, pp. 33-9.

[8] Included in *Meine ungehörigen Träume*, pp. 77-87

[9] This is a clear allusion to the work by Milan Kundera, *The Unbearable Lightness of Being*. A further allusion to this work can be found in Helga Königsdorf, *Gleich neben Afrika* (Berlin, 1992), p. 81: 'Wir waren Kreuzritter, denen der Glaube abhanden gekommen war. Und ohne den Glauben war der Mord plötzlich Mord'. Such a statement can be seen as an echo of Kundera's words in *The Unbearable Lightness of Being*, London, 1985 (first published 1984), p. 176: 'Anyone who thinks that the Communist regimes of Central Europe are exclusively the work of criminals is overlooking a basic truth: the criminal regimes were made not by criminals but by enthusiasts convinced they had discovered the only road to paradise. They defended that road so valiantly that they were forced to execute many people. Later it became clear that there was no paradise, that the enthusiasts were therefore murderers'.

[10] Helga Königsdorf, *Über die unverzügliche Rettung der Welt* (Berlin and Weimar, 1994).

[11] Ibid, p. 122

[12] See Helga Königsdorf, *Respektloser Umgang* (Berlin and Weimar, 1988) (first published in 1986), p. 94.

[13] See also Helga Königsdorf, *Respektloser Umgang*, p .93 and *Über die unverzügliche Rettung der Welt*, p. 38.

[14] Included in *Der Lauf der Dinge*, pp. 159-179.

SECTION TWO

THE VISUAL ARTS

Wilfried van der Will

INTRODUCTION

In looking back at the legacy of art in the former GDR it is obvious that it was not exclusively beholden to the dogmas of socialist realism. The fundamental tenets of that prescription kept being repeated by the cultural ideologues of the GDR throughout its history. Irrespective of periods of 'thaw' and perceived leniency towards 'deviant' artistic practices in both art and literature, an atmosphere of taboo pervaded the consciousness of all practitioners. This remained in place even when at times any such taboos appeared officially to be revoked. Artists and writers, reluctant to understand themselves as dissidents, tried to preserve for their creativity spaces of relative autonomy. Naturally this posed problems since creative individuals were having to work within an envelope of ideological hegemony formatted by the organs of the state and the representatives of the ruling party in the spheres of art and literary criticism. The more that these agencies monotonously repeated the official articles of faith, the more tempting it was for independent spirits to test their validity and inherent limits of tolerance. The creative intelligentsia's idea of socialism deviated increasingly from that of 'really existing socialism'. Although writers and artists by and large felt committed to socialist-humanist positions and hence had no difficulty testifying to anti-capitalist sentiments, a cat-and-mouse game arose between the authorities and the artists over the latter's styles of depiction. Strategies of outwitting the never officially acknowledged presence of censorship inevitably brought the artists close to acting in seeming conformity with it. However, the heritage of early twentieth-century European modernism, from impressionism to expressionism, dada and surrealism – indicted as movements of bourgeois decadence and symptoms of capitalist societies in decline – proved a remarkably strong source of inspiration for visual art in the GDR. Official expectations of party-political partisanship, the projection of positive socialist heroes, the glorification of the world of material production, the pictorial constraints of realism, socialist or otherwise, were undercut or ignored to such an extent that at least for tactical purposes the state was constantly forced to moderate the potential fierceness of its negative sanctions. While it is clear that examples of abstract art, so prevalent in the West, were rare or absent in the GDR, modes of representation and depiction inspired by early and high modernism were very common. The large exhibition in the Altes Museum in Berlin (3 October to 31 December 1979), celebrating the 30th anniversary of the GDR, is good evidence for this. It was organised by the Ministry for Culture, the Association of Visual Artists of the GDR and the top echelons of the East German Trade Union Federation. Apart from obligatory examples of socialist realism (e.g. *Monteur* by Karl Erich Müller, 1964; *Chemiearbeiter am Schaltpult* by Willi Sitte, 1968; *Schweißer* by Volker Stelzmann, 1971) the catalogue, *Weggefährten, Zeitgenossen. Bildende Kunst aus drei Jahrzehnten*, amply illustrates the propensity towards stark mythical symbolism and allegory (e.g. *Kain*, 1965, *Die Flucht des Sysiphos*, 1972, and *Liebespaar*, 1970, by Wolfgang Mattheuer) as well as the presence of Ernst Barlach (e.g. Theo Balden, *Zeitungsleser*, 1967) and Wilhelm Lembruck (e.g. Hans Steger, *Aufsteigende*, 1968) in sculpture, Käthe Kollwitz in drawing (e.g. Max Uhlig's *Fischerfrauen bei der Arbeit*, 1966) or impressionist techniques in the paintings of Willi Sitte.

Yet despite a certain pluralism of styles in the GDR the relationship between artists and the state remained precarious and could all too easily result in isolation or departure to the West, as is demonstrated by the two essays that follow.

Astrid Ihle

FRAMING SOCIALIST RECONSTRUCTION IN THE GDR: *WOMEN UNDER SOCIALISM* – A DISCUSSION OF THE FRAGMENTS OF A DOCUMENTARY PROJECT BY THE PHOTOGRAPHER EVELYN RICHTER

This paper will discuss a documentary project by Leipzig-based photographer Evelyn Richter, focussing on the lives and working conditions of women under socialism, with particular emphasis on the female industrial worker. This independent documentary project, which Richter initiated herself and embarked upon in the late 1950s – motivated by the wish critically to evaluate socialist imperatives against individually experienced reality – will be analysed in terms of the conditions of photographic practice within GDR visual culture in the late 1950s/early 1960s. In particular, Richter's photographs of female industrial workers will be discussed in relation to official images of womanhood, as they were being propagated by the East German press and mass media at that time. Sketching out its original framework of production, this paper attempts to highlight the work's inherent, if not explicitly articulated, challenge to officially endorsed state culture.

In the late 1950s Leipzig-based photographer Evelyn Richter (b.1930) embarked upon a long-term photographic exploration of the lives and working conditions of women under socialism, with particular focus on the female industrial worker. This documentary project, which Richter, then working free-lance as a commercial photographer, initiated herself – motivated by the wish critically to evaluate socialist imperatives against individually experienced reality – did not go unnoticed by the cultural authorities. Disregarding the photographer's critical ambition, Richter was asked by a publishing house to collaborate on the publication of a state-commissioned book documenting the lives of women under socialism.[1] With the building of the Berlin Wall in 1961, however, this project came to an abrupt end, dismissed by the official authorities as no longer a political priority. As a consequence, Richter's photographs of women in the new state-owned industry were never published in that form. It was not before the late 1970s, early 1980s – when photography officially emancipated itself from its subservient role as 'ideological tool' and was granted the equally problematic status of an autonomous means of 'artistic creation' – that some of these photographs were re-discovered and made available to a wider public, albeit in a very different form and context: as single unrelated photographs, serving different curatorial agendas, either on museum walls or in revisionist surveys of the history of GDR photography, appropriating and legitimising a certain strand of humanist documentary work, into which Richter's photographs were unquestionably assimilated.[2]

Singled out and 'iconised', the photograph *An der Linotype* (Fig. 1) has since then become one of Richter's most widely publicised images, lauded today as a forceful symbol for what is now considered the highly problematic discourse and practice of the socialist emancipation of women.[3] But what, if anything, does this picture tell us about its original meaning(s), i.e. the terms of its reception and ramifications, the conditions of photographic practice within GDR visual culture, or the actual lives and working conditions of women under socialism? Taking this photograph as my point of departure for a closer analysis of Richter's documentary work, I intend briefly to sketch out and analyse its original framework of production, in order to pose the question: what made such an independent project *different*, challenging and possibly subversive of officially endorsed state culture?

Set in relation to an emerging photographic tradition in the GDR, as it was articulated through the normative discourse of socialist realism, Richter's work will be analysed in terms of the conditions of photographic practice within East German visual culture as they presented themselves to a young woman photographer who came of age during the 1950s, and, committed to a socially engaged documentary practice, appropriated the camera for an exploration of her own interests and concerns. In terms of subject matter – the female industrial worker – Richter's photographs would have been easy to assimilate into the official canon of socialist images of womanhood that were propagated by the East German press and mass media throughout the 1950s and 1960s: from the *Trümmerfrauen* of the immediate post-war period to the socialist work brigades of the new state-owned industry, encompassing the agrarian worker of the LPG[4] as well as the now legendary female 'tractorist' – representations of women proliferated across a wide range of discourses and signifying systems, constantly converging, interacting, and cross-referring to create a dense texture of meaning for the terms 'woman' and 'socialism' (Fig. 2). While seemingly adhering to the imagery of socialist reconstruction that was officially encouraged and rewarded, Richter's photographs of female industrial workers distinguish themselves through a subtle disruption of accepted codes and conventions, producing unexpected slippages and shifts of meanings, which – inadvertently or not – allow the viewer to peer beneath the veneer of socialist rhetoric, and articulate the photographer's privileged subjective perception.

1.

Richter's photographic beginnings in Leipzig fall into the highly dichotomised cold-war climate of the 1950s which saw the streamlining and (re-)politicising of culture in the GDR on a hitherto unprecedented level under the doctrine of Soviet-style socialist realism. Its ideological and aesthetic principles, as laid down by Andrei Zhdanov at the Soviet writers' congress in 1934, were indiscriminately applied to all areas of cultural production, including the mass media and photography. Photography's field of signification was thus clearly delimited, on the one hand, by the proper socialist content – as defined by the triad of *ideinost, partiinost,* and *narodnost* – and by restrictive aesthetic codes, based on the principles of 19th century realism, on the other.[5] Modernist avant-garde traditions of the 1920s and early 1930s, which had explored the medium's inherent visual and technical possibilities, were branded as 'formalist' and banned from the official context, surviving only in certain niches.[6] The formalism-realism debate, which determined cultural policies throughout the 1950s, imposed on photographic practice formal and practical constraints which had important consequences for the medium's application, function and status within GDR visual culture. On the one hand, photography subsisted in the form of a second-rank 'artistic', popular amateur pastime; on the other, its seemingly 'evidential

Fig. 1

Evelyn Richter
An der Linotype
B/w photograph
Berlin, c. 1959
Photo: courtesy of the artist

Fig. 2

Walter Arnold
Traktoristin
Bronze
1952
Photo: Staatliche Galerie Moritzburg Halle,
Landeskunstmuseum Sachsen-Anhalt

force', as Roland Barthes puts it, was fully exploited to serve explicitly defined political ends in the service of cold-war propaganda.[7] Photography's ostensible immediacy, as well as its persuasiveness to act as an authentic historical record made it seem predestined to play a critical role as 'ideological tool'. Bound up in the cold war context, GDR photojournalism of the 1950s was expected to produce positive forward-looking images to help promote the blueprint of a new socialist society. Following the Stalinist legacy of staged and manipulated photomontages, based on Anatoly Lunacharsky's definition of photography as 'not merely a chemically treated plate – but a profound act of social and psychological *creation*',[8] photography was self-consciously used, in the hands of the party, to give visual expression to a predetermined notion of 'social(ist) reality' set by firm social, political, and ideological codes. Independent initiatives, which set out to stretch the rigid framework of photography's field of signification, were viewed with suspicion by the cultural authorities. Photography's potential not only to create but also disrupt the monosemic consensus that constituted 'socialist reality' – what Barthes refers to as 'the fundamental polysemy of photographic images'[9] – especially made the realist documentary mode seem a precarious form. Discredited as 'naturalistic', the socially engaged documentary style of the immediate post-war period was no longer encouraged due to its perceived lack of a clearly defined sense of *Parteilichkeit*. Instead, photographers were exhorted to make a 'critical and creative selection of reality' based on firm Marxist-Leninist principles.[10] Still there were, at least for a short period of time, concentrated efforts among young GDR photographers who came of age during the 1950s, such as Arno Fischer in Berlin or Ursula Arnold in Leipzig, to forge a photographic practice which was felt to be more authentic and truthful to life, freed from restrictive aesthetic codes and the instrumental demands of political propaganda.

After a private training at the studio of traditional portrait photographer Pan Walther in Dresden, and brief professional experience as a photographer for an optical company, Richter enrolled in 1953 at the *Hochschule für Grafik und Buchkunst* in Leipzig, the only art academy that offered a photographic training at that time. However, the *Hochschule*'s programmatic emphasis on socialist realism, as well as the course's practical orientation towards the medium's reproductive and illustrative function, constituted a source of conflict and frustration for Richter.[11] The realisation that 'realism' in photography did not mean to search for what is new in socialist society through a close observation of everyday life, but to illustrate what was postulated as 'typical' by means of staged and manipulated images, was unacceptable to Richter who rejected what she perceived as the falsification of reality in official discourse. Formal experimentation as well as the photographer's proclaimed interest in developments in the Western part of Germany, in particular Otto Steinert's *Subjektive Fotografie* in Essen, finally prompted Richter's premature dismissal from the *Hochschule* in 1956. Disillusioned with her educational experience, she then joined together with other like-minded photographers in Leipzig to form the group *action fotografie* in 1956 which drew its inspiration, both stylistically and conceptually, to a large extent from international developments – such as *magnum*'s 'human interest' photography – which were filtered through to them through catalogues and exhibitions. Notably Edward Steichen's *The Family of Man*, which toured West Berlin in 1955, left a strong impression on young GDR photographers.[12] Although the group was short-lived, sabotaged by state-administered interventions and control, it was enthusiastically received while it was around as written comments both by the general public (who saw it as 'liberating and inspiring'), and the press (who lauded its 'courage to experiment') seem to suggest.[13]

2.

Richter's photographic work of the late 1950s should be seen in terms of the photographer's development of a highly personal, conceptually-minded realist style which was stimulated by the perceived necessity to break up the positivism of official discourse and introduce a subjective, possibly critical view into photographic practice. After her ex-matriculation from the *Hochschule*, Richter earned a living with routine assignments for the theatre and the industrial fair in Leipzig. Working full-time as a commercial photographer, Richter's personal work was often directly inspired by and carried out in those same locations to which she was sent as a free-lance photographer. These included 'semi-public' spaces such as the industrial sector to which she would not normally have had access. Before long, Richter started to invest these routine assignments with personal interests and concerns. In the case of the industrial sector her focus of attention were the overworked women toiling at dangerously outdated machines. So, while officially Richter produced photographs that were meant to celebrate state-owned industry and its products, in her personal work the photographer concentrated on the apparent gaps between official propaganda and individually experienced socialist reality.

Parallel to, but totally independent of the political-aesthetic programme of the *Bitterfelder Weg* which was introduced in 1959 calling upon artists and intellectuals to enter the factories to further cultural exchange and communication with the work force, Richter pursued her documentary project by spending her free time in the factories, talking to the female workers, familiarising herself with their work, and photographing them. However, without a legitimising official framework, such as the *Bitterfelder Weg*, Richter's activities were viewed with suspicion by the authorities, and although she enjoyed the confidence of the women, official permission to take photographs of members of the female work-force was only reluctantly granted to the photographer, which made the project a very time-consuming and insecure enterprise. When asked about her personal motivations, Richter has said: 'Ich fühlte mich zwar emanzipiert, aber so richtig zufrieden war ich nicht; da wollte ich herausfinden, wie andere Frauen lebten, was andere Frauen fühlten'.[14] Thus, while the photographer's preoccupation with the female work force squarely fits into contemporary discourses and practices, her independent documentary initiative was clearly inspired by a subjective, critical examination of socialist imperatives and their impact on the quality of female life. Propelled by her own concerns and experiences as a woman in the newly-founded socialist society of the GDR, Richter thus embarked on a long-term photographic exploration of the conditions of female emancipation and self-realisation under state socialism. By choosing to focus on the female industrial worker, however, Richter appropriated a socialist 'icon' whose signification went well beyond its immediate didactic function, to imply a whole set of notions, representations and structures through which state socialism defined itself. Not surprisingly then, Richter's independent work soon attracted the attention of the official authorities, and before long the photographer was asked by a Leipzig-based publishing house to submit her photographs for publication in a state-commissioned book documenting women's life under socialism – on condition that she would from now on collaborate and only take photographs at officially designated places. Needless to say, such restrictions were at odds with the imperatives of Richter's independent project. At the same time, however, the publishing deal provided the photographer with the much needed official framework to pursue her work, as well as giving her the prospect of making her photographs public.

3.

Stylised as an 'activist heroine' by the socialist press, the female industrial worker of the new state-owned industry was meant to epitomise, during the course of the 1950s, the successful realisation of the proletarian revolution, not only in terms of the redistribution of the means of production but with regard to the emancipation of women. Following selective instrumentalist interpretations of the 'woman question', as originally formulated in the writings of Friedrich Engels and August Bebel, female emancipation 'socialist-style' was largely premised upon women's massive entry into the industrial workforce.[15] In 1959 Walter Ulbricht, the SED's first secretary, proudly proclaimed that 'die Arbeiter- und Bauernmacht – erstmalig in der Geschichte des deutschen Volkes – [...] den Frauen nicht nur die formale Gleichberechtigung gegeben [hat], sondern auch die ökonomische Gleichberechtigung, die in dem Recht auf Arbeit, in dem Grundsatz "Gleicher Lohn für gleiche Arbeit" und im Recht auf Bildung ihren Ausdruck findet'.[16] Although there can be no doubt that, at least initially, there was genuine and exemplary commitment on the part of the GDR to emancipating women – socialist legislation in regard to women's rights was indeed path-breaking – it is equally important to stress that during its 40 years of existence gender equity in the GDR remained primarily defined in economic terms. Employment thus became an important factor in terms of women's self-esteem and social recognition. By the late 1980s, 91% of working age women in the GDR were engaged in paid employment, with the bulk of the female labour force concentrated in light industry.[17] However, the ideological emphasis on the female labour force's participation as a precondition for female emancipation ultimately prevented a more differentiated discussion of gender equity and women's self-determination, based on the recognition of sexual difference and individual autonomy. As Barbara Einhorn has succinctly stated, 'from the linkage between socialist revolution and women's emancipation emerged the conceptually reductive notion that labour force participation was not only a necessary, but also *the sufficient* condition for women's emancipation'.[18]

Meanwhile, photography played a crucial role in popularising new models of female identification that accompanied and helped legitimise this process of social transformation. Through its production and persistent reiteration of certain female stereotypes, which were mutually reinforced by repetition and circulation in diverse forms across many other sites of signification, photography seemingly 'naturalised' the ideological workings behind those representations and helped perpetuate a limited – and limiting – range of female role models. Personified in representations of activist-heroines or subsumed into the iconography of a uniform collective body dedicated to the enterprise of socialist reconstruction, the female worker was textually encoded into socialist realist discourse. (Fig. 3, 4) Similar to the popular *Aufbau* literature, which proliferated during the early years of the GDR, the didactic function of these images, as they appeared in magazines such as *Für Dich* or the short-lived *Die Arbeiterin*, was primarily to persuade 'reluctant husbands' and women themselves that women should join the socialist workforce.[19] Articles such as 'Die Maschine – der Freund der Arbeiterin' were meant to

Fig. 3

Cover of
Die Arbeiterin.
Zeitschrift für die
Interessen der
werktätigen Frau
1/1960
Photo: Staatsbibliothek
Berlin, Preußischer
Kulturbesitz

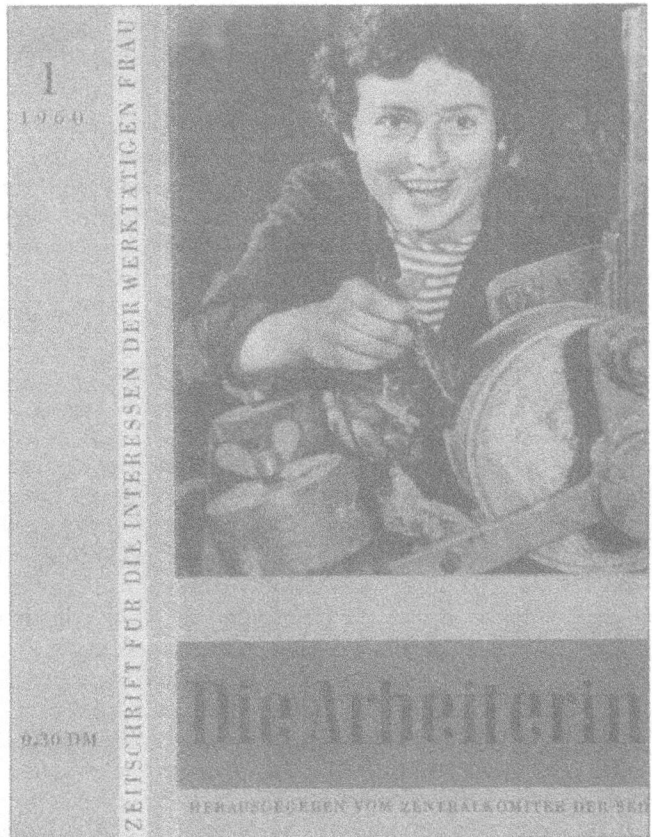

Fig. 4

Die „beste Näherbrigade im inner-
betrieblichen Wettbewerb" im VEB
Feinstrumpfwerk Oberlungwitz,
Bezirk Karl-Marx-Stadt, 15.2.1954
Photo: Deutsches Historisches
Museum, Berlin

break down inhibitions and slowly introduce woman to her new role in socialist society where 'the new machine, the mechanised and automated apparatus, is the woman's true friend. [...] The qualified woman worker controls the new machine, she masters the new technology.'[20] Statements such as these hardly disguise an early modernist longing for a mechanised utopia in which not only men, but also women and machines, live together in harmony. This aspiration was given powerful expression in photographs of industrial themes which presented both male and female workers as productive and well-functioning elements of a larger social apparatus. While in early photographs women workers can still be seen to betray a sense of awkwardness when handling heavy machinery, these representations quickly gave way to photographs which came to determine the official image of socialist women by making, as Irene Dölling has pointed out, the 'unquestioned nature of female employment [...] graphically vivid through completely unspectacular depictions of competent, productive women routinely and skilfully working while radiating a self-evident confidence in their abilities.'[21]

4.

At first view, Richter's photographs of female industrial workers do not seem to differ significantly from those official representations in that they, too, present a rather unspectacular view of women's daily work in the new state-owned industry. The photograph *An der Linotype* (Fig.1) shows a young woman of whom it can certainly be said that she is 'routinely and skilfully working while radiating a self-evident confidence in [her] abilities'; in fact, she is operating the heavy printing press with such self-effacing 'naturalness' that she almost seems to have become one with the machine – an integral part of the socialist apparatus. Yet, upon closer inspection, Richter's photograph thwarts the socialist consensus by a subtle disruption of accepted codes and conventions. The picture's formal composition, with the women's position echoing the different components of the machinery, underlines the idea of an organic fusion of worker and machine; in fact, it seems graphically to reiterate one of the basic tenets of socialist ideology with regard to gender equity whereby women's emancipation cannot be divorced from her participation in socialist production. However, by focussing on the massive printing press, with its complex technical apparatus – which could be seen to bespeak a rationalist 'masculine' logic – a shift of emphasis occurs: Dwarfed by the enormous bulk of the machinery, the woman appears to be stuck in her position, imprisoned in a 'harness of torture' from which only her face, hands, and feet protrude as incongruously human details, as Karl Gernot Kuehn has remarked.[22] As we have seen, officially, women were recognised primarily as workers, as indispensable elements of socialist economy, and only secondarily as autonomous and gendered subjects. Through its reversal of standard iconographic codes – according to which the worker had to dominate the composition – Richter's photograph raises the fundamental question as to female autonomy within such a reductionist paradigm, thereby anticipating the crux of later feminist critiques of the socialist emancipation of women.

In terms of rhetorical conventions and codes of portraiture, too, Richter's photograph has little in common with the smiling prototypes of socialist realist iconography. Obviously, Richter was not interested in providing socialist propaganda with 'typical' female role models for emulation when she was photographing members of the female industrial work-force. The woman at the linotype lacks the enthusiastic zeal which lends meaning to similar official portraits (Fig. 3); in fact, her seemingly concentrated gaze could also be seen to betray a sense of fatigue or even absent-mindedness. Equally, the image's internal textual signifiers, such as its black-and-whiteness, the graininess of print, as well as the weakening of certain stereotypes of femininity, reiterate tropes more commonly associated with the depiction of anonymous collective labour rather than individual portraiture. (Fig. 4) Significantly, the woman at the linotype does not answer to the viewer's gaze which renders identification difficult, but instead grants the depicted worker a certain independence and resistance to political instrumentalisation. Clearly, Richter's photographic project was informed by a different agenda, aimed at a critical examination of socialist rhetoric with regard to the conditions of female emancipation as experienced by the majority of GDR women. As a consequence, the viewer is presented not with a 'typical activist heroine' but with an anonymous worker who despite – or precisely because – she cannot be readily identified comes across as threateningly 'real'. The unobtrusive style of Richter's portraiture, which distinguishes itself through a subtle play of light and shade and a levelled viewpoint, sharply contrasts with the often aggressive frontality that characterised official 'shots'; it also helps create a sense of authenticity and unmediated directness, as opposed to the hardly disguised staging of official photographs. Needless to say, Richter's photograph is no less a construction than any other photographic record, its 'evidential force' based on a skilful exploitation of the camera's technical competencies, rhetorical devices, and codes (colour, focus, texture, grain, etc.). Still, the impression of 'authenticity' that emanates from Richter's photograph cannot (or should not) be exclusively ascribed to a mastery of technique, as it is also, significantly enough, the result of an intensive, personally motivated, and time-consuming working relationship between Richter and her photographic subjects, which clearly distinguishes such an independent project from impersonal journalistic work bound by tight deadlines. Not least, it bespeaks a complicity and trust between the photographer and her subject which would become a trademark of Richter's work.

5.

While Richter's documentary work was to a great extent inspired by the photographer's belief in the 'transformative' powers of a humanist photographic practice, Richter also self-consciously exploited the conceptual aspect of realist photography in order to help clear the mystifying veil of ideology. The motif of a woman working at a linotype – a machine that commands both physical and intellectual skills – is in itself rather exceptional within the socialist realist iconography of the female worker, not least because it positions woman at a strategic point of symbolic intervention, i.e. in (potential) control of the word. With this photograph, taken in the printing office of the newspaper *Neues Deutschland*, the SED's mouthpiece, Richter could also be seen commenting on women's passivity, or even complicity, as regards their active participation in reproducing their own terms of subjection. The ostensible lack of any concrete textual signifier which would allow the viewer to extract the 'right' meaning from a photograph such as *An der Linotype* introduces a subtle textual ambiguity into Richter's work which, in turn, reaffirms photography's inherent polysemic aspect. In the end, this polysemy presented the real challenge to official socialist realist discourse, based on a monosemic conception and construction of 'reality'. As David Bathrick has pointed out in his discussion of 'dissident' writers in the GDR, artists' and intellectuals' fall from grace often resulted (at least initially) not so much from a direct expression of deviant political views in their work but rather from a 'sometimes unintended fall into "polysemic" modes of address that, by virtue of their multiplicity of meaning, were perforce understood and evaluated as negative, that is, as subversive of the official "monosemic" mode of discourse.' Works of art that 'explicitly or implicitly encouraged or enabled ambiguity' – or, in other words, the production rather than the consumption of meaning – 'were, by that very fact alone, lacking a clearly articulated sense of *Parteilichkeit* (political commitment)'.[23]

As we have seen, Richter's independent documentary project was self-consciously motivated by the photographer's wish critically to evaluate the discrepancy she witnessed between socialist aspirations and socialist reality, with special regard to the conditions of female life and self-realisation. It originated at the intersection between public and private discourses, official propaganda and personal concerns, and represents one of the first attempts by a GDR photographer to articulate a privileged subjective perception in photographic practice.[24] Given the rigid cultural and political guidelines of that period it seems, however, doubtful whether Richter's photographs would eventually have qualified for publication in a state-commissioned book. With the building of the Berlin Wall in 1961, which initiated an altogether new political era in the history of the GDR, the project was dismissed by the authorities as no longer fitting the state's political agenda. Significantly, Richter was from now on no longer permitted entry into the factories which set an end to her personal investigations as well. Still, one cannot help wondering what would have been the outcome of such a collaboration, or if a collaboration would ever in fact have taken place. Given Richter's personal investment in that project, as well as her uncompromising stance in terms of her photographic vision, it seems unlikely that she would have been willing to accept changes and alterations to her initially independently conceived project to accommodate socialist imperatives both on an aesthetic and ideological level. This leads us to reconsider the project from a different angle: what was the political incentive behind commissioning Richter, a renowned individualist who had been expelled from the *Hochschule* for failing to conform to the norm, with providing illustrations for a book that would have made her work available to a wider public? In the end, was this assignment a form of 'state intervention', a preventive measure seeking to control what could have been a possibly disruptive enterprise, detrimental to the socialist project? We have to remember that Richter was effectively appropriating one of state socialism's most powerful ideological 'icons' – the female industrial worker – submitting it to a critical revision as to its actual meaning and function within the state socialist discourse. In so doing, Richter's work ultimately questioned the acceptance of wider social, political, and ideological structures which, as Irene Dölling has suggested, effectively 'anchor the division of the world into the powerful few and the powerless mass, into the responsible and the dependent'.[25] The photograph *An der Linotype*, with its subliminal criticism of state socialism's patriarchally-biased power structure, can therefore be seen not only as a forceful symbol for the problematic nature of women's emancipation under socialism, but as a Cassandra-esque 'warning' relating to the larger socialist project as it articulates some of the inherent contradictions and ideological shortcomings which would eventually help to disrupt the socialist enterprise. Although the state-commissioned documentation of the lives of GDR women was never actually realised, Richter pursued her photographic exploration of the quality of female life under socialism – highlighting the rift between official rhetoric and individually experienced reality – on an independent basis, as far as she could, until well into the 1970s and 1980s, which clearly bespeaks the photographer's personal commitment to that matter. Her series of portraits of anonymous women from all strands of life, taken at work, at home, as well as in public spaces, today presents the viewer with a highly personal and yet widely understood document of women's daily life in the GDR, beyond the sloganising and rhetoric of official propaganda.

NOTES

[1] This book was to be part of an envisaged series treating specialised themes (e.g. women, children) in a propagandistic fashion to celebrate and represent to an international audience the achievements and progress of human life under socialism.

[2] One of the first major revisionist surveys of the history of photography designed for a GDR audience was A. Hüneke, G. Ihrke, A. Neumann, U. Wallenburg (eds.), *Medium Fotografie* (Leipzig, 1979).

[3] The photograph *An der Linotype* was first published in 1973 in a book by Berthold Beiler and Heinz Föppel, *Erlebnis, Bild, Persönlichkeit* (Leipzig, 1973), which presented the work of five GDR photographers (Evelyn Richter, Helga Wallmüller, Arno Fischer, Walter Danz, Eberhard Klöppel) from a stringent Marxist-Leninist viewpoint.

[4] LPG – *Landwirtschaftliche Produktionsgenossenschaft* (agricultural working collective).

[5] Stylistically based in 19th history painting Soviet-style socialist realism had its ideological foundation in Andrei Zdhanov's writings of 1934, which had emphasised 'ideological commitment' (*ideinost*), 'party-mindedness' (*partiinost*) as well as 'national/popular spirit' (*narodnost*) as indispensable elements of socialist art. Set up in opposition to various forms of pre-war modernism which, denounced as 'formalism', served as examples of an alternative reactionary political framework, socialist realism in the GDR came to be identified with all that was perceived as progressive in German culture. The campaign for socialist realism reached its most aggressive and overtly politicised articulation in a declaration by the Central Committee of the SED on 17 March 1951 entitled 'Der Kampf gegen den Formalismus in Kunst und Literatur, für eine fortschrittliche Kultur' in which formalism, identified as 'American cultural barbarism', was made directly responsible for the 'destruction of national consciousness and indirect support of the war policies of world imperialism.' See David Bathrick, *The Powers of Speech. The Politics of Culture in the GDR* (Lincoln and London, 1995), p. 90.

[6] See, for example, Edmund Kesting, *Ein Maler sieht durchs Objektiv* (Leipzig, 1958).

[7] In his posthumously published book *Camera Lucida* (London, 1982), Roland Barthes appears to reinstate the notion of the photographic record as 'evidence' based on what he sees as the medium's alleged phenomenologically-based 'power of authentication' (pp.88-89). Barthes here not only seems to depart from his own prior writings but also decidedly contrasts with preceding theoreticians (Benjamin, Brecht) who described the photographic record before all as an ideological construction contingent on specific historical and institutional practices for meaning. For a critique of Barthes' later position see John Tagg, *The Burden of Representation. Essays on Photographies and Histories* (London, 1988), pp. 1-5.

[8] Anatoly Lunacharsky, in Jo Anna Isaak, *Feminism and Contemporary Art. The Revolutionary Power of Women's Laughter* (London and New York, 1996), p. 126. Lunacharsky's emphasis.

[9] Roland Barthes, in Abigail Solomon-Godeau, *Photography at the Dock. Essays on Photographic History, Institutions, and Practices* (Minneapolis, 1991), p. 184.

[10] Karl Gernot Kuehn, *Caught – The Art of Photography in the German Democratic Republic* (Los Angeles, and London, 1997), p. 39.

[11] Socialist realism's programmatic emphasis on 19th century history painting led to highly grotesque results at the photographic department of the *Hochschule für Grafik und Buchkunst*, as photography students were encouraged to stage photographic scenes modelled after 19th century Russian history painting. See Peter Pachnicke and Klaus Lieblich, 'Reproduction und Eigenausdruck. Geschichte der Abteilung Fotografie', in *Hochschule für Graphik und Buchkunst 1945–1989* (Leipzig, 1989), p. 51.

[12] Organised by Edward Steichen, Head of Photography at the Museum of Modern Art, New York, in 1955, *The Family of Man* was conceived as an internationally touring exhibition of photography which heavily capitalised for its popular appeal on a distorted and decontextualised multinational humanism, from which 'history' was carefully excluded. For a critique see Barthes, 'The Great Family of Man' in *Mythologies* (London, 1973), pp. 100-102.

[13] For a discussion of the history and activities of *action fotografie* see, for example, Ulrich Domröse, 'action fotografie', in *Evelyn Richter – Zwischenbilanz. Fotografien aus den Jahren 1950–1989* (Moritzburg and Halle, 1992), pp. 11-15.

[14] Evelyn Richter, conversation with the author, Leipzig, 2 March 1997.

[15] Friedrich Engels, *The Origin of the Family, Private Property and the State*, 1884; August Bebel, *Women under Socialism*, 1879 (revised 1909).

[16] Walter Ulbricht, 'Zum Geleit', in *Die Arbeiterin. Zeitschrift für die Interessen der werktätigen Frau*, Zentralkomitee der SED, Berlin, No. 1/1959, p. 1.

[17] Hildegard Maria Nickel, 'Women in the German Democratic Republic and in the New Federal States: Looking Backward and Forward (Five Theses)', in Nanette Funk and Magda Mueller (eds.), *Gender Politics and Post-Communism. Reflections from Eastern Europe and the former Soviet Union* (New York and London, 1993), p. 139.

[18] Barbara Einhorn, *Cinderella Goes to Market. Citizenship, Gender and Women's Movements in East Central Europe* (London and New York, 1993), p. 20.

[19] ibid., p. 232.

[20] F. Brock, W. Uhlemann, Abt. Maschinenbau und Metallurgie beim ZK der SED, in *Die Arbeiterin*, Berlin, No.2/1959: 'In unserer Gesellschaftsordnung ist die neue Maschine, die mechanisierte und automatisierte Anlage, ein wirklicher Freund der Frau. (...) Die qualifizierte Arbeiterin meistert die neue Maschine, sie beherrscht die neue Technik.', p. 34.

[21] Irene Dölling, '"But the Pictures Stay the Same..." The Image of Women in the Journal *Für Dich* Before and After the "Turning Point"', in Funk and Mueller, op. cit., p. 169.

[22] Kuehn, p. 69.

[23] Bathrick, p. 16.

[24] Mention should be made here of Arno Fischer's independently conceived photographic project documenting the divided city of Berlin which was to be published but eventually suffered a similar fate as Richter's work for obvious political reasons. With the building of the Berlin Wall his photographs were considered obsolete, as they were no longer corresponding to official reality. For a discussion of Fischer's work see Kuehn, op. cit., pp. 88-95.

[25] Dölling, p. 175.

Jennie Hawksley

CONTINUITY OF PRACTICE VERSUS CHANGE IN CIRCUMSTANCE: GDR VISUAL CULTURE AND THE EAST GERMAN ARTIST. AN EXAMINATION OF THE WORK OF VIA AND PINA LEWANDOWSKY

This paper examines the work of artists Via and Pina Lewandowsky. As young artists, trained in the GDR but entering post-educational practice just a year or two prior to the Wende, *their artistic activity spans this turbulent period. They have successfully entered and negotiated the field of professional artistic practice during the decade since then. This examination of a small part of their work situates their continuing artistic practice in the broader context of issues concerning the place of the visual cultural heritage of the GDR in the current and future culture of a politically and economically unified Germany.*

Following the events in the GDR of November 1989 and the subsequent decision in favour of unification, a contradiction between continuity of practice and change in circumstance emerged as a very real conflict for many artists working in East Germany. The demands of change in terms of basic survival frequently reduced artistic practice to an unaffordable luxury. Many artists who had practised in the days of the GDR succumbed to these new practical obstacles. However, those who resolved to try to overcome them, then found themselves facing ideological hurdles erected during the heated debates over art, artists and their relationship to the GDR state apparatus, which followed the opening of the Wall. These practical and ideological difficulties are, on the one hand, confronted by the artist as an individual, but on the other hand it is, in part at least, through individual responses that these conflicts are transposed onto the broader cultural plane. To ask what it means to have been an artist in the GDR continuing to practice after 1989, is also to ask what impact the heritage of visual culture in the GDR is having on the culture of a unified Germany. It is to ask what the future holds for the visual culture of the GDR.

This article will examine these questions and their implications firstly by exploring some of the responses to changing circumstance made in the work of Via and Pina Lewandowsky; and secondly, by discussing some aspects of the cultural climate and context, since 1989, within which they continue their collaborative artistic practice.

1.

The Lewandowskys belong to a generation of artists whose development, training and early post-educative practice occurred in the GDR. As such they represent a group of people who are old enough to have experienced the impact on artistic and intellectual development of visual cultural conditions in the GDR, but young enough for this analysis not to be concerned with the differing issues raised by those older artists who had more fully established their relationship to the state. The Lewandowskys had, in actual fact, decided that they wanted no relationship with this state. Via Lewandowsky, whose lack of identification with the GDR only marginally preempted its dissolution, left for the West only months before the Wall was opened, Pina Lewandowsky followed soon after. And so their biographies, almost ironically, seem peculiarly resonant of the fate of their native country at that time.

Via Lewandowsky made his first trip to West Berlin in 1989.[1] His work was to be included in the exhibition *Neue Kunst aus Dresden* (BASF-Feierabendhaus, Ludwigshafen 1989). He describes this first crossing into West Berlin as a revelatory experience 'everything looked better and it was just a few metres away'. He describes it as 'stepping behind [his] lines of consciousness'. In August 1989 Lewandowsky made a further trip to West Berlin but this time he had decided that he would not return to the East. Within three months it became apparent that Lewandowsky's decision had anticipated the immediate future, the Wall was opened and all East Germans were free to travel to the West. In the meantime Lewandowsky had been preparing works for his first exhibition as a citizen of West Berlin, which opened in December 1989 under the title *Sie können nichts schreien hören. Acht Porträts zur Euthanasie (*Neue Gesellschaft für bildende Kunst). The eponymous work consisted of eight canvasses, each delicately tinted and streaked with a pale translucent yellow and bearing a precisely inscribed human head. Acrylic and urine on canvas, these paintings exhibit Lewandowsky's 'reproductive painting' technique; this is the meticulous combination, projection and reinvention of pre-existing images, medical textbooks provide a favourite source, which emerge from the process as seamless but subverted. 'Euthanasia' here is Lewandowsky's metaphor for life in the GDR, and it is calculated to make ironical reference to the National Socialists' euphemistic use of the word ('euthanasia' rather than 'murder'). Yet as a metaphor it also evokes subtler processes of suggestion, reorientation, indoctrination, perhaps the procedures of delimitation that define the 'lines of consciousness' which, when first he had come to West Berlin, Lewandowsky felt he had 'stepped behind'. What is immediately apparent in these eight portraits is that the mouth is the primary site of torture and concealment. The first in the series, *Der zu einer glücklichen Stunde Geborene* (8 Porträts...1989 Nr.1), shows the tongue firmly clamped between two bound rods reminiscent of medieval torture (fig.1). In the last, *Man sieht, daß es nie zu Hause ankommen wird* (8 Porträts...1989 Nr.8), the rods reappear strapped to a face whose uncentred gaze remains unexplained by a complete facial expression; the mouth falls beneath the lower edge of the canvas. These mouths cannot comment. In the accompanying catalogue the portraits are juxtaposed with photographic stills, largely from Via Lewandowsky's 'Autoperforationartist' performances made before his move to West Berlin in 1989.[2] These offer up a relationship between Lewandowsky's performance art whilst living in the East and his artistic reflection on those conditions of living, yet made in, and for an exhibition in, West Berlin. Lewandowsky has described the Euthanasia project as extending from both his immediate anger at life in the GDR and his sense of freedom at living in the West. Though he has also described the project as his 'final statement' on life in East Germany, a thematic continuity nevertheless spans the change in circumstances of 1989. Themes of handicap, helplessness and fatigue continue as fundamental to the Lewandowskys' work.

In May/July 1992 Via Lewandowsky's work *Counterselection* was shown at the Corcoran Gallery of Art, Washington DC, as a part of the group exhibition *Interface: Berlin Art in the Nineties*. *Counterselection* included six hundred photocopies, meticulously inscribed works which share the linearity of the Euthanasia portraits, and which again draw on anatomical illustrative sources. The title of the work is characteristically rich in suggestion, evoking some sense of opposition, a selection running counter to the 'norm', to natural selection. Furthermore, Darwinism is raised as an issue. Images display anatomical parts strangely combined or congealed, often rendered apparently 'helpless' or 'useless'. But these are no ordinary handicaps: two hands still appear but their exceptional effectiveness when combined as a pair is subverted and withdrawn, each hand now protrudes from the other. An obliquely gazing head is presented, onto which seems grafted or bandaged what appears as an outsized representation of the balance organ (which in actuality is embedded in the inner ear); script is shown on panels either side (fig.2). The balance alluded to here is implied as a mental state. It is an image of a 'view', an unsettling image of a 'balanced view'. Mental balance is 'normal', and 'imbalance' runs counter to that norm. But language is at stake here, where the physiological fitness of the balance organ is necessary for effective bodily movement, the property of 'balance' is transposed from the physical to the mental plane, mental fitness is also 'balance'. Yet the composition of that fitness is more subtle, less easy to define. Themes of the use, restriction and manipulation of language raised in the Euthanasia project are raised here. If that language of fitness should prove to be the 'enemy' then how can that enemy be described? Lewandowsky's images formulate the possibility that something may indeed be wrong.

Later in 1992 images from *Counterselection* reappeared in Pina & Via Lewandowsky's contribution to Documenta IX. The title of this work, *Anomalie Normaler Dauer,* introduces us to the oxymoronic possibility that the anomalous, that which by definition exceeds the scope of the paradigm, the norm, might somehow be subject to standardisation, in this case restrained by duration. But at the same time the necessity of anomaly in delimiting the norm is underlined. Hence the Lewandowskys do not so much reverse the terms – the anomalous becoming normal, the normal becoming odd – as set them in motion, estranging reality by inducing perpetual oscillation. *Anomalie Normaler Dauer* Part 1 consisted of 48 panels under the title *Vermehrung von Täuschung* (fig.3).[3] The Lewandowskys' interest in reiterating peculiar, largely anatomical images seems not to be confined to the instantiation of particular anomalies but is extended to the idea of anomaly itself. Multiple images are presented simultaneously and weighted equally by uniform panel size. Yet they extend filamentous links across the rigid grid of panel divisions, and, of necessity, the uniform grid co-extensively fragments them. These processes are identical, extension and fragmentation. The visual matrix of simultaneous events is contained by a process of uniform, regularising fragmentation. The *Counterselection* gazing balance head reappears among the many panels of *Vermehrung von Täuschung,* querying the origin of that particular species of normalcy and containment which is 'the balanced view'.

Despite their characteristic initial outlandishness the Lewandowskys' representations are very much tied to the everyday and the mundane. Recurring themes of handicap, helplessness, fatigue are not asking the viewer to address her/himself to an experience of life outside, or at least at the margins, of normal experience; we are not being invited to enter strange new worlds. Handicap, helplessness, fatigue are suggested instead as very much our own, as implicit in 'normal' experience. In this respect, the use of images from medical textbooks is no surprise. Any philosophical exploration of the

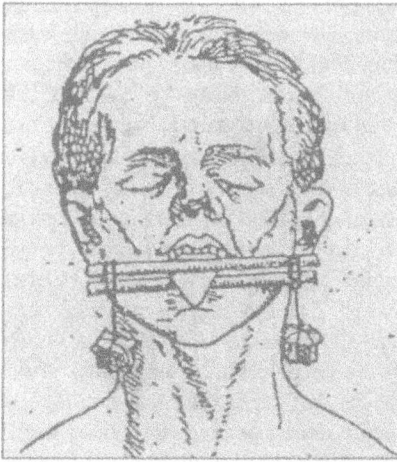

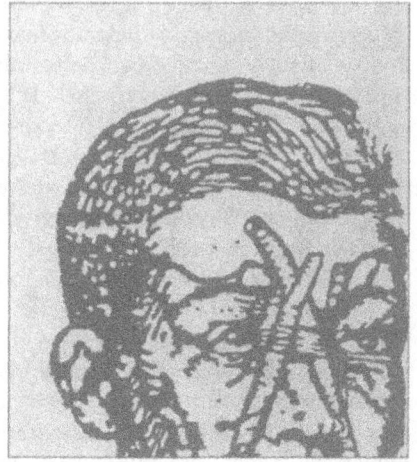

Figure 1. Sie können nichts schreien hören. No's 1 & 8 (1989)

Figure 2. From Counterselection (1991)

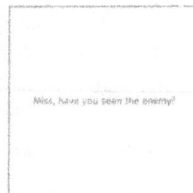

relationship between the aesthetic mobilisation of the human body in art and the use in science of the artist's technique for the purpose of medical illustration is of secondary relevance. What the Lewandowskys' reinventions declare first and foremost is that science, and more pertinently medicine, in defining and circumscribing the human body, fragments it, takes it apart. The Lewandowskys' images deduce from that, using the same constituent parts, science's images, the fragmentary experience of human being. But where science seeks to zip the body back up, having pinned it down, the Lewandowskys show a singular disdain for such efforts. Their work *Über den toten Punkt hinausgeschossen* consists of the complete works, in nine volumes, of physiologist Ivan Pavlov, comprehensively shot through with a gun.[4]

With regard to a conjunction between art and science's representations of the human body, Via Lewandowsky's approach is strident, extending far beyond an illuminating but abstract juxtaposition of images. In a recent installation, *The Artist's Brain*, at the Deutsches Museum, Bonn (March-June 1998), Lewandowsky projected onto the wall of the darkened room a large image of his own head in profile. This image was manipulated such that a segment of the scalp appears peeled back to reveal the artist's brain beneath. In addition to this a metal column stands in the centre of the room surmounted by a small glass dome. The periphery of the dome displays a circulating neon text supplied by Lewandowsky's frequent collaborator, the poet Durs Grünbein. Within the dome, head-sized in contrast to the large projection on the wall, is a magnetic resonance image of a lateral slice through the centre of the brain. Lewandowsky has described this installation as being in part about a particular difficulty he has encountered in his negotiations and investigations concerning the final consummation of this idea and piece of work. This difficulty is one of obtaining the medical, scientific and ethical sanction to recover his own brain, with the necessary collusion of physicians, after death for the purposes of sculpture. The resonance image in the dome stands as a substitute for the artist's brain and a reference to the practical difficulty. Brains bequeathed to science may occupy jars of formaldehyde standing in rows for the purposes of research, but for art? In response to those who view this proposed artwork as purely spectacular, Lewandowsky states his interest in creating sculpture using his own body as 'to break through certain limits of sculptural ideas... to write new laws in terms of how to deal with art... the project is about the *limitation* of art'. Here it appears that for Lewandowsky the handicap, helplessness and fatigue of art is not just similar to but indivisible from the handicap, helplessness and fatigue in human terms exposed in so much of his and Pina Lewandowsky's work.

Many artists and commentators from the East refer to having sensed the disappointment, post-1989, on the part of those in the West who had tried to find evidence of an organised underground artistic culture working away in opposition to the state. The recognition that artistic activity in the GDR could not simply be divided into 'state' and 'anti-state' would have to be succeeded by an openness to examining a subtle variety of positions in relation, rather than opposition, to the machinery of state control. Where official ideology asserted fundamentally the didactic and illustrative function of art, 'unofficial' positions were frequently manifested by some form of rejection of the ideological use of visual art. Yet Lewandowsky remarks that in terms of his practical techniques even those in the subcultural scene, such as it was, seemed unable to assimilate with his method of reproductive painting. Where the basic subcultural artistic position in the GDR has been described as neither for nor against the state but *outside*,[5] Lewandowsky's comment would seem to situate his work as radically outside - outside even the usual possibilities for 'outsiderness' extended in the GDR. His formal methods bear this out in terms of at least two basic tendencies in artistic practice which resisted being completely subsumed by state ideology. Simplifying for the sake of brevity, the first is an adherence to a *l'art pour l'art* aesthetic, asserting the autonomy of art as against its ideological manipulation (oppositional perhaps, but passively so), and the second is an expressionist style, harking back to the early twentieth century avant-garde, pregnant with an individualism at odds with the communist ethos. The Lewandowskys' methods, however, interrogate the possibility of expression at the same time as refusing to let the viewer off the hook by allowing her/him an easy retreat into a purely aesthetic appreciation. In contrast to one delusory ideal of expressionism that the gesture bypasses mediation, presenting instead a hotline to the emotive soul, the Lewandowskys' work announces its construction. The transfer, appropriation and reinvention of images displays its meticulous calculation. Like mythical beasts, the Lewandowskys' constructions are an accumulation of parts which in themselves are usually recognisable, mundane, and often banal. The possibility of expressing the intangibles of thought and sensation is explored in the Lewandowskys' work by a combination of language and visual substitution. Words and titles do not comment upon objects and images in an explanatory way, but rather combine with them in offering up equivalents. The Lewandowskys link elements of their visual vocabulary in an ongoing series of sequences of equivalents which refuses to extend to an explanatory conclusion. Explanation is defied and deferred. And if the hindering of explanation can threaten to render art effectively meaningless, then the Lewandowskys in response are entering onto the paradoxical territory of examining what it means to be meaningful. They refuse to enter a state of denial concerning the difficulty of expression but instead encounter it in a calculated way. As a result their art is peculiarly accessible, no particular brand of aesthetic sensibility or accumulated knowledge of art is necessary. Their quasi-linguistic combinations of largely familiar objects, images, words are recognisable, and so clearly displayed that there is no danger that expressive melodrama might obscure the frequent, and often deeply sinister, humour which attests to the critical commitment of the Lewandowskys in their approach to art. The Lewandowskys' insistence on deferring and confounding explanation seems also to be a refusal of a false solidification of meaning which would label and delimit their artistic practice. But if we should consider this as one effect of the initial conditions of artistic development under a regime which sought to control artistic culture precisely through labelling and delimitation, then we should also take note that the Lewandowskys' particular practice is not only continuing but maturing under the subsequent liberal conditions of cultural life in the West.

2.

That euphoria should be followed by scepticism, that freedom should prove to have limitations is not surprising; what is significant is how those limits are experienced and interpreted. From a practical point of view – for the Lewandowskys' life post-GDR has extended opportunities to travel and professionally pursue their creative practice in ways that the regime is extremely unlikely to have afforded them – they had, as we know, already made their decision to leave before the *Wende*. The change for artists of the

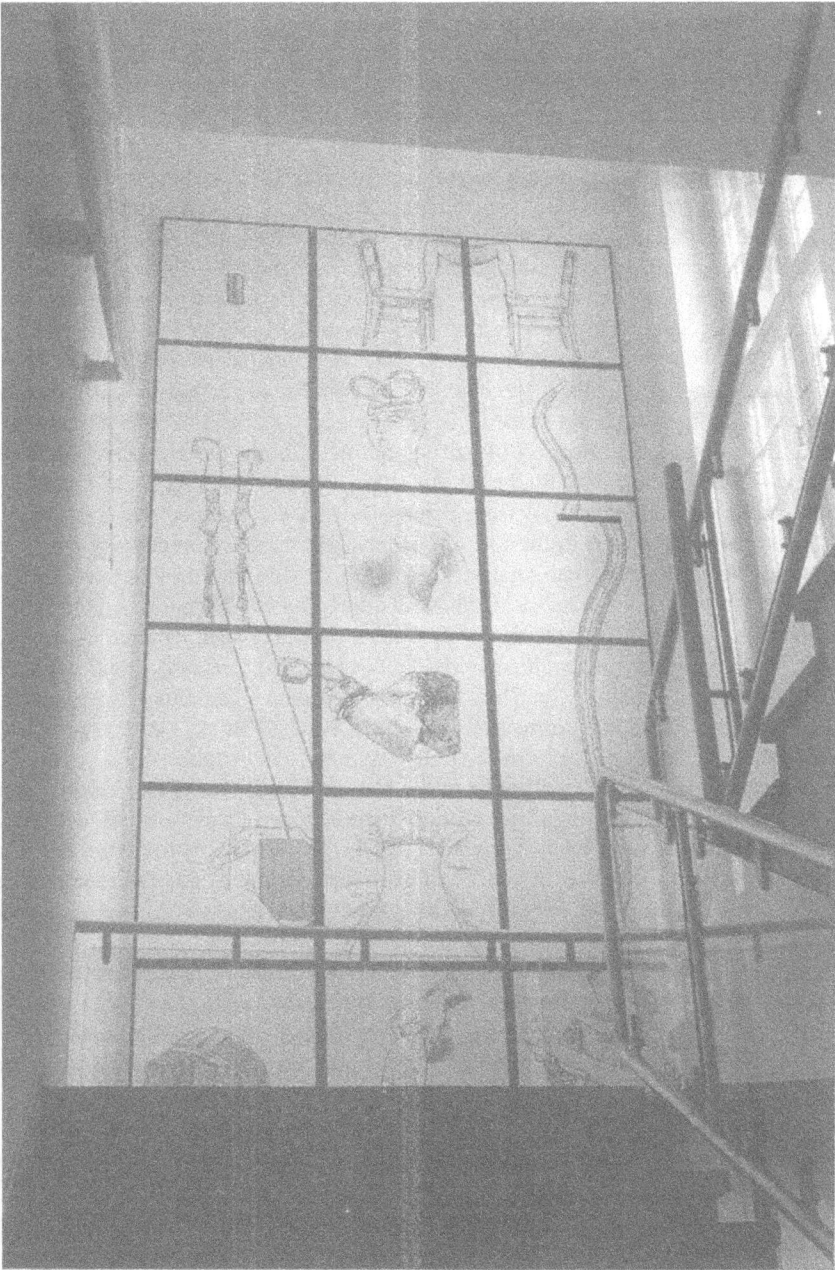

Figure 3. From Documentation IX (1992)

Lewandowskys' generation may well have come at a point in their artistic development where, for those who are succeeding, it could be accommodated as part of that development; in other words, change itself may be perceived as absorbed within an overarching personal developmental continuity. The pertinent question remains as to whether and how an early developmental history in the GDR impacts on the continuing practice of these artists from 1989 to the present day. And it is a question which directly concerns both the possibility of cultural continuity and the personal experience of change.

Considering the individual aspect first, the question as to the impact upon current artistic output of an early developmental history in the GDR may be phrased as follows: what are the meanings or consequences of a GDR background for artists practising from 1989 to the present day? Or, what does it mean to be, or have been, an East German artist? Lewandowsky's response to this question indicates a double-edged scenario. On the one hand, at a time when initial curiosity concerning 'unorthodox' art in the GDR combined with frequent disappointments at the character of 'unofficial' activity, Via Lewandowsky has remarked that he was often treated 'like a stranger' by critics in West Germany. They seemed to him better able to accept the visual culture of other Eastern Bloc countries than that of the GDR. Though with hindsight this seems explicable in terms of a confounding of expectations on both sides, not least perhaps in that those expectations may not have been fully formed or informed, there is a broader issue here. Lewandowsky's perceptions on this point stand as anecdotal support for the proposition that the relationship between the West German cultural establishment and other Eastern European states had as its model the polite and politic exchange of cultural interest between nations. However, after 1989 the relationship between culture in the GDR and West Germany could not be one of nationally distanced interest, and it had no precedent. Lewandowsky's experience signalled the problems of unification in practice in Germany that continue to be encountered in the cultural field. On the other hand there is undoubtably a certain kind of kudos to be had from being an artist from the former GDR. This is dependent largely on the swift and enterprising recognition of the potential commercial value of 'differentness' – entrepreneurship as firstly survival and secondly success. In many respects these two possibilities may be viewed as two sides of the same coin, they are twin symptoms of a process of exoticisation, the exotic object is fascinating and marginalised, invited but estranged.

However, this GDR 'exoticism' is inevitably a transitory state. Artists with GDR childhoods, but post-*Wende* training entering the arena even now have experienced conditions of artistic development very different from those of the Lewandowskys' generation. Whatever the ongoing problems and dilemmas posed by unification across the cultural field, that process of basic cultural amalgamation seems set to advance with every successive generation of artists. As Via Lewandowsky has wryly remarked, 'I am a fossil'. Even now anecdotal evidence would suggest that the emphasis in visual culture is swinging towards accenting regional difference rather than polarising in terms of a historical cultural differentiation between West Germany and the GDR – and there are many possible interpretations of this.

This volume is presented under the title *East Germany: Continuity and Change*. Given the present circumstances, as indicated here, what is the future for GDR culture? What are the possibilities for an ongoing continuity? In other words, is it possible to have a German culture in which the alternative cultural heritage of the GDR, however complex and difficult to assess, is duly recognised? As yet continuity is maintained in the personal histories of those who experienced life in the 'other' state. But as time goes on if that experience of an alternative way of living is to be more than a now concluded episode in history, then that continuity must be expressed at a supra-individual level. In time the genuinely East German artist, and by this I mean those who as artists experienced life in the GDR, will be a figure of the past. If the heritage of GDR visual culture is only to be represented by these genuinely East German practitioners then it will inevitably be relegated to the museum, partially represented by selected images, objects and documents which will bear its trace like the petrified footprints of an extinct species. But if the heritage of GDR visual culture is to have a living continuity, then it returns us to the question of impact raised earlier on. If the impact of artistic development under conditions in the GDR should prove to be productive of qualitative difference, then a position could be struck which would refuse either ethnographical relegation to the museum or the total absorption of East German artistic and critical potential. The latter might open up the temptation of simply imposing the visual cultural heritage of West Germany as the only valid one. If such a position were to be established, then for visual culture in East Germany the balance between the change of western cultural appropriation and the continuity of playing a productive, dialectical, negotiative, part in the visual cultural future of Germany could be tipped in favour of the latter.

It remains to be assessed whether artists from the former GDR are making a contribution to contemporary art which is marked by qualitative difference. In terms of artistic compromise and concession to change the Lewandowskys appear to be striking a convincing position of refusal. Through the discussion here of some of their work – and it should be noted that this small selection does little justice to its breadth and variety – I have tried to indicate how the Lewandowskys have maintained an artistic identity, method and approach through which they have intelligently and selectively utilised the artistic and technical opportunities and possibilities available to them since 1989, rather than allow these to be the agents of their transformation. Combining humour with gravity, enigma with accessibility, the Lewandowskys address the viewer with a directness that seems refreshingly sympathetic.

At the beginning of this discussion I suggested a slight irony in that the Lewandowskys might be viewed, biographically, as representative of their country precisely because they chose to leave. I will conclude this essay by extending that suggested irony. In refusing to capitulate artistically to the pressures and demands of the change, the Lewandowskys may prove to be representative of a productive visual cultural continuity not least because they refuse to identify themselves particularly as 'East German' artists. I have suggested that the present phase of the East German artist will be relatively short, the Lewandowskys astutely set their sights on a future much longer than this. If the *Artist's Brain* installation should reach its final completion then Via Lewandowsky will assure his personal artistic longevity in an extraordinarily direct way. But if the Lewandowskys' particular approach to art and the human condition should prove to have a difference in semantic quality, then it may contribute significantly to assuring and legitimating the role, in a combined German cultural continuity, of the complex visual cultural heritage of the GDR. Whether such a qualitative step is being taken and exactly how it is seen to be inflected by artistic developments in the GDR, remains, as ever, a problem for art history and social analysis. What is certain is that the

Lewandowskys' work does raise these questions, among many others, and this cannot help but be healthy provocation.

NOTES

[1] Factual information regarding the Lewandowskys, and Via Lewandowsky's quotations, in this paper derive from an interview with the author, conducted in March 1998.

[2] The *Autoperforationartists*, members Via Lewandowsky, Micha Brendel, Else Gabriel, Rainer Görss, was a performance art group formed in Dresden and active 1987–89. Highly visceral public performances included the simulated physical and psychic mutilations that the group name implies.

[3] The *Documenta* exhibitions, held every four to five years in Kassel, Germany since 1955, showcase German and international contemporary art. *Anomalie Normaler Dauer* included the two further parts: *Am Ende eines Raumes (Gebeinkiste und Spruchkammer)* (artistic intervention in memorial to the Unknown Soldier, Kassel: a wax cast simulating the 'unknown soldier' was placed inside a glass topped crate and positioned over the memorial stone) and *Neigung zu ungehemmter Löslichkeit*. Lewandowsky arranges for smoke to issue from the roof of the Staatstheater at fifteen minute intervals. See Pina and Via Lewandowsky *Alles Gute! Good Luck!* (Leipzig, 1995).

[4] Pavlov presented a view of the brain as simply the site of neuronal activity designed to produce variously complicated physical reflexes in vertebrate animals including humans. This kind of highly reductive scientific treatment of human beings figures either implicitly or explicitly in much of the Lewandowskys' work.

[5] Sascha Anderson, 'Nicht für, nicht gegen, sondern außerhalb' quoted in Christoph Tannert 'The Illusion of art in the GDR', in *Europe Without Walls*, ed. by. James Aulich and Tim Wilcox (Manchester, 1993), p.134. Anderson's is a complex case; he had actively participated in the 'unofficial' scene but was later discovered to have been an *MfS* informer and as such was a part of that extensive network of intelligence-gathering observers, which meant that the 'unofficial' could never be significantly beyond the official gaze.

SECTION THREE

VARIETIES OF NON-CONFORMITY

Ian Wallace

INTRODUCTION

The collapse of the GDR in 1989, as sudden as it was unstoppable, took almost everyone by complete surprise. Ever since, commentators have striven to identify reasons for the demise of both the GDR and the wider communist system of which it was a key part.

The five chapters in this section may be seen as a valuable contribution to this process. They focus on specific social and political tensions within the GDR which helped to undermine the experiment in socialism set up in post-war eastern Germany in 1949. Building largely on extensive researches in previously inaccessible archives (notably those of the Stasi, aka the Ministerium für Staatssicherheit), the authors offer a series of perceptive insights which enrich our reading of the GDR's short history. In choosing to investigate the increasingly vocal disillusionment of 'ordinary' citizens in the late 1980s Jonathan Grix illuminates a relatively neglected phenomenon, using two particular examples to document its importance and offering strong evidence that it was not, as has been suggested elsewhere, a factor of only short-term importance. By establishing the existence of right-wing extremism in the GDR a decade *before* unification, Gordon Charles Ross is able to challenge the widespread perception that unification was the cause of this phenomenon rather than simply the occasion for its public self-assertion. While the number of GDR activists may have been relatively small and strikingly young (Ross speaks arrestingly of the 'juvenilisation' of extremism), their very existence is significant in a state which claimed to have eradicated fascism and militarism. Stephen Brown's contribution points up the paradox that the *rapprochement* between Church and state in 1978 in practice promoted the transformation of relatively low-level disaffection into active dissent among Church supporters, although the latter failed to construct an effective political vehicle for expression of that dissent. In pointing to the organisational structures of the state and of the Protestant churches as at least part of the explanation for the particular forms of interaction which characterised their difficult relationship, Brendan de Silva emphasises the crucial role of the State Secretary for Church Affairs as an intermediary between the churches and the real decision-makers in the SED, arguing that the latter received only misleading reports which played down the churches' real dissatisfactions while the former had an unrealistic belief that the politically weak State Secretary in fact had the power to help them achieve their goals. Michael Ploetz highlights the important but hitherto largely neglected role of the Peace Council of the GDR in the Cold War confrontations of the early 1980s and shows how the dogmatic inflexibility of the Marxist-Leninists served to split the peace movement. Ironically, this meant that they thereby played a not unimportant part in the ultimate demise of the communist system.

Taken as a whole, the section throws interesting new light on aspects of GDR history which have only recently become fully accessible to the demands of rigorous research.

Jonathan Grix

NON-CONFORMIST BEHAVIOUR AND THE COLLAPSE OF THE GDR

Using a bottom up approach, this paper traces the decomposition of citizens' loyalty towards the SED-state in the years prior to 1989. The banning of the Sputnik *journal and the deterioration of the economy are cited as major factors in fuelling existing dissatisfaction with the regime among citizens. Furthermore, insights are offered into the relationship between the ruled and rulers, as the focus is on the internal social dynamics of dictatorship and not on the so-called 'opposition' and power-wielding elites. Citizens' reactions to the crumbling economy and state* Bevormundung *are discussed by drawing on unpublished official documents.*

Introduction

This paper analyses some of the lesser known forms of non-conformist behaviour among the general population in the GDR leading up to the *Wende* of 1989. It thereby attempts to cover an area not dealt with by contemporary academic accounts which tend to be on either the so-called 'opposition' or power-wielding elites. In doing so, it discusses the sources behind the dissatisfaction which provoked such behaviour, the forms the articulation took and the effect of these actions on the overall collapse of the GDR itself. The state's relative stability, achieved to a great extent by widespread societal integration and participation, was undermined by the population's shift from private and individual acquiescence to the public and ever more collective expression of their grievances in the years *prior* to 1989. Two clear factors behind citizens' increasing willingness to voice their dissatisfaction with the regime are discussed, as are the forms this expression took. The examples used to analyse the move from stable continuity to regime-threatening change are as follows:

1.   Firstly, the SED's attempt at preventing the reform processes in the Soviet Union and its satellite states from spilling over into the GDR, culminating in the ban of the *Sputnik* magazine in November 1988. This sent a shock wave resonating throughout society which fuelled the decline of conditional loyalty among the GDR citizenry and brought about various forms of non-conformist behaviour, some of which were similar, if not identical, to the responses to 2. below.

2.   The effect of the catastrophic deterioration of the GDR economy in the last years of the GDR on the population, taken from unpublished Stasi *Stimmungsberichte* of workers in a number of different places of work.[1] Among the non-conformist responses to the economic stagnation (and 1. above) was the huge increase in *Eingaben* to the authorities, which presents a clear indication of the readiness of the population to begin openly to express their long-standing dissatisfaction. Additionally, the act or threat of non-

voting – usually in written form as an *Eingabe* – is introduced, as this was often the form taken to 'warn' the authorities of people's intentions.

Public reactions to the ban of *Sputnik* and its long-term consequences for the GDR

Von der Sowjetunion lernen, heißt siegen lernen [2]

According to a study undertaken by two political scientists in Potsdam, the ban of the *Sputnik* magazine on 19 November 1988 – inextricably linked to the GDR's refusal to take on any of the reforms coming out of the Soviet Union – caused a wave of protest throughout society.[3] Furthermore, they contest that the protest associated with the ban 'ebbed' after only a few weeks. My own findings in an in-depth case study of Schwerin support their claim that 'the majority of GDR citizens had in 1988/89 already internally taken leave of socialism', for socialism East German style was unpopular and not accepted by the population long before 1989.[4] Equally, the link between the 'dangers' of reform from the Soviet Union and the ban of *Sputnik* are also clear in the analysis of Schwerin. The present paper, however, differs from the Potsdam study on one crucial point: this is in its assessment of the long-term significance of the ban for the collapse of the country and the erosion of conditional loyalty among workers, intellectuals and deep into the ranks of the SED itself.[5]

Perestroika and glasnost

The GDR gerontocracy had little sympathy with the notion of reform, as they became encrusted in their conservative form of socialism on German soil. Gorbachev and the reforms closely associated with him were seen for what they were: a call for the restructuring of the economic sphere accompanied by liberalisation in the political sphere, and, therefore, a danger to the conservative GDR. By late 1988 – the time of the *Sputnik* ban – it became absolutely clear that the restructuring processes in the Soviet Union and the other countries of the socialist block were not to be allowed to spread to the GDR. By the time of Gorbachev's accession to power in the Soviet Union, the SED-state had already set about trying to stop the influence of both *Perestroika* and *Glasnost* spilling over into the GDR. The East German populace, however, was kept up to date with events via the West German media and they criticised the fact that in the GDR 'a considerable information deficit exists on the restructuring in the socialist brother countries'.[6] Gorbachev and his policies had been the source of great hope for many in the GDR, notably intellectuals and SED members, whose dream of a humane socialism seemed possible. The reform process was eventually reported by the Stasi to be widely discussed by the population, from 'below' and far beyond the rank and file SED members.[7] Hitherto Stasi reports from Schwerin were characterised by a *lack* of references to the population's interest in events happening in neighbouring socialist countries.

In June 1988 the police reported that the summit meeting between George Bush and Michael Gorbachev was 'seen as a great hope by many for liberation, especially in travel' in the GDR. Six months later in December the 'vast majority of citizens spoke of Genossen Gorbachev with great respect', whilst venting their anger over the *Sputnik* ban, for 'one cannot avoid heated discussions in the long run by a ban'.[8] By the end of November a reformed GDR seemed like an attractive prospect for many, as the possibility of unification with West Germany remained remote. The wider reform processes taking place elsewhere, together with the withdrawal of *Sputnik*, had a profound effect on GDR citizens as a whole, going well beyond the 5,300 subscribers and the 1,455 individual purchasers of the magazine in Schwerin.[9] The masses had had the achievements of the Soviet Union constantly drummed into them from a very early age. Thus, the apparent U-turn on GDR-Soviet policy, which reached its height with the ban of *Sputnik*, a magazine popular for its choice of topics, written in German and produced in the Soviet Union, came as a total shock to many. The wider appeal of this magazine was evident in the GDR from 1985 onwards, as it was regularly copied, photocopied and passed from hand to hand.[10] Astonishment and dismay did not stop with regular readers alone, but it went far beyond this into factories and offices throughout Schwerin *and* up and down the country, whether party members or not.[11] This was also the case on the national level, for the Stasi were unable to distinguish between arguments made by SED members and non-members.[12] Back in Schwerin the party reported to the Central Committee (ZK) informing them that they had received over 600 *Eingaben* relating to the *Sputnik* incident – approximately one tenth of the readership. At the same time the police reported to the *Bezirksleitung* on the desire for reform among the population and their discussions on the *Sputnik* ban, whilst management at the *PMS* (*Plastmaschinenwerk* – Plastic Factory) wrote – in increasingly frank language – that 'the answers to why it [the magazine] was banned are not accepted' by the workers at their plant.[13]

The words *unmündig* and *Unmündigkeit* are found most often in describing the population's reaction to the authority's ban of *Sputnik*. In the *Bezirkskrankenhaus* (*BKH*) employees 'feel they are having their decisions made for them [*bevormunden*] and are not in agreement with the fact that they are not given the opportunity to judge certain articles themselves'.[14] Equally, the words *Vertrauensverlust* (loss of trust) and *Unverständnis* (lack of understanding) have a predominant role in reports. Without exception the news of the ban was received in all spheres of the population with dismay.[15] Teachers responded by calling this a 'muzzle-policy', whilst members of the second largest mass organisation in the GDR, the DSF (*Gesellschaft für Deutsch-Sowjetische Freundschaft* / German-Soviet Friendship Society), threatened to leave the association.[16] Employees in shipping and waterways described the ban as an 'over-reaction and presumption' by the authorities responsible. These and 10 workers from the *PMS* were no longer ready to pay the DSF contributions and were already leaving the association.[17] Additionally, several anonymous telephone calls were registered by the district committee/board of the DSF, along with several intentions of leaving the organisation,[18] an undertaking which would indicate a clear distance to the ruling elite and their state.[19] Doctors at the *BKH* talked of a further 'incapacitation of citizens and an undermining of the people's trust in the party' whilst others went further still, suggesting that the ban was an astonishing contribution to and distortion of history, as up till now we have, as the GDR, only learnt from the Soviet Union.[20]

Equally infuriating to many citizens was the SED's statement that the Minister for Post, Rudolph Schulze, was responsible for striking *Sputnik* off the list of newspapers and periodicals. Mr. Schulze confirmed after the collapse of the GDR that he had in fact first learnt of his decision by reading the SED mouthpiece *Neues Deutschland*.[21] It was in a leading article in this paper that the SED attempted to justify the ban almost five days after the actual event, leading to citizens complaining about the party's late reaction.[22] In just under a year's time the leadership's intransigence in the face of an obvious need for action was to push many people into direct political action.

The ban sparked off spontaneous and heated discussions, and, according to workers and employees of the *Deutsche Post*, signified that 'the trust relationship between the citizens and the party cannot be consolidated, if the SED trusts citizens so little and attempts to cut them off from unpleasant information'. As a result of dissatisfaction with the GDR's media and information policy, which constantly glossed over current and apparent deficits and important events, an increased amount of rumours, speculation, half-truths, political jokes and misinformation against SED policies circulated throughout society.[23] In a move toward making his grievances with the ban public, a worker put up a 'wall newspaper' at his place of work with the title 'like a herd of sheep' in which he openly expressed his opposition to the state's measures, referring also to the 5 Soviet films banned by the state.[24] This example is indicative of many incidents of public voice following the SED ban of *Sputnik*, an incident which led to the 'mood in the GDR [becoming] increasingly[...]marked by desperation and despondency'.[25]

Hand written flyers, banners and the 'wall newspaper' in factories, firms etc. were used widely to express citizens' dissatisfaction with the *Sputnik* incident and other grievances.[26] Other reactions include the sending of individual and collective *Eingaben* to the authorities (around 200,000 republic-wide[27]) and the collection of signatures against the SED's decision. Many people left or threatened to leave the DSF and even the SED,[28] an action which would almost certainly bring with it sanctions and disadvantages in the all encompassing, all inclusive authoritarian state. Thus the *Sputnik* ban was the tail end of a period of *Abgrenzung* (demarcation) from the Soviet Union which had included the economic minister's, Kurt Hager's, well known and well quoted phrase referring to the reform process in the Eastern Bloc and its inapplicability to the GDR in April 1987: 'would you feel duty bound to change the wallpaper in your flat if your neighbour changes his?'[29] This statement shocked the GDR population, because it was a public rejection of the notion of reform. The more the GDR population became interested in the wider reform process, the more the authorities distanced themselves from it.[30]

The move by the SED to prevent the spread of reform processes filtering from the Soviet Union and other East European communist countries through to the GDR was seen at the time by citizens as a political *Fehlentscheidung* (wrong decision).[31] In one report Erich Honecker is personally made responsible for the political mistake 'and it is about time that a successor was found'. This is a surprising find in the backwaters of Schwerin and with almost a year to go before Honecker's own enforced resignation. For, as academics working on the national Stasi documents insist, 'the demand, that Honecker stand down as SED general secretary *is never mentioned in the Stasi files before his fall*'.[32] This example is indicative of the dissatisfaction felt by many out in the provinces. At a time when dissatisfaction at the workplace was at an all time high and provisions for consumer and other goods at an all time low (see below), the decision was suicidal. It bolstered and supported the decline in conditional loyalty toward the regime among all levels of society. Citizens were officially not allowed to read newspapers from the West 'and now the newspapers from the East [were] being banned' as well.[33] Many citizens were well aware that further societal developments would be seriously restricted 'by an ever deepening crisis of trust and by conflict situations coming to a head'.[34] Thus, the end of 1988 saw a clear erosion of conditional loyalty among wide sections of the ruled *and* the rulers, with the *Sputnik* event fuelling existing dissatisfaction with a number of different things, ranging from freedom of speech to the workplace and consumer goods.

Far from 'ebbing' after a few weeks, the resonance of this obvious breach of trust had lasting, significant consequences for the East German dictatorship.

Economic deterioration as a catalyst for non-conformist behaviour
The GDR economy began to run into serious trouble at the end of the 1970s and especially the beginning of the 1980s. The GDR began a 'forced export effort' coupled with the throttling of imports, including crucial spare parts, in order to combat a massive foreign debt.[35] The consequences of these actions for both the quality of exported goods, plant and machinery, especially those used in the production of consumer goods, were devastating. The degree of obsolescence led to growing stoppages and damage of plant.[36] This was, in part, due to the inability of the state's productive capacity to sustain Erich Honecker's social programme of subsidisation of costs for a wide range of basic goods and his massive housing programme, the realisation of which was to end in 1990.[37] The rationale behind this massive social policy programme was to compensate for the freedom denied the people and the lack of democratic legitimacy of the regime, whilst at the same time attempting to secure mass loyalty, albeit conditional.[38] This 'arrangement' or pragmatic coexistence – part of the so-called *Sozialvertrag* – began to breakdown as the economy stuttered. The result of this economic downturn was an increase in the chronic lack of spare parts for machines, tractors etc., shortages in consumer goods and the continuing shortage of raw materials. Worker dissatisfaction increased as a direct result of the state of the economy, because the workplace in the GDR, and with it the associationism based on work collectives and trade unions, had the function of filling the gap between the private and the public sphere in socialist everyday life. Everything from child care, medical care and shopping to holidays and sports clubs was arranged through the workplace.[39] The firm in the GDR, around which the SED focused its activities, was on the one hand central to the ideology of Marxism-Leninism, and on the other it took over a social function in which employees were members of work collectives, brigades and so on. This was both essential for the stability of the dictatorship and looked upon by many workers as one of the more positive aspects of socialist life. As dissatisfaction set in at the workplace, essentially a social microcosm of society, it therefore touched on many other aspects of people's lives, far beyond that usually experienced in the West.[40]

Expressions of dissatisfaction
Citizens' reactions to the decomposing economy in Schwerin *Bezirk* took on many forms that fall outside the attention of scholars working on the so-called 'opposition'. Although initially the various acts of non-conformist behaviour were of an individual nature, their rapid increase in number during the latter years of the East German dictatorship constituted a common desire for change which gradually manifested itself in collaborative efforts. These ranged from the rise in critical and usually unpublished or unanswered petitions (*Eingaben*) to the authorities and readers' letters in regional newspapers to the increased use of companies'/factories' 'wall newspapers' to relay information critical of the state, incidences of graffiti, anonymous telephone calls and the burgeoning growth of critical discussions at the workplace. All of these represent a break with the previous conformity of the masses and constitute a common desire for a public sphere in which dialogue could take place.

The Stasi reported clearly on the effects of the decaying economic situation on workers' morale, suggesting that discussions at the workplace were becoming more and more openly critical of the state.[41] Central to workers' discussions was the widespread dissatisfaction with their current economic situation. The permanent dissatisfaction with the supply situation,[42] the subject that attracted the bulk of written and verbal complaints from workers, was compounded by the scarcity of spare parts, for this choked the stuttering GDR economy into fits and starts leading to periods of stoppages becoming longer and longer.[43] Stoppages were increasingly used by workers in Schwerin for personal shopping and other private work, usually involving using the firm's equipment and sometimes its materials. This went so far as to include people selling off company goods in order to obtain other goods otherwise not available. Many workers were found to have goods including wine, spirits and food stuffs stored in their cellars for the purpose of exchange in the flourishing black economy.

This chaotic planning resulted in a stop and go of working activity and more importantly the throttling of innovation, whilst factories were placed under increasing pressure to meet unrealistic targets with inadequate supplies of goods and parts and an increasingly demoralised work force.[44] Under these circumstances and conditions, firms could no longer produce their products, unleashing a knock-on effect to the wider economy.

By publishing positive reports on the state of the economy, which stood in stark contrast to the personal hands-on everyday experience of workers,[45] the SED effectively provoked non-conformist reactions from citizens. The GDR media policy affected the mood of the population by deepening indifference, leading to both falling working morale and a decline in general work discipline. Ordinary workers who had hitherto kept well within the parameters of the dictatorship were gradually being alienated from the regime by economic deterioration and unrealistic media propaganda. The stagnation of the economy toward the end of the 1980s was accompanied by a rise in all the non-conformist activities mentioned: critical discussions at the workplace, the distribution of hand-written flyers, the use of both banners and the 'wall newspaper' in factories, firms etc. to express citizens' dissatisfaction with the supply situation in Schwerin *Bezirk* and the wider republic. The Area Hospital (*BKH*), the largest employer in the region, had a lively wall newspaper which, according to Dr. Georg Diederich, was well read and acted as a focal point for those seeking information outside of the official propaganda. These pockets of public expression of dissatisfaction grew significantly during 1987-1989 *throughout* the republic.[46]

In 1988 the Stasi noted that the 'the workers' relationship to their place of work had experienced a marked change in recent years'.[47] It was this very change in attitude that created the preconditions for the swift collapse of the GDR only one year later. Along with dissatisfaction came disaffiliation and alienation. The gap between the rulers and the ruled had increased still further *before* the fatal year of 1989. Thus one of the most powerful driving forces behind the change of attitudes, behind the shift from passive to active citizens, from individual grumbling to collective grumbling was economic deterioration, its effect on the population *and* the leadership's inability to address it.

Eingaben and the refusal to vote

The elections in the GDR were usually preceded by a rise in *Eingaben*.[48] The local/municipal elections in May 1989, which acted as a catalyst in the wider context of the collapse of the GDR, were not only paid special attention by grass-roots dissident groups, but also by many ordinary citizens as well. In March 1989 many *Eingaben* contained criticisms and complaints of problems at the municipal level. Again the main factors were housing problems followed by the supply situation and the service industry, refused travel applications and criticism of local councils and representatives.[49] Citizens now threatened with *Nichtteilnahme* (non-participation) at the forthcoming local election if the above grievances were not addressed. Even Church officials 'are making the fact whether they vote or not dependent on demands they have made on the state being fulfilled'.[50] The authorities were well aware that *Eingaben* were used as a way of forcing the state to address certain problems, for in one report they stated that 'the threat of not voting is often accompanied by letters and criticism to the local councils'. These should be looked upon as 'a sort of application of pressure in order to achieve personal advantages'.[51] Schwerin recorded an increase in non-participation of some 3.5 fold over 1986 when, as in 1989, the majority of people who threatened with non-participation worked in trade, industry, the service industry and agriculture. People with higher education – with the exception of would-be exit applicants and Church personnel – were in the minority.[52] In the small area of Ludwigslust alone, a *Kreis* to the south of Schwerin, the number of potential non-voters who had reported their intentions to the authorities had gone from 425 on 12.4.89 to 482 on 19.4.89.[53] In Lübz the authorities had received 211 *Eingaben* and 175 threats of non-participation in the election. The main problem was again housing and housing policy, and the number of complaints is reported as constantly changing, for the authorities 'are trying in the short-term to hold discussions with citizens and bring about changes'.[54] This is indicative of the state's attempt at actually trying to address citizens' problems at the local level, a fact underpinned by numerous examples in the in-depth study of Schwerin.

Subsequently the forthcoming election was actively used by Schwerin citizens to provoke discussions on the problems they faced at the local level. The link between the election and the solving of problems was well known to the authorities.[55] In the *Grundorganisation* (the lowest level of SED organisation in the GDR) at the *PMS* a working group was set up with the inventive name of 'election' and with the purpose of providing 'information on colleagues who for particular reasons do not wish to vote'.[56] The deterioration of the economy, workplace and supply situation – and the lack of discussions on the current political situation[57] – in the years prior to the election had combined with other aspects to force the dissatisfaction of the population through the safety valve of *Eingaben* and non-voting. In Schwerin this channel of voice had increased everywhere and the city council had already received 314 *Eingaben* by 1 January 1989. Half of these touched on the subject of housing, an indication of the state of living conditions at the time.[58] Some citizens even used the threat of non-participation to protest against the ban of the *Sputnik* magazine (discussed above), which was not back on GDR shelves until late October 1989.[59] By 27 April 1989 the number of *Eingaben* to the authorities in Schwerin *Bezirk* had risen to some 2,643,[60] an indication of the growing use of one of the few channels through which citizens could air their grievances under the dictatorship.

The act of speaking out against undemocratic procedures in the GDR was perceived by the authorities as a move toward the political by previously passive citizens. These political elements were creeping into the reasons for not wanting to vote, for 'in comparison to previous years an increase in the number of non-voters with political motives can be discerned'.[61] These ranged from not being in agreement with the freedom, democracy and the planned economy in the GDR, to not accepting the GDR's voting law (*Wahlrecht*). These political motives are representative of the change from passive to more vocal citizens.

Concluding remarks

This short paper has attempted to give an insight into some of the less glamorous forms of non-conformist behaviour and non-participation by the population of the former GDR. The brief examples presented here, which have not attracted the scholarly attention of those concerned with the so-called 'opposition', took place on a republic-wide scale in most *Bezirke*. It is the author's contention that this process of change from passive individual suffering of grievances to the active, collective expression of the same constitutes a major, underestimated factor behind the internal collapse of the GDR. Umbrella organisations, such as *Neues Forum*, were able to tap into this broad existing discontent and offer a focal point to which such people turned in the hope of change. Two major catalysts behind the release of pent-up *existing dissatisfaction* were discussed: the SED's attempt at preventing the reform processes affecting most of eastern Europe and the Soviet Union from catching on in the GDR and the effects of the economic deterioration in the late 1980s on the population's mood. Existing grievances, held in check by the unspoken *Sozialvertrag*, manifested themselves in the variety of non-conformist activities or acts of non-participation described above. The increasing frequency of such activities taken collectively *throughout* the republic can be seen as the burgeoning of a nascent civil society, in which the desire to discuss problems openly and vent discontent about society was common to all. This phenomenon, barely given attention in the academic literature, took place at the same time as the expansion of a replacement public sphere in and around the Church. Together, these long evolutionary developments (along with the activities of would-be emigrants) facilitated the avalanche of protest in the fatal year of 1989. The rapid increase in incidents of non-conformist behaviour constituted a 'movement' of individual actions, which, in the long run, facilitated the shift to collective action. It was this very shift in attitudes and perceptions that mobilised citizens to take direct, political action and effect change.

NOTES

[1] As the GDR was officially a 'workers' and peasants' state' employees are almost exclusively referred to as simply 'workers' (*Werktätige*, literally 'the working people'). I have kept to this for clarity and only use 'employees' when it is clear that the reports refer to a non-industrial sector.

[2] Cited in: S. Wolle, *Die heile Welt der Diktatur. Alltag und Herrschaft in der DDR 1971-1989* (Berlin, 1998), p. 293.

[3] See an article on the report in *Nordkurier*, 6.9.97, p.23. Interestingly enough the said edition of *Sputnik* did not discuss reforms of socialism but contained a controversial article 'critical of the German Communist

Party during the 1920s'. See J. Torpey, *Intellectuals, Socialism and Dissent. The East German Opposition and its Legacy* (London/Minnesota, 1995), p. 121.

[4] The case study was part of a wider project analysing the collapse of the GDR from the perspective of the masses. See: Jonathan Grix, 'The Role of the Masses in Regime Transformation: Exit, Voice and Loyalty and the Collapse of the GDR' (unpublished PhD.), Institute for German Studies, Birmingham University, October 1998

[5] The concept of conditional loyalty, developed in full in Grix., is loyalty toward the state conditioned by various factors, depending on which stratum of society one came from. In the case of the general population it can be seen as encompassing the unspoken *Sozialvertrag* between the rulers and the ruled, which exchanged social welfare for lip-service to the SED's ideology and acknowledgement of the party's leading role, among other things.

[6] BStU Aust. SN, Außenstelle Schwerin, AKG 15a, report 175/88 from 25.11.88, p. 53. (See the end of these notes for an explanation of archival abbreviations).

[7] BStU Aust. SN, Außenstelle Schwerin, AKG 14c, report 155/88 from 31.11.88, p.1/2; AKG 07, report 155/88 from 26.10.88, p.188; also *Nordkurier* from 6.9.97, p. 23. Mr. Schmidt, an employee at the BstU subsidiary in Schwerin, stated in an interview with the author on 24.3.98 in Schwerin that the most discussed topic in his factory was that of *Perestroika* and *Glasnost.*

[8] MLHA BPA SED SN, IV F-2/3/215, Police reports from 8.6.88, 12.12.88 (p.47 and p. 81); and BStU Aust. SN AKG 5a, KDS Güstrow, report 23/89 from 16.6.89, p.13.

[9] The figures are from: MLHA BPA SED SN, IV F-2/3/216, report from 7.11.88, p. 105.

[10] Interview with Mr. Dorn, BStU employee, Schwerin 23.3.98.

[11] Exemplary for Schwerin *Bezirk* is BStU Aust. SN AKG 18a, KD Parchim, report 37/88 from 2.12.88, p.129/130; MLHA BPA SED SN, IV F-2/5/90, *VEB Baustoffmaschinen Ludwigslust, Information über Stimmung und Meinungen zur Außen - und Innenpolitik,* from 28/11/88, p. 237; MLHA BPA SED SN, IV F-2/5/91, *VEB Fernmeldewerk Neustadt-Glewe, Bericht über Meinungen und Stimmungen* from 9.12.88, p. 148. For the wider picture see: MfS ZAIG, BStU, ZA, ZAIG 5352, report from 2.3.89 cited in: E. Kuhrt (ed.), *Die SED-Herrschaft und ihr Zusammenbruch* (Opladen, 1996), p.251.

[12] BStU, ZA, ZAIG 4244, printed in: G-R. Stephan (ed.), *'Vorwärts immer, rückwärts nimmer!' Interne Dokumente zum Zerfall von SED und DDR 1988/89* (Berlin, 1994), p. 54.

[13] The files are, in order: MLHA BPA SED SN IV F-2/5/88, report from 8.11.88, p.69; MLHA BPA SED SN IV F-2/3/216, *Informationsbericht der Polizei* from 7.11.88, p.92 and MLHA BPA SED SN IV/7/259/032, report from 14.11.88, p.2.

[14] MLHA BPA SED SN, BKH file IV 7/230/024, report from 29.88, p.1.

[15] BStU Aust. SN, KD AKG 18b, report 63/88 from 23.11.88, p. 106.

[16] ibid, p. 121. On the size of the DSF see C. Kumpf, *Faktoren des Zerfalls: Die Regimekrise in der ehemaligen DDR* (Frankfurt/M., 1995), p. 124.

[17] BStU Aust. SN, AKG 46a, BV SN, report 348/88, from 25.11.88, p.109; also BStU Aust. SN, AKG 15b, report189/88 from 30.12.88, p. 121. Interestingly, the *PMS* workers 'are not considering leaving the FDGB as this would mean the loss of material advantages, such as wage group, holiday place etc.', see AKG 15b p. 121.

[18] BStU Aust. SN, AKG 46a, BV SN, report 348/88, from 25.11.88, p. 106

[19] Ilko-Sascha Kowalczuk, 'Artikulationsformen und Zielsetzungen von widerständigem Verhalten in verschiedenen Bereichen der Gesellschaft', in: Deutscher Bundestag (ed.) *Materialien der Enquete-Kommission, 'Aufarbeitung von Geschichte und Folgen der SED-Diktatur in Deutschland'*, Volume VII,2 (Frankfurt/M,1995), pp.1203-1284, here p. 1242.

[20] BStU Aust. SN, AKG 46a, BV SN, report 348/88, from 25.11.88, p.107.

[21] S.Wolle, *Die heile Welt der Diktatur. Alltag und Herrschaft in der DDR 1971-1989*, p 295.

[22] BStU Aust. SN, BV, AKG 15b, report 180/88 from 9.12.88, p. 19.

[23] ibid, report from 11.11.88, p. 94. One such joke runs: A police officer stops a man who is carrying a large sack on his back and asks him what is inside. The man replies that the politburo is inside. On opening the sack on request the policeman said, 'there is only rubbish in here', to which the man replied, 'you said it!' This and other examples in: BStU Aust. SN. AKG 6b, KD Sternberg, report 19/89 from 17.10.89, p. 213.

[24] BStU Aust. SN AKG 46a, report 9.12.88 *Reaktion von Werktätigen des Bezirkes Schwerin auf die 7. Tagung des ZK der SED*, p. 149 and BStU Aust. SN Department XVIII 35, report 7.3.89 for period 1.1.89-1.3.89, p. 3.

[25] J. Torpey, *Intellectuals, Socialism and Dissent*, p. 121.

[26] The *BKH* had a lively wall newspaper which, according to Dr. Georg Diederich, was well read. See: 5 Mecklenburg-Vorpommern, Vol. III, *'Leben in der DDR, Leben nach 1989 - Aufarbeitung und Versöhnung'*, 'Veranstaltung zum Thema 'Die Geschichte der Wende',(Schwerin, 1st edition 1996), contribution by Georg Diederich, p. 133.

[27] C. Kumpf, *Faktoren des Zerfalls: Die Regimekrise in der ehemaligen DDR*, p. 162.

[28] BStU, ZA, ZAIG 4244, reprinted in Stephan, G-R. (ed.), *Vorwärts immer, rückwärts nimmer!*, p. 56.

[29] S. Wolle, *Die heile Welt der Diktatur. Alltag und Herrschaft in der DDR 1971-1989*, p. 292.

[30] W. Süß, *Taz* newspaper from 12.8.87, p.9, nr.2281.

[31] BStU Aust. SN, ZA, ZAIG 4244, report from 30.11.88: 'The majority of opinions expressed ....that this decision was politically wrong'.

[32] Cited in: E. Kuhrt (ed.), *Die SED-Herrschaft*, p.253. The emphasis is mine.

[33] BStU Aust. SN AKG 15a, report from 25.11.88, p.57.

[34] BStU Aust. SN AKG 18b, report 63/88 from 23.11.88, p.116.

[35] C. Flockton, 'The Declining Performance of the East German Economy', 1992 (unpublished manuscript), p.17.

[36] M. Haendcke-Hoppe-Arndt, 'Wer wußte was? Der ökonomische Niedergang der DDR', *Deutschland Archiv*, No. 6, 1995, pp.587-602, here p. 599.

[37] K. Schroeder, *Der SED-Staat. Geschichte und Strukturen der DDR* (München, 1998), p. 307.

[38] For a good discussion on the GDR's legitimacy see: J. Wiegohs/M. Schulz,'Die revolutionäre Krise am Ende der achtziger Jahre und die Formierung der Opposition', in: *Enquete-Kommission*, op. cit., Volume VII.2, pp.1955-1968.

[39] See: K. Schroeder, *Der SED Staat*, p. 515; also A.Pickel/H. Wiesenthal, *The Grand Experiment. Debating Shock Therapy, Transition Theory, and the East German Experience* (Boulder, Colerado, USA, 1997), p. 27.

[40] K. Schroeder, *Der SED Staat*, p. 515.

[41] BStU, AKG 7, 109/88, report from 3.8.88, p. 134.

[42] G-R. Stephan (ed.), *Vorwärts immer, rückwärts nimmer!*, p. 36f.

[43] MLHA, IV/7/259/032, report from 9.1.89, p. 2.

[44] MLHA, IV/7/259/032, report from 14.11.88, p. 1.

[45] BStU Aust. SN, AKG 14c, report 169/88 from 11.11.88, p. 153.

[46] See: Landtag Mecklenburg-Vorpommern, Volume II, *'Leben in der DDR, Leben nach 1989 - Aufarbeitung und Versöhnung'*, p. 133.

[47] BStU, AKG 7, 155/88, report from 26.10.88, p. 200.

[48] Interview with Thomas Helms, printer, in Schwerin, 17 August 1997.

[49] This example is taken from KD Ludwigslust in BStU Aust. SN, AKG 5c, *Die Lageeinschätzung in Vorbereitung der Kommunalwahlen am 7.5.89*, report 11/89 from 30.3.89, p. 46.

[50] MLHA BPA SED SN, Z 10/90 8, report from 9.5.89 for March/April 1989, p. 4.

[51] BStU Aust. SN, AKG 5c KD Ludwigslust, report 14/89 from 28.4.89, p. 58.

[52] Information in: A. Mitter, / S. Wolle (eds.) *Ich liebe Euch doch alle..., Befehle und Lageberichte des MfS Januar - November 1989* (Berlin: 1990), p. 103; and BStU Aust. SN, Leiter 2b, BV Schwerin from 13.6.86.

[53] ibid, p.57.

[54] BStU Aust. SN AKG 5c, KD Lübz, report 4/89 from 17.4.89, p. 11-12.

[55] BStU Aust. SN AKG 46b (no date), p. 27.

[56] MLHA BPA SED SN, Plastmaschinenwerk: 1987-89, IV/7/259/032, report from 17.4.89, no page number.

[57] BStU Aust. SN AKG 5c, KD Lübz, report 4/89 from 17.4.89, p. 12.

[58] BStU Aust. SN AKG 46b, KD Schwerin (no date), p. 27.

[59] *Schweriner Volkszeitung*, nr. 248, 21/22.10.89, front page. This was just one day before Schwerin's big demonstration.

[60] BStU Aust. SN, AKG 2a, BV Schwerin, report (no number) from 5.4.89, p. 89.

[61] BStU Aust. SN, AKG 5c KD Ludwigslust, report 14/89 from 28.4.89, p. 59.

Files Cited in the Text:

Files from the State Commissioner for the Documents of the State Security Service of the Former German Democratic Republic (BStU), subsidiary (Aust.) Schwerin (SN):

BStU Aust. SN, AKG 07, report 109/88 from 3.8.88; ibid., report 155/88 from 26.10.88
BStU, Aust. SN, Department XVIII 36
BStU Aust. SN, AKG 18b, report 75/88 from 28.12.88
BStU Aust. SN, AKG 10b report 21/88, 5.2.88
BStU Aust. SN AKG 14a, report 133/88 from 21.9.88
BStU Aust. SN AKG 11a report 38/88 from 2.3.88

Files from the Mecklenburg Area Main Archive (MLHA), area party archive section (BPA) in Schwerin:

MLHA BPA SED SN, IV/7/259/032, *Plastmaschinenwerk*: 1987-89, , report from 14.11.88; ibid., report from 9.1.89
MLHA BPA SED SN, IV 2/3/215, *Informationsbericht der Bezirksbehörde der deutschen Polizei zu Stimmungen und Meinungen der Bevölkerung zur 6. Tagung*, report from 17.6.88
MLHA BPA SED SN IV 2/3/213, *Information der Lage und zum Verhalten der Gesuchsteller* from 23.3-30.3.88
MLHA BPA SED SN IV F-2/5/86, *BL Schwerin an ZK über besondere Vorkommnisse*, 1988, report from 11.8.88

MLHA BPA SED SN IV F/2/3/216, report from 8.12.88
MLHA BPA SED SN IV F-2/5/86, *BL Schwerin an ZK über besondere Vorkommnisse*, 1988, report from 11.8.88

Gordon Charles Ross

THE SWASTIKA IN SOCIALISM: RIGHT-WING EXTREMISM AND MILITANT NATIONALISM IN THE GDR

Based on empirical research in the former GDR state archives as well as interviews with right-wing extremists, this paper reconstructs and discusses the nature of right-wing extremism and militant nationalism in the GDR between 1980-1990. A discourse analysis of statements made by right-wing youths in the GDR, extracted from the Stasi *files, shows that many of the arguments they put forward equate closely to those put forward by the far-right and militant nationalists in Germany today.*

Introduction

Recent revelations about right-wing activity in the *Bundeswehr*, the startling electoral success of the far-right DVU in recent *Landtag* elections in Sachsen-Anhalt and the recorded rise in extreme right-wing related activism in the Federal Republic in 1997,[1] show that the problem of right-wing extremism in Germany continues to occupy public and political discourse. Furthermore, discussion since the *Wende* over whether right-wing extremism and racism are more or less prolific in the east or west of Germany continues to undermine collective German understanding. Not surprisingly, most responses to the problem of right-wing extremism in Germany tend to focus on the problems associated with unification; on the socio-economic, political and cultural transformation of Germany, in particular on the advent of massive unemployment in the new *Länder* (e.g. Husbands 1991; Heitmeyer 1991a/b; Grill 1991). Whilst this perspective is not misplaced, I would argue that it is ultimately short-sighted in that it overlooks the existence and development of a militant right-wing movement before unification, in the German Democratic Republic (GDR).

With this perspective in mind, three interrelated tasks will be carried out in this paper. First, right-wing extreme activity, as it manifested itself in the GDR in the 1980s, will be reconstructed from empirical data and subjected to critical analysis. The aim of this historical reconstruction is to provide an impression of the nature and extent of right-wing extremism in the GDR, as well as to demonstrate continuities between right-wing extremism both *before* and *after* the *Wende*. Second, statements made by right-wing extremists will be analysed in the search for the motivation behind right-wing extremism in a state that described itself as 'socialist' and 'anti-fascist'.[2] Third and last, some conclusions will be drawn for the present situation in Germany. My argument is that it has been a reversion to an exclusionist ethno-nationalism, which right-wing extremists refer to as 'Germanness', rather than an explicit neo-fascism, that has mobilised right-wing extremism both in the GDR and in Germany today. In this context, it will also be argued that Germany, east or west, cannot be seen as a *Sonderfall*.

The swastika in socialism: right-wing extremism in the GDR

Manifestations of right-wing extremism in the GDR present a diverse picture.[3] The archival material contains examples of anti-Semitism, racism and xenophobia; a virulent anti-communism and the glorification of the National Socialist past; the desecration of Soviet war memorials and Jewish cemeteries; the possession and dissemination of neo-fascist literature and regalia such as swastikas; the celebration of Hitler's 'birthday'; attacks on foreigners and guest workers living in the GDR; and finally assaults on punks and left-wing opponents as well as other acts of violence and vandalism with an extreme right-wing ideological motivation. One may question whether this type of behaviour can be called right-wing extreme at all but there are clear indications in the archives that this was politically motivated behaviour. This is reflected in statements in the files: 'A number of the members of the sub-group of the skins have a very clear right-wing extreme orientation.'[4] Whilst many of these incidents were probably spontaneous, unplanned and carried out by random individuals, there is a lot of evidence to suggest that not all incidents involving right-wing extremism in the GDR were simply the product of drunken yob behaviour. On the night of 17 October 1987, for example, twenty-five skinheads, including three from West Berlin, attacked a concert in the *Zionskirche* in East Berlin, organised predominantly by church and alternative groups. The skinheads had met in a pub before the attack and planned their action. They shouted anti-Semitic, anti-Communist and neo-fascist abuse and physically assaulted members of the audience. The fighting was finally broken up by the police but not before there were several injuries, one person being taken to hospital.[5]

Although there were no legal right-wing political parties in the GDR, right-wing groupings and organisations were beginning to form at the end of the 1980s. The *Lichtenberger Front* for example was founded in East Berlin in 1986 and *Die Bewegung 30. Januar* was a neo-nazi party founded in 1988 by Ingo Hasselbach and André Riechert. The group was dissolved by the *Stasi* in March 1989 but its hard-core members became leading members of extreme right-wing groups in East Germany after unification (Hasselbach/Bonegel 1993: 41). *Operative Vorgänge*[6] were made by the *Stasi* into a series of incidents involving youths who were attempting to establish paramilitary groups in the 1980s. The results of these investigations revealed a whole range of activities, including military training, the dissemination of National Socialist literature, singing 'fascist songs' in public, plans to break into Sachsenhausen concentration camp to steal nazi uniforms and regalia, the celebration of Hitler's 'birthday', hostile activities towards Soviet soldiers and (failed) attempts to acquire fire-arms. A similar group was uncovered in 1985 and its activities were investigated by the MfS.[7] The importance of the formation of these groups cannot be overstated because the emergence of clandestine neo-nazi groups and *Kameradschaften* in the GDR in the 1980s allow one to speak of the beginnings of a right-wing political movement. According to Hasselbach, for example, the foundation of the *Bewegung 30. Januar* was the 'birth of the neo-nazis in East Germany.'[8]

Stasi files also show that the GDR right-wing movement was increasing in size and activities in the 1980s. Criminal and violent acts of an extreme right-wing nature rose five-fold in the GDR between 1983-1987 (Weiß 1989: 5i; Wagner 1993: 2). In 1984 the MfS department in charge of political incidents of a right-wing nature, *Sektion HA/XXII*, estimated that right-wing agitation encompassed 13.5 per cent of all anti-state offences.

According to the report, this type of offence had risen significantly in comparison to the previous year.[9] There were ten incidents per month involving right-wing skinheads recorded by the *Stasi* until August 1988.[10] These are significant figures for a state that claimed to have eradicated fascism and militarism 'for ever'.

Nevertheless, the GDR right-wing extreme movement itself remained comparatively small. This is supported both by official GDR statistics as well as unofficial (observer) estimates. In 1988, for example, sociologists and church leaders in the GDR estimated the number of 'hard-core skinheads and neo-fascist youths' to be between one thousand and one thousand eight hundred with a concentration of activists in East Berlin (Hockenos 1993: 84). In 1988, Erich Mielke's deputy produced a document that reported eight hundred extreme right-wing activists and thirty-eight extreme right-wing groups. The last study of right-wing extremists made by the *Deutsche Volkspolizei* (the GDR police) in November 1989 estimated around one thousand five hundred 'known right-wing extreme skinheads and *Faschos*' in the GDR (Kriminalpolizei 1989). Based on this evidence it is clear that right-wing extremism in the GDR was only populated by a small number of activists. Nevertheless, empirical evidence suggests that the *militant* right in Germany today is still organised in the same kind of loose structures as it was in the GDR (cf. Willems/Würtz/Eckert 1993).

Further parallels can be drawn between right-wing extremism before and after unification. For example, several studies show that the recent wave of right-wing extremism in Germany is predominantly made up of male youths aged between fifteen and twenty-five. Studies for 1992 show that only 2.5 per cent of those arrested for racist violence were over thirty years of age.[11] It is therefore possible to speak of the juvenilisation of right-wing extremism. This juvenilisation also applies to the situation in the GDR (Kokoschko 1990: 7). Right-wing extremism in the GDR was largely a phenomenon populated by young men aged under twenty-five. The 'entrance age' into the right-wing scene was estimated to be as young as sixteen.[12] On the whole both the primary and secondary sources suggest that neither right-wing extremists in the GDR nor in the new East German *Länder* today are over-represented by actors from the lower social classes or the so-called 'victims of modernisation' (Heitmeyer 1992; Leggewie 1990; Klönne 1989). On the contrary, all the evidence suggests that right-wing extremism in the GDR was populated mostly by what one can call 'normal' and 'average' GDR youths, who worked conscientiously and whose social status is not indicative of a high level of social marginalisation. Studies undertaken of criminal acts with an extreme right-wing background suggest that all classes of GDR society were represented (Madloch 1990: 11). In 1986/1987, for example, at least eighty per cent of the GDR extreme right held what was considered to be a socially respected status in their society. More than three-quarters had professional training and almost half were *Facharbeiter*.[13] (Wagner 1993: 9). There were a total of seventeen known trials of skinheads in the GDR between the end of 1987 and mid-1989 (Neubacher 1994).[14] The majority of the accused were workers and *Handwerker*. Only a minority had previous convictions and, according to Arenz's study, the majority were 'normal, inconspicuous youths' (Arenz 1989: 806). 'All in all,' claim Ködderitzsch and Müller, 'these were the children of an orderly, clean, disciplined world [...] the children of forty years of anti-fascist education.'[15]

Neither is there any convincing evidence to show that right-wing extremists in Germany today are drawn disproportionately from socio-economically disadvantaged groups. This is true of both extreme right-wing criminals as well as extreme right-wing voters. Between 1991 and 1993, for example, 33.6 per cent of extreme right-wing activists arrested by the police were either school pupils, students or apprentices, 28.7 per cent were skilled workers, 11.3 per cent were unskilled workers and just 11.3 per cent were unemployed[16] (Verfassungsschutzbericht 1993: 21). The socio-economic background of the members of extreme right-wing mainstream political parties makes the 'victims thesis' seem even less convincing. Here, it is possible to talk of a middle class stratum (Stöss 1993; Ladwig 1993). Until the spectacular success of the DVU in Sachsen-Anhalt in 1998, the mainstream right-wing parties achieved their best results in the more affluent *Bundesländer*, such as Baden-Württemberg and Bayern, and have fared worse in the impoverished East German *Länder* with their high levels of unemployment (Ladwig 1993). Clearly then, one must search for the motivation for right-wing extremism in Germany in other areas.

Militant defenders of 'Germanness'
What was the motivation for right-wing extremism in the state-socialist, anti-fascist state? An analysis of the *Stasi* files suggests that for the GDR right-wing extremists the notion of 'Germanness', or what they called *Deutschtum*, was a central item in their value repertoire. This kind of ethno-nationalism was not just related to racism or chauvinism but was an expression of an 'exclusionary identity politics' (Eric Hobsbawm) based on an ethno-centric claim to identity. According to Bernd Wagner, for example, the main ideological goal of right-wing extremists in the GDR was not the resurrection of the Third Reich, but a desire 'to gain recognition from an unstructured majority of the population to prove themselves *militant defenders of German interests*' (Wagner 1993: 12, italics added). This line of argument is supported empirically in repeated references to 'Germanness' throughout the archival material, for example: 'The historically unreflected *Deutschtum* is a conspicuous slogan in the skinheads' vocabulary.'[17] Furthermore, right-wing skinheads' 'moral values are, in the most part, characterised by views such as the 'honour and loyalty of a German'.[18]

What did the GDR right-wing extremists understand by 'Germanness'? In their view, being 'German' meant being hard-working, productive, orderly, clean, disciplined and strong. Values such as strength and power, national pride, discipline, order and the heroism of the German soldier in the Second World War were idealised.[19] Typical 'German' values frequently recorded by the *Stasi* were punctuality, loyalty, decency and awareness of duty.[20] '*Verpfeifen*' (snitching) on friends and other group members was viewed not only as an offence in itself but also as 'unworthy of a German' and 'damaging to loyalty and comradeship.'[21] In the words of one GDR right-wing extremist, the best aspect of the National Socialist regime was its 'German order'.[22]

According to the GDR constitution, 'German militarism' had been eradicated in the GDR,[23] yet right-wing attitudes towards the military were generally very positive. It is known that the GDR right-wing extremists were fascinated by the special contingents of the armed forces and that they saw them as embodying typical militaristic values of order, comradeship and discipline. Consequently, many of them volunteered for extended military service and many were recruited into the *Nationale Volksarmee* (NVA) and the *Gesellschaft für Sport und Technik* (GST), finding a niche in an army which they saw above all as a 'German army' (Siegler 1991). According to a report made by the MfS in

1988 the right-wing extremists were 'of the view that military training is part of being German.'[24]

The right-wing youths themselves placed great value on their hard work and industriousness. This gave them a sense of pride and allowed them to draw a clear distinction between themselves, foreigners and rival groups, in particular the 'un-German' punks and Goths. Thus, in the words of an eighteen-year-old skinhead:

> I do my work regularly, consider myself hard-working and produce
> quality work. This is the point that distinguishes a real skin. I belong to
> a group in which every member behaves and thinks this way. In general,
> we are hard-working and can't stand shirking and scroungers.[25]

Punks were therefore rejected and singled out for abuse because they were seen as anarchic, dirty and 'un-German'.[26] A right-wing youth working in the building trade explained his attitude towards the punks; 'I just think that there has to be order in a state and not anarchy. That's why I reject punks. They can live in the dustbin [sic]' (Engelstädter 1991: 5). In the words of another GDR skinhead: 'A German is clean and ought to be clean. Even what the punks and Goths wear is un-German.'[27]

The right-wing extremists' 'positive' attitude towards work, the military and discipline was frequently praised by work colleagues and the MfS. The *Stasi* officers observing right-wing activity in the GDR were aware of the importance of their ethno-nationalist views. According to MfS trainee officer Torsten Gruhn, for instance:

> One can assume that the 'hard core' of the skinheads regard the punks,
> Goths, foreigners and homosexuals as a threat (un-German, lazy, anti-
> social) because they do not fit into their glorified ideology of
> *Deutschtum.*[28]

In fact, the MfS shared the view that such ideological beliefs, values and morality were instrumental in the formation of the GDR's right-wing groups. Thus we find the statement in another file that 'The similarity of attitudes to work, violence vis-à-vis other persons (e.g. foreigners, homosexuals) condition the [group] formation'.[29] There is evidence in the files that shows that the MfS was prepared to adopt right-wing values itself in an attempt to infiltrate and subvert right-wing groups. One *Stasi* file reviewed contains a report on how *Inoffizielle Mitarbeiter* (IMs) could be best trained to infiltrate right-wing groups. According to the author, certain typical values could be discerned, such as 'punctuality, loyalty, decency and awareness of one's duty'.[30]

An ethno-nationalist claim to identity also represented the justification of and motivation for racist sentiments amongst the GDR extreme right. They frequently justified their racist views by claiming that foreigners represented a threat to the 'German people'.[31] Again, this argument is reflected in statements found in the archives:

> The ideological position of the hardcore of these [extreme right-wing]
> youths is characterised by virulent nationalist and racist influences.
> These manifest themselves especially in terms of xenophobia and the
> glorification of acts of violence, as well as against social conditions in
> the GDR[32]

The right-wing extremists often referred to groups who exploited the social welfare benefits of the GDR economic system as *Schmarotzer* (parasites). A rejection of foreigners living in the GDR was based on the politics of social envy because of the belief that foreigners enjoyed certain privileges that were not generally available to GDR citizens. Stereo-typical impressions of foreigners as 'lazy, parasitic and stinking' were continually contrasted with stereo-typical images of 'Germans' as 'clean, hard-working and disciplined.' This is reflected in a statement made by a GDR skinhead, describing himself as belonging to the 'neo-nazi trend':

> I'm against foreigners 'cause they're taking our places at university and
> stealing our girls and cause trouble...they should go back to where they
> came from. I am also in favour of going to work regularly [....] 'cause I
> believe that the Germans have always been hard workers[33]

This statement suggests that socio-economic factors within the relative affluence[34] of the GDR were important as a source of justification for right-wing action. In this statement, for instance, the right-wing youth is excluding foreigners from the 'benefits' of state-socialism, e.g. free places at universities, free child-care, etc. There is also an obvious perceived sexual threat embedded in the statement 'our girls' which smacks of a male chauvinism in which German women are seen as the property of German men, to be protected from 'non-Germans'.

In many ways such criticisms are not dissimilar to those expressed on the far right in Germany and other parts of Europe today in which some sections of the conservative and far-right politicise the 'crisis' of the welfare state and exclude certain groups, especially foreigners, asylum-seekers, single mothers, etc., from its benefits (Betz 1991; Glennerster 1991). Foreigners and outsiders are not merely seen as a threat to the welfare state but also as a threat to the right-wing extremists' sense of identity as Germans. In this context, it would make more sense to define right-wing extremists as the 'chauvinists of identity' rather than the 'chauvinists of affluence' (Ladwig 1993; Rommelspacher 1991).

Ethno-nationalism has also motivated right-wing groups since the *Wende*. Studies show that the racist attacks that took place in Germany between 1991 and 1993 have been less motivated by an explicit neo-nazi motivation than a diffuse ethno-nationalism. Willems et al's empirical study of right-wing and racist activism after 1990, for example, came to the conclusion that xenophobic violence in Germany had little to do with an explicit neo-nazism but was largely motivated by 'diffuse feelings and images of a general threat and disadvantage of Germans' (in: Merten/Otto 1993: 103). A study of right-wing extremism sponsored by the *Land* Brandenburg in 1997 found that right-wing violence was rooted in 'hatred of foreigners and intolerance of anything different'. Most were not militant neo-nazis but 'normal' east German youths who 'want to be part of a popular national community governed by "German values."'

Conclusions: lessons from the past
What lessons can be learnt from this for today's situation? First, the evidence presented suggests that right-wing extremism in Germany has been *exacerbated* rather than *caused* by German unification. This is not to claim, of course, that right-wing extremism in the GDR and in Germany since the *Wende* are exactly the same. In comparison with the explosion of right-wing related violence that took place in Germany after unification, manifestations of right-wing extremism in the GDR were less prolific, less organised and obviously less spectacular. Whilst this quantitative and qualitative rise after 1990 must be borne in mind, it is nevertheless possible to discern continuities between right-wing extremism before and after the *Wende*. 'In sum,' as Minkenberg argues, 'unification only

reinforced those dynamics which had already begun before 1989 while adding the insecurities and imponderabilities of the massive transformation process in the East' (Minkenberg 1994: 188).

Second, the right-wing problem, as the GDR case shows, has not been caused by massive immigration, or large numbers of foreigners, or the problems associated with asylum.[35] Clearly then, the motivation for right-wing extremism has to be sought in other determinants; determinants, moreover, that span the *Wende*. I have tried to argue that this might be found in the question of ethnicity and how it should be defined. This line of argument, moreover, applies to both the GDR and the five new *Länder*. Whilst an exclusionary ethnic nationalism is not, of course, the *only* cause of right-wing extremism, it helps explain the motivation for right-wing extremism that today is often based on the theory of an imaginary 'nation'. In fact, I would argue that the concept of the ethnic nation is implicitly exclusive and serves, in one form or another, as a source of legitimisation for Europe's far right ideologies. In this context, one is not necessarily dealing with individual pathological cases but with the process by which the boundaries or normative limits of ethno-nationalist and racist sentiments become constructed and serve as a basis for right-wing extreme political activism and ideology. It goes without saying that Germany is not a special case in this context. Ethno-nationalism is the major motivating factor for the extreme-right and militant nationalists in Europe today. What *is* special about Germany is that re-unification is taking place not only against a backdrop of economic restructuring and mass unemployment, but also at a time of globalisation and the gradual erosion of national sovereignty.

Third, with the incorporation of seventeen million East Germans into the new Republic in 1990, what took place in Germany was not just the economic and political take-over of the former GDR, but a process that has been called the 'reconstruction of Germanness' (Räthzel 1990). This reconstruction could only be successfully carried out, I would argue, by demarcating 'insiders' and 'outsiders' in terms of citizenship. This, of course, is a nation-building process common to all nascent states. In Germany, after unification, the authorities in Bonn and sections of the mass media played upon fears of 'swarms' of asylum-seekers and immigrants flooding into Germany when the 'boat' was supposedly already 'full'. Such claims were largely bogus, however, as official Federal figures for 1987 show that only 9.6 per cent (57,379) of immigrants to Germany were asylum-seekers and nearly half (46.8 per cent) were defined as 'Germans' (*Übersiedler, Aussiedler*). In addition, official statistics show that the German population as a whole had decreased, not increased (Räthzel 1990: 35).

Lastly, and until the new SPD-Green government changes the law, citizenship in the Federal Republic will still be based on article 116 of the *Grundgesetz*, which establishes citizenship predominantly in terms of blood rights (*jus sanguinis*). This way of defining citizenship is a remnant of the Reich Citizenship Law of 1913. Thus, it can be seen that the notion of the *Volksgemeinschaft* has survived the transition from Weimar, through the nazi dictatorship, through the GDR, till today (Fulbrook 1995: 19). There is still no automatic right to German citizenship for non-Germans unless they fulfil a number of conditions such as the requirement to have been resident in the FRG for at least ten years, being able to speak German, having a flat, etc. These citizenship rules have led to the perverse situation where *Volksdeutsche* from Eastern Europe, who speak no German and have never lived in Germany, can claim automatic rights to German citizenship, whilst

Gastarbeiter and their children, who have lived and worked in Germany all their lives, have no such rights unless they meet the conditions listed above.[36] These conditions and the high cost of naturalisation in the FRG are two reasons why only 2.9 per cent of the Italian, 2.8 per cent of the Spanish and 0.75 per cent of the Turkish population have been naturalised.[37] All these facts suggest to me that it was the politicisation of the asylum question, rather than the actual number of asylum-seekers and immigrants coming into Germany, that mobilised right-wing and racist activity after unification.[38]

NOTES

[1] The *Kriminalpolizei* (the Federal Republic of Germany's equivalent of the CID) recorded a total of 5,173 extreme right criminal offences in Germany in 1997. This was an increase of fourteen per cent over 1996. It also recorded the first rise in the number of extreme right-wing activists (47, 000) since 1993.

[2] The empirical data fall into two general categories: first, my own archival research in the FDJ, SED and MfS archives in East Berlin. Second, semi-structured interviews with members of extreme right-wing groups and experts in the field of right-wing extremism undertaken mostly during fieldwork in Germany 1993-1994.

[3] In this paper, the term right-wing extremism is used as an umbrella term for political activism and ideology with a traditional right-wing motivation (neo-nazism, militant nationalism, racism, etc.).

[4] SED file IV 2/2.0.39/246: 55 (Anhang 3)

[5] SED Hausmitteilung, in: SED file IV 2/2.039/313: 2

[6] *Operative Vorgänge* were secret operational proceedings carried out by the *Stasi* on all citizens of the GDR suspected of anti-state activity or leanings.

[7] MfS file VVS JHS o001-403/85: 30ff

[8] Interview with former East German neo-nazi Ingo Hasselbach in (West) Berlin 14.06.1994.

[9] Information der HA/XXII vom Mai 1985: Über Erkenntnisse aus der politisch-operativen Aufklärung und Bearbeitung von Vorkommnissen der staatsfeindlichen Hetze (streng geheimes Material - Reg. Nr. 377/85), in: MfS file VVS JHS o001-403/85: 32

[10] MfS file VVS-JHS o001-337/89: 3

[11] Source: '*Fragenund Antworten zum Rechtsextremismus*' on website:
http://www.uni. marburg.de/dir/material/doku/statist/farecht.html.

[12] MfS file VVS JHS o001-300/89: 27

[13] Note: skilled workers and artisans enjoyed a high level of social status and respect in the GDR due to their training and skill.

[14] Note: in some of these trials an extreme right-wing background was not established, cf. Ammer 1988: 804.

[15] Source: Ködderitzsch/Müller 1990: 23

[16] A government-sponsored study undertaken in 1993 on the social background of those arrested for acts of extreme right-wing and racist violence found that unemployment might be more significant in the new *Länder*. Twenty-six per cent were unemployed in the eastern *Länder* compared with eighteen per cent for Germany as a whole, in: *Tatsachen über Deutschland* 1993: 368.

[17] MfS file VVS JHS o001-486/89: 106

[18] MfS file VVS JHS o001-337/89: 29

[19] MfS file VVS JHS o001-300/89: 21

[20] MfS file VVS JHS o001-337/89: 30

[21] MfS file VVS JHS o001-337/89: 29

[22] MfS file VVS JHS o001-337/89: 63

[23] Article 6 of the Constitution of the GDR, 06 April 1974

[24] MfS file HAXX, 02.02.1988

[25] Cited, in: Engelstädter 1991: 92

[26] MfS file VVS JHS o001-337/89: 62

[27] MfS file VVS JHS o001-486/89: 12

[28] MfS file VVS JHS o001-300/89: 47

[29] MfS file VVS JHS o001-300/89: 32

[30] MfS file VVS JHS o001-337/89: 30

[31] MfS file VVS JHS o001-300/89: 21

[32] MfS file VVS JHS o001-337/89: 8

[33] MfS file VVS JHS o001-337/89: 62

[34] It is worth remembering that the GDR was *relatively* wealthy compared with its poorer Slavic neighbours, in particular Poland, Romania and Czechoslovakia.

[35] In 1989, foreign nationals made up only 1.1% of the East German population, compared to 7.3% in West Germany. Cf. Ursachen, Umfang und Auswirkungen von Ausländerfeindlichkeit auf dem Gebiet der ehemaligen DDR und Möglichkeiten ihrer Überwindung. Eine Untersuchung der ISG-Sozialforschung und Gesellschaftspolitik im Auftrag des Bundesministers für Arbeit und Sozialforschung, Köln 31.12.1990.

[36] Since 1987, almost fifty per cent of migrants to (West) Germany have been either ethnic Germans from Eastern Europe (*Aussiedler*) or Germans from the GDR (*Übersiedler*) cf. Räthzel 1990: 32

[37] Cited in Räthzel 1990. Note: Räthzel does not cite a period for these figures though it is likely they refer to West Germany in the late 1980s.

[38] This, for example, has been shown empiricially in: Koopmans 1995

SOURCES

Primary
MfS files: Archives of the Ministerium für Staatssicherheit der DDR, (MfS), Berlin
VVS JHS o001-403/85: Diplomarbeit: Darstellung operativ-bedeutsamer Erscheinungen und Handlungen neonazistischer Potentiale des Operationsgebietes, deren Auswirkung auf die DDR und daraus resultierende Schlußfolgerungen: Major Jürgen Dalski, Oltn. Dieter Jerie, JHS Potsdam, Frankfurt (Oder), 03.01.1986

VVS JHS o001-300/89: Diplomarbeit zum Thema: Ursachen und Bedingungen für das Entstehen operativ bedeutsamer Personenzusammenschlüsse jugendlicher und jungerwachsener DDR-Bürger - bezogen auf Skinheadgruppierungen im Bezirk Potsdam sowie der von ihnen ausgehenden sozial-negativen operativ bedeutsamen Handlungen - und sich daraus ergebenden Konsequenzen für die politisch-operative Arbeit der BV Potsdam. Offiziersschüler Torsten Gruhn, JHS Potsdam, Potsdam 21.04.1989

VVS JHS o001-337/89: Diplomarbeit zum Thema: Erfordernisse der Erziehung und Befähigung von inoffiziellen Mitarbeitern (IM) zur operativen Bearbeitung von rechtsextremistischen Erscheinungen unter Jugendlichen der Hauptstadt: Offizierschüler Rainer Taraschonnek, BV Berlin Abteilung XX/2, Berlin 27.04.1989

VVS JHS o001-486/89: Diplomarbeit zum Thema: Untersuchungen zum Stand der Erfüllung der politisch-operativen Aufgabenstellung zur vorbeugenden Verhinderung und Bekämpfung von Skinheads im Verantwortungsbereich der Kreisdienststelle Oranienberg: Bartl, Joachim, Hptm. Oranienberg, 13.10.1989

VVS o008-14/88: Einschätzung über in der DDR existierende Jugendliche, die sich mit neo-faschistischer Gesinnung öffentlich kriminell und rowdyhaft verhalten sowie Schlußfolgerungen zu ihrer weiteren rigorosen Zurückdrängung und zur Verhinderung von derartigen Jugendlichen ausgehenden Gefährdungen der Sicherheit und Ordnung. HA XX. No date

SED files: Zentral-Parteiarchiv der Sozialistischen Einheitspartei Deutschlands (SED), Berlin
Source Books (*Findbücher*): Büro Egon Krenz, Abteilung Staats-und Rechtsfragen

Abteilung Kirchenfragen, Bezirksparteien Archiv (BPA) Berlin bis 1981

SED file IV 2/2.0.39/246

SED file IV 2/2.0.39/313

SED file ZK IV. B2/14/56

BPA file IV D - 2/4/397

Secondary
Ammer, Thomas (1988): 'Prozesse gegen Skinheads in der DDR', in: *Deutschland Archiv*, 8/1988

Arenz, Waltraud (1989): 'Skinheads in der DDR'. *Gesamt-Institute, Analysen und Berichte*, Nr. 8, 1989

Autorenkollektiv (1993): Un-Heil über Deutschland: Fremdenhaß und Neofaschismus nach der Wiedervereinigung. Hamburg

Betz, Hans-Georg (1991): Post-modern politics in Germany. The politics of resentment. New York

Bodewig, K./R. Hesels/D. Mahlberg, Hrsg. (1990): *Die schleichende Gefahr, Rechtsextremismus heute.* Essen

Engelstädter, Heinz (1991): 'Der Aufbruch neofaschistischer Gruppen in der früheren DDR', in: *1999*, 6 Jg. H.2, pp. 88-103

Falter, Jürgen W. (1994): Wer wählt rechts? Die Wähler und Anhänger rechtsextremistischer Parteien im vereinigten Deutschland. München

Fulbrook, Mary (1995): Anatomy of a Dictatorship. Inside the GDR 1949-1989. Oxford

Gabriel, Oscar W. (1996): 'Rechtsextreme Einstellungen in Europa: Struktur, Entwicklung und Verhaltensimplikationen', in: Jürgen W. Falter, Hans-Gerd Jaschke und Jürgen R. Winkler, Hrsg. *Rechtsextremismus. Ergebnisse und Perspektiven der Forschung (Sonderheft 27)*, Opladen, 344-360

Glennerster, Howard, ed. (1991): The Radical Right and the Welfare State: An International Assessment. Hertfordshire

Grill, Bartholomäus (1991): 'Auferstanden aus Ruinen. Der Rechtsradikalismus in Ostdeutschland ist der extreme Ausdruck einer zerstörten Gesellschaft', in: *Die Zeit*, Nr. 25/14.06.1991, p.3

Hasselbach, Ingo/Winfried Bonegel (1993): *Die Abrechnung.* Berlin-Weimar

Heise, Joachim/Jürgen Hofman (1988): *Fragen an die Geschichte der DDR.* Berlin (Ost) 1988

Heitmeyer, Wilhelm (1991a): 'Einig Vaterland - Einig Rechtsextremismus? - Sortierungsüberlegungen zu unübersichtlichen Rechtsextremismuspotentialen im Vereinten Deutschland', in: Butterwegge, Christoph & Horst Isola, Hrsg. *Rechtsextremismus im Vereinten Deutschland.* Bremen-Berlin, 1991, 120-142

Heitmeyer, Wilhelm (1991b): 'Der Eisberg im Osten. Zu den Ursachen des jugendlichen Rechtsradikalismus und der wachsenden Gewaltbereitschaft in den neuen Bundesländern', in: *Die Tageszeitung*, 18.06.1991

Heitmeyer, Wilhelm (1992): Die Bielefelder Rechtsextremismus-Studie. Erste Langzeituntersuchung zur politischen Sozialisation männlicher Jugendlicher. Weinheim/München

Hobsbawm, Eric (1994): The Age of Extremes. The short Twentieth Century 1914-1991. London

Hockenos, Paul (1993): Free to Hate. The Rise of the Right in post-Communist Eastern Europe. London

Howard, David, ed. (1991): The Radical Right and the Welfare State: An International Assessment. Hertfordshire

Husbands, Chris (1991): 'Neo-Nazis in East Germany - The New Danger?', in: *Patterns of Prejudice*, Vol. 25, no. 1, 3-17

Klönne, Arno (1990): 'Aufstand der Modernisierungsopfer', in: *Blätter für deutsche und internationale Politik*, Heft 5, 545-548

Ködderitzsch, Peter/Leo Müller (1990): *Rechtsextremismus in der DDR.* Göttingen

Kokoschko, Ray (1990): Sozialisationsleistungen rechtsextremer Gruppierungen und ihre Beziehungen zur sozialen Umwelt in der DDR. Diplomarbeit. Humboldt-Universität, Berlin

Koopmans, Ruud (1995): *A burning Question: Explaining the Rise of Racist and Extreme Right Violence in Western Europe.* Wissenschaftszentrum Berlin für Sozialforschung GmbH, FS III 95 -101, Berlin, Juni 1995

Koopmans, Ruud/Paul Statham (1997): 'Ethnic and Civic Conceptions of Nationhood and the Differential Success of the Extreme Right in Germany and Italy', forthcoming in: Guigni M., McAdam D., Tilly C., eds. *How Movements Matter: Theoretical and Comparative Studies on the Consequences of Social Movements.* Wissenschaftszentrum Berlin für Sozialforschung (WZB). Berlin

Kriminalpolizei (1989): Studie über Erkenntnis der Kriminalpolizei zu neofaschistischen Aktivitäten in der DDR. Berlin. Unveröffentlichtes Manuskript

Ladwig, Bernd (1993): 'Ursachen des Rechtsextremismus', in: *AMI,* Heft 10, 1993, 4-18

Leggewie, Claus (1990): Die Republikaner - Phantombild der neuen Rechten. Berlin

Madloch, Norbert (1990): 'Rechtsextremistische Orientierungen in der DDR-Jugend: wie sind sie entstanden?', in: Magistratsverwaltung für Jugend, Familie und Sport (n.d - 1990), 9-19

Madloch, Norbert (1995): Studie: Rechtsextremismus und das Superwahljahr 1994 in den neuen Bundesländern. Daten und Interpretationsversuch.

Merten, Roland/Hans-Uwe Otto Hrsg. (1993): Rechtsradikale Gewalt im vereinigten Deutschland. Jugend im gesellschaftlichen Umbruch. Opladen

Minkenberg, Michael (1994): 'German Unification and the Continuity of Discontinuities. Cultural Change and the Far Right in East and West', in: *German Politics,* Vol. 3, No. 2 (August 1994), 169-192

Neubacher, Frank (1994): *Jugend und Rechtsextremismus in Ostdeutschland vor und nach der Wende.* Godesberg.

Räthzel, Nora (1990): 'Germany: one race, one nation?', in: *Race and Class,* 32 (3), 1990, 31-47

Rommelspacher, Birgit (1991): 'Rechtsextreme als Opfer der Risikogesellschaft. Zur Täterentlastung in den Sozialwissenschaften', in: *1999,* Heft 2/1991, 75-87

Schöpflin, George (1995): 'Nationhood, communism and state legitimation', in: *Nations and Nationalism,* Nr. 1, 1995, 81-91

Siegler, Bernd (1991): Auferstanden aus Ruinen. Rechtsextremismus in der DDR. Berlin

Stöss, Richard (1993): 'Rechtsextremismus und Wahlen in der Bundesrepublik', in: *Aus Politik und Zeitgeschichte,* B11/1993, 12.03.1993, 50-61

Süß, Walter (1993): *Zu Wahrnehmung und Interpretation des Rechtsextremismus in der DDR durch das MfS.* Der Bundesbeauftragte für die Unterlagen des MfS der DDR, Nr. 1/93

Tatsachen über Deutschland (1993): *Tatsachen über Deutschland.* Bonn

Verfassungsschutzbericht (1993): *Verfassungsschutzbericht für 1993*. Bundesministerium des Innern. Bonn, 1994

Wagner, Bernd (1993): Politisch motivierte Gewalt in Ostberlin. Berlin

Waibel, Harry (1994): Jugendlicher Rechtsextremismus in der DDR. Neofaschismus, Antisemitismus und Xenophobie. Unveröffentlichtes Manuskript einer Doktorarbeit. Berlin

Weiß, Konrad (1989): *Die alte neue Gefahr – junge Nazis in der DDR*. Berlin Ost. Nur für den innerkirchlichen Gebrauch, March 1989

Willems, Helmut/Stefanie Würtz/Roland Eckert (1993): *Fremdenfeindliche Gewalt; Eine Analyse von Täterstrukturen und Eskalationsprozessen*. Vorgelegt dem Bundesministerium für Frauen und Jugend und der Deutschen Forschungsgemeinschaft.

Stephen Brown

THE PROTESTANT CHURCHES AND POLITICAL OPPOSITION: CONTINUITY AND CHANGE 1978 TO 1989

The basic policy of the GDR Protestant churches between 1978 (the year of the summit meeting between Erich Honecker and the Protestant churches in the GDR) and 1989, the year of the Wende, *contained many elements of continuity, summed up by the phrase 'church within socialism'. However, there were also significant changes, particularly because of the growth of alternative groups within the churches. The church-sponsored 'conciliar process for justice, peace and the integrity of creation' helped to transform this disaffection into dissent but failed to lead to the development of an explicitly political movement, something which contributed to the division and marginalisation of the opposition after the* Wende.

The Protestant churches in the GDR

The GDR was the only state in central and eastern Europe in which a Soviet-backed government confronted a nominally Protestant society. Initially organised on an all-German basis, the churches (both Roman Catholic and Protestant) in the GDR were the only institutions not formally integrated into the system of 'democratic centralism' controlled by the SED. However, in 1969, following pressure from the GDR authorities on the East German *Landeskirchen* to separate from the all-German EKD, the Federation of Protestant Churches in the GDR *(Bund der Evangelischen Kirchen in der DDR)* was founded as a federation of the eight legally independent *Landeskirchen* on the territory of the GDR.

The *Kirchenbund* received official recognition by the GDR authorities only in 1971, just months before Erich Honecker replaced Walter Ulbricht at the head of the SED. The history of the *Kirchenbund* is thus intimately connected to the developments of the Honecker era and can be divided into two periods: pre-1978 and post-1978. From 1971 to 1978 there was an increasing rapprochement between the *Kirchenbund* and the GDR authorities, with a significant role played by the concept of *'Kirche im Sozialismus'* (church within socialism), an idea that was developed following the *Kirchenbund* synod in Eisenach in 1971: the church should neither be 'alongside, nor against, but within socialism' *(Nicht Kirche neben, nicht gegen, sondern im Sozialismus)*. In the years that followed, the term 'church within socialism' was used to describe a political strategy, which it was claimed avoided the extremes of total assimilation or outright resistance to the policies of the SED.[1]

The emergence of 'disaffection' within the Protestant churches in the GDR

The first 'summit' meeting between the leaders of the *Kirchenbund* and Erich Honecker took place on 6 March 1978, becoming the basic point of reference for both the *Kirchenbund* and the state. However, from 1978 there was increasing dissonance, not least because the limited recognition and legitimacy conferred by the meeting of 6 March 1978 meant that the *Kirchenbund* began to act in a more self-confident way. The programmes of pre-military education introduced into schools in 1978 led to the development of peace education programmes in Protestant parishes,[2] which in turn provided a catalyst for the development of an alternative youth-based subculture under the umbrella of the church. That the growth of politically disaffected groups within the churches should have started with peace groups is no coincidence. The GDR was the only state in central and eastern Europe with a tolerated alternative to armed military service. The *Bausoldaten* (soldiers in construction units), introduced in 1964 after representation from the churches, were integrated within the National People's Army (NVA) but freed of the obligation to carry arms. *Bausoldaten,* in many cases, could not expect professional advancement or even higher education. Many turned to the church, training as pastors, creating a 'reserve army' of activists within the church able to provide resources and support to such peace groups.[3] The fact that the issue of peace provided a *focus* for the development of groups also subverted the official ideology, which insisted that the GDR was a *Friedensstaat* as well as creating links to western European peace movements (particularly to the peace movement and to the Greens in the Federal Republic) and to the dissident Marxist left in the GDR. Increasingly, the formation of peace groups within the Protestant Church was followed by the formation of ecology, civil liberty and even gay and lesbian groups.

One way of analysing these developments is the distinction made by Ramet between *dissatisfaction, disaffection* and *dissent.*[4] *Dissatisfaction* is 'discontent with the way in which certain parts of the system operate [...] without necessarily calling into question the legitimacy or optimality of the system'. *Disaffection* is discontent with the system without necessarily entailing belief in an ability to change the system, possibly expressed in social non-conformism or deviance. *Dissent* is discontent with the system coupled with a belief in one's ability to effect change. If the basic position of many church members vis-à-vis the GDR was one of *discontent*, the emergence of the groups marked the growth of *disaffection* within the church, not part of a formal organisation imposed from above, but as an informal decentralised network within the framework of the church.

The transformation of disaffection into dissent
Among the developments in the 1980s that helped transform disaffection into dissent were the foundation of the network *Konkret für den Frieden* (KfdF), and the development of the 'conciliar process for justice, peace and the integrity of creation'. Based around an annual seminar hosted by one or other of the *Landeskirchen* in the GDR, *Konkret für den Frieden* (also known as *Frieden-Konkret*) became one of the most significant networks of peace, environmental, third-world, human rights and women's groups in the GDR, linking groups that were based within the Protestant Church by conviction, those that operated within the structures of the church by necessity and those, such as the *Initiativ Frieden und Menschenrechte,* that rejected the idea of seeking 'protection' from the churches. These efforts were regarded with considerable suspicion by the GDR authorities,[5] seeing in them an attempt to create an organisational structure for the independent peace movement in the GDR. From 1985 the network established a 'continuation committee'[6] (*Fort-setzungsausschuss*) to prepare the next year's seminar and to co-ordinate activities in the intervening twelve months, which increasingly took on the characteristics of a spokespersons' group (and included people such as Heino Falcke, Joachim Garstecki,

Markus Meckel, Rainer Eppelmann, Hans-Jochen Tschiche, Bärbel Bohley, Vera Wollenberger). During this period the network was also brought into the organisation of the 'conciliar process' which culminated in the Ecumenical Assembly of 1988 and 1989, gathering representatives from both the hierarchies of the main Christian denominations in the GDR and the grass-roots groups.

The 'conciliar process' was initiated by the World Council of Churches following its assembly in Vancouver in 1983 which, responding to a proposal from the GDR delegates, called on the WCC 'to engage member churches in a conciliar process of mutual commitment (covenant) to justice, peace and the integrity of creation'.[7] The 'conciliar process' envisaged that 'the churches at all levels – congregations, dioceses/synods, networks of Christian groups and base communities'[8] should become active and see the issues of justice, peace and the environment as central issues of the Christian faith. The GDR Protestant churches picked up the 'conciliar process' at a relatively early stage (1984-85) not least because of the efforts of Heino Falcke, who had played a major role at Vancouver in getting the idea of a 'conciliar process' adopted by the assembly, and who, as moderator of the *Kirchenbund*'s committee on church and society, had a significant role within the GDR church structures. Falcke was already well-known in the GDR for his key-note speech at the *Kirchenbund*'s 1972 synod in Dresden, in which he called for a 'socialism capable of being improved' (verbesserlicher Sozialismus) and for greater freedom of discussion in the GDR:

> Would the leading role of the Party not be enhanced, its authority strengthened, if that authority were seen to be the source of liberty which helped people to stand on their own feet? A common purpose will only emerge when people trust each other, respect each other in genuine partnership and allow all points of view to be put in free discussion, argument pitted against argument. Does not the very life of socialism depend for its survival on striving to attain such maturity?[9]

Although the GDR authorities successfully put pressure on the church leadership not to include Falcke's speech in the official proceedings of the synod, copies of the speech continued to circulate unofficially in the GDR. Falcke, who was involved in *KfdF*, was also an outspoken exponent within the *Kirchenbund* of the need to take seriously the grass-roots groups. The influence of the conciliar process, with its threefold linkage of justice, peace and creation, could already be seen at the *KfdF* seminar in Stendal in 1985, where the organisers invited – for the first time – environmental and third-world groups to the meeting.[10] Not only did the conciliar process provide a framework to give a sense of coherence to disparate groups and initiatives throughout the GDR, its ecclesiological content also functioned to allow groups to see the church structures as an immediate (albeit surrogate) target for their demands, in the absence of a space within society in which they could function.

In the GDR, the high point of the conciliar process was the Ecumenical Assembly, which met in three sessions in 1988 and 1989,[11] following a proposal made by the *Stadtökumenekreis Dresden* in 1986 that the 'conciliar process' should culminate in a gathering to focus on the issues of justice, peace and the integrity of creation within the context of the GDR. Not least because of the influence of Falcke (who was appointed moderator of the *Kirchenbund*'s co-ordinating committee for the conciliar process), representatives of *Konkret für den Frieden* were co-opted into the preparations for the

Ecumenical Assembly. One of the most significant results of co-opting *KfdF* into the preparations for the Ecumenical Assembly was the transformation of the discourse of 'justice'. As envisaged at the WCC's 1983 Vancouver assembly, the conciliar process was intended to link the issue of peace, a concern for WCC member churches in the northern hemisphere, with that of global justice, which was the overriding issue for its member churches in the Third World. In the course of preparations for the Ecumenical Assembly in the GDR, however, the discourse of justice and injustice was appropriated and applied to GDR society itself, something which can be seen from an analysis of the *Eingaben* (petitions and statements) received by the organisers of the Ecumenical Assembly. Of the 7,000 out of the 10,000 *Eingaben* received which could be evaluated before the Ecumenical Assembly began, 2,772 were related to the issue of justice (1,650 to problems in GDR society; 650 to problems of global justice and 472 to the issue of justice within the church); 2,194 were linked to the issue of peace (220 to the question of deterrence, disarmament and other issues of war and peace; 945 on military service and the possibility of conscientious objection; 1,065 on peace education; and 261 which challenged the churches to become churches of peace); and there were 1,459 on the environment, with almost all relating in some way to the GDR (energy, air, water, lifestyle and so on).[12] Even where the *Eingaben* concerned the issues of peace or the environment, they often reflected concern about the actual conditions within the state. It was from this starting point that the Ecumenical Assembly was able to produce a catalogue of changes which were deemed to be necessary in the GDR,[13] described by Werner Jarowinsky, the SED Politburo member and Central Committee secretary responsible for church affairs, in an internal SED discussion, as 'ein komplettes Programm der Installierung einer Oppositionsbewegung'.[14] According to Wolfgang Rüddenklau, a prominent opposition activist:

> Die dort verabschiedeten Texte, die viele Anliegen der Basisgruppen, wenn auch sehr gemäßigt, aufnahmen und gewissermaßen allen Religionsgemeinschaften empfahlen, hatten teilweise fast revolutionäre Brisanz. So hieß es in einem Texte über die Totalverweigerer: ‚Sie handeln im Vorgriff auf eine zukünftige Weltfriedensordnung und leisten damit einen prophetischen Dienst'.[15]

The timing of the Ecumenical Assembly was also of great significance. Its first meeting took place in March 1988 soon after the wave of protest that swept the GDR in the wake of the arrest (and later expulsion from the GDR) of a number of the key peace and human rights activists in January 1988. Its final session took place just before the communal elections in May 1989, and the unprecedented opposition to the policy of single-lists organised by the National Front. The disaffection manifested by the groups was being transformed into explicit dissent, that is, not only discontent with the system but also a growing belief in the ability to effect change. It was a major objective of the Stasi to bring protest groups of whatever kind into the structures of the church – so that the groups would be subject to discipline and control by the church hierarchy and that the groups might be enmeshed into theological or internal church discussions and away from political debate about changes in society. However, the integration of *KfdF* into the conciliar process seems to have had the opposite effect. Rather than disciplining the groups, it led to a radicalisation of the Ecumenical Assembly, and thus a church gathering that was notably less under the control of the church hierarchy. Moreover, the resonance that the Ecumenical Assembly generated in the parishes meant that many issues which had previously been raised by the groups became linked to the life of parishes, from which developed the potential for their role during the *Wende*.[16]

Political change and the *Wende*
The Ecumenical Assembly was a manifestation of the fact that demands by the groups for fundamental changes within the GDR represented a much wider spectrum of discontent and dissatisfaction in the GDR. The assembly also marked a shift from dissatisfaction into explicit dissent, with demands for fundamental political change. What was lacking, however, was a political vehicle to effect change. If the Ecumenical Assembly marked the high point of the influence of *Konkret für den Frieden* within the Protestant churches, it also marked the start of its final phase, in which it was unable to make the transition from being a loose network of groups to become a more explicitly political organisation which could respond to the crisis of GDR society. The 1988 *KfdF* seminar which took place in Cottbus just after the first meeting of the Ecumenical Assembly marked growing uncertainty about the future direction of the network. The issue of the relationship between the seminar and the hierarchy of the Protestant church had not been settled; the *Fortsetzungsauschuss* was increasingly becoming a 'spokesperson' for the groups, which raised the issue as to whether *KfdF* was primarily an annual seminar or an association with a common programme; new groupings were springing up alongside *KfdF*: the *Umweltbibliothek*, the green-ecological network *Arche*, *Arbeitskreis Solidarische Kirche* and *Kirche von unten*. Moreover, the 'conciliar process' was absorbing the energies of some of the most active members of the *KfdF* and the Ecumenical Assembly was itself becoming a parallel institution to *KfdF*. In this context Hans-Jochen Tschiche (the director of the Evangelical Academy in Magdeburg) drew up a 'consensus paper' listing the points on which he believed the groups were united. This paper called for a 'public and open debate' about the crisis in the state, a 'pluralistic, democratic and decentralised organisation of economic and social life' in the GDR, the abandoning of technologies which were destructive to the environment, the dismantling of consumerist goals of the socialist society, total disarmament and the creation of nuclear-frees zones in Europe, a change in the world economic system in favour of the poor, the 'demilitarisation of public life' in the GDR, the 'de-ideologisation' of education and the 'de-bureaucratisation' of relations between the state and citizens.[17] Although this programme received, according to the Stasi, the unconditional support of Bishop Gottfried Forck of Berlin-Brandenburg[18] it proved impossible to gain a consensus at the Cottbus seminar. In part this was the result of the presence at the gathering of a vocal group from the Christian Peace Conference (CFK), which aligned itself with the official policies of the GDR, and a number of IMs (*inoffizielle Mitarbeiter*) - such as Wolfgang Schnur. But another reason was also the strongly independent nature of many of the groups.

In Greifswald in 1989,[19] Tschiche again attempted to make *Frieden-Konkret* adopt a more political perspective, by suggesting that instead of being a loose network of groups, it should form the nucleus of an 'Association for the Renewal of Society'. This idea again failed to reach consensus but formed one of the sources for the later development of *Neues Forum*. Markus Meckel outlined his idea for the creation of a 'Social Democratic Party', while the *Evangelische Studentengemeinde* from Karl-Marx-Stadt proposed that the network should call for a 'Gesamtgesellschaftliche Dialog' along the lines of the Round Table in Poland. It was thus becoming increasingly clear that the critical situation in the

GDR required a more formal structure than a loose network of groups. However, the participants at the Greifswald seminar were unwilling to transform the seminar and/or its *Fortsetzungsauschuss* into such an association or forum. In this situation the key participants within *KfdF* fell-back on other, informal, structures through which they attempted to create new associations, movements and political parties, the programmes and statements of which were themselves influenced by the conciliar process.[20] Nevertheless, the fact that it had been unable to create a single movement bringing together the groups contributed to the weakening of the influence of the opposition during the *Wende*.

If *KfdF* was incapable of transforming itself into a vehicle for explicit dissent which could pursue political change in the GDR, the same is true for the Protestant church leadership as a whole, which played a remarkably low-key role during the *Wende*, seeing its task as one of mediation. The effect of the *Wende*, however, was to expand civil society outside the structure of the *Kirchenbund* into society. In this process, parishes and local groups were well placed to play a significant role. However, the church leadership was no longer needed as an intermediary or a surrogate addressee of demands from below. With the migration of this partial civil society into society as a whole, the political function of the church leadership declined in importance.

Conclusion

Throughout its existence, there was a continuity in the basic policy of the GDR *Kirchenbund* towards the GDR authorities, summed up by the phrase 'church within socialism', avoiding the extremes of total assimilation or outright resistance to the policies of the SED. The policy was only possible, however, because the GDR authorities themselves were prepared to tolerate the existence of a church which was not fully integrated into the SED dominated system of 'democratic centralism'. However, the 'summit meeting' of 6 March 1978, rather than sealing the role of the Protestant church as a loyal church within socialism, strengthened the independent internal structures of the church. This created a space for the development of a limited 'civil society' and the growth of political disaffection, and initiatives such as *Konkret für den Frieden* provided the means to network the various groups throughout the GDR. The threefold linkage of 'justice, peace and the integrity of creation' in the 'conciliar process' gave a sense of coherence to the disparate demands of the groups. In particular, it provided an opportunity, legitimated by the church, to apply the discourse of justice to GDR society itself. The high point of the 'conciliar process', the Ecumenical Assembly, marked the transformation of disaffection within the structures of the church into explicit dissent. The conciliar process also provided the basis for a stronger identification with dissent in the parishes, enabling them to become focal points for disaffection by those outside the church. However, neither *Konkret für den Frieden* nor the structures of the *Kirchenbund* were able to provide a political vehicle for the expression of this dissent. As a result, a number of distinct, and, in part, competing groups, movements and associations were founded in 1989. Although many of these groups picked up the discourse of the conciliar process in their programmes and appeals, the failure to develop an explicit vehicle for political change which could bring together all these initiatives was a significant factor leading to the division, and ultimately, the marginalisation of the opposition after the *Wende* of 1989.

NOTES

[1] There was one issue which could not be touched by this debate, and that was the 'German Question', or, in other words, the continued existence of the German Democratic Republic itself.

[2] For a description of how these programmes developed, see Fritz Dorgerloh, 'Schwerter zu Pflugscharen: Wie die Friedensdekaden begannen', in *aej information 5/97*, October 1997.

[3] See Stefan Herbst, 'Das ökumenische Friedensseminar in Königswalde' in *Orientierung*, No. 15, Vol. 60, 31 December 1996, p. 254.

[4] Sabrina Petra Ramet, *Social Currents in Eastern Europe: The Sources and Meaning of the Great Transformation*, 2nd edition (Durham, NC, 1995) p. 6.

[5] Thus *Konkret für den Frieden* was described as the 'Bildung eines Sammelbeckens negativer und feindlicher Kräfte im Umkreis von Pfr. Eppelmann': see Information über Verlauf und Ergebnis der 5. Synode der Evangelischen Kirche Berlin-Brandenburg, S APMO-BA ZPA IV B2/14/123, quoted in Gerhard Besier, *Der SED-Staat und die Kirche: Höhenflug und Absturz* (Berlin-Frankfurt, 1995), p. 510, note 235.

[6] *Konkret für den Frieden* was closely monitored by the MfS, and despite the changes in the *Fortsetzungsausschuss* from year to year, the lawyer Wolfgang Schnur, later to be one of the co-founders of *Demokratischer Aufbruch* and an IM for the Stasi, remained a member of the committee throughout its existence.

[7] David Gill, *Gathered for Life: Official Report VI Assembly of the World Council of Churches* (Geneva: WCC Publications/Grand Rapids: Wm. B. Eerdmans, 1983) p. 255. The text of the proposal by the GDR delegates can be found in Bund der Evangelischen Kirchen in der DDR, *Gemeinsam Unterwegs: Dokumente aus der Arbeit des Bundes der Evangelischen Kirchen in der DDR 1980-1987* (East Berlin, 1989) pp. 264-268.

[8] Gill, *op. cit.*, p. 89.

[9] Heino Falcke, 'Christus befreit – darum Kirche für andere. Hauptvortrag bei der Synode des Kirchenbundes in Dresden 1972', reprinted in Heino Falcke, *Mit Gott Schritt halten* (West Berlin: Wichern-Verlag, 1986), pp 24ff; English translation (slightly adapted) from Trevor Beeson, *Discretion and Valour: Religious Conditions in Russia and Eastern Europe* (London, 1982), pp. 200-1.

[10] Ehrhart Neubert, *Geschichte der Opposition in der DDR 1949-1989* (Berlin, 1997) p. 573.

[11] For a more detailed discussion of the Ecumenical Assembly see Christof Ziemer, 'Der konziliare Prozess in den Farben der DDR', in *Materialien der Enquete-Kommission, "Aufarbeitung von Geschichte und Folgen der SED-Diktatur in Deutschland"* (Baden-Baden, 1995), Volume VI, 2, pp. 1430-1635.

[12] See the transcript of a speech by Heino Falcke at a conference on the conciliar process at the Evangelische Akademie Hofgeismar, 22 to 24 February 1988, in the Pressearchiv der Evangelischen Kirche in Berlin-Brandenburg, Berlin (Ordner: Falcke*)*.

[13] For the texts produced by the Ecumenical Assembly, see *epd-Dokumentation*, 6/89, 6a/89, 21/89.

[14] Frederic Hartweg (ed) *SED und Kirche: Eine Dokumentation ihrer Beziehungen*, Band 2: SED 1968-1989, bearbeitet von Horst Dohle (Neukirchen-Vluyn, 1995), p. 504.

[15] Wolfgang Rüddenklau, *Störenfried: DDR-Opposition 1986-1989* (Berlin, 1992), p. 277.

[16]The symbol of the conciliar process – a dove breaking the chains of injustice – was turned into a badge for the 'prayers of renewal' in Wittenberg and became the symbol of the *Wende* in Wittenberg for instance.

[17] The consensus paper is reprinted in Stephan Bickhardt, 'Die Entwicklung der DDR-Opposition in den achtziger Jahren', in *Materialien der Enquete-Kommission, op. cit*, Vol. VII, 1, pp. 501-503. Bickhardt describes the consensus paper as the 'bedeutendste Verständigungs- und Konsenspapier der Gruppen', *ibid.,* 485

[18] 'Information Nr. 113 des MfS über einige aktuelle Aspekte der Situation in den Kirchenleitungen der evangelischen Landeskirchen', reprinted in Gerhard Besier/Stephan Wolf (eds.) *'Pfarrer, Christen und Katholiken': Das Ministerium für Staatssicherheit der ehemaligen DDR und die Kirchen*, 2nd edition (Neukirchen-Vluyn, 1991), p. 549

[19] Neubert, *op. cit.*, pp. 798-799

[20] Ziemer, *op. cit.*, pp. 1488 - 1489

Brendan de Silva

THE PROTESTANT CHURCH AND THE EAST GERMAN STATE: AN ORGANISATIONAL PERSPECTIVE

Though long recognised by German scholars as an integral part of GDR history, the role of the East German churches has received insufficient attention in the GDR scholarship of the English speaking world. This paper argues that the stance of the Protestant Church towards the communist State was influenced not only by practical and theological considerations, but also by the organisational structure of the Church and the ideological views of Church leaders.

Introduction

The path chosen by the Protestant Church in its interaction with the SED-State has often been called the road *zwischen Anpassung und Opposition*. The apparent vacillation of the Church between conformity and opposition, and the variety of views that existed among Church pastors and leaders, make it difficult for the scholar of Church-State relations in the GDR to develop a clear and coherent picture. This paper addresses this contentious issue firstly by demonstrating how differences in the organisational structure of Church and State shaped their mode of interaction. Secondly, it points to some of the theological dichotomies which created tension regarding the Church's stance towards the SED-State. Thirdly, it examines ideological considerations such as the Church leaders' view of socialism. Seen together, these factors can help to explain the perceptions and actions of the Church leaders towards the SED-State, and also the variation among them.

On the whole, the Church in the 1980s moved towards an increasing acceptance of socialism and the pursuance of a policy of 'small steps' rather than calls for radical change; however, increasing radicalism at the grass roots level and the activities of vocal pastors threatened this position.[1] The State meanwhile adhered to its inherently flawed *Kirchenpolitik*: a policy which focused almost exclusively on the Church leadership and sought to effect a *Differenzierungsprozess*, whereby reactionary elements within the Church would be gradually separated from and isolated by progressive elements. An examination of the organisational structures of Church and State, and how these affected their mode of interaction, helps to explain how the two institutions came to their above positions.

Organisation of the Church

The two key elements which defined the organisational structure of the Protestant churches in the GDR are independence and democracy. Unlike the hierarchical organisation of the Catholic Church, for example, each *Landeskirche* answered to itself and not to any higher ecclesiastical authority. At the same time, however, this ecclesiastical independence was tempered by dependence on the state. Both this independence and dependence stem from the historical development of the churches, whereby each *Landeskirche* was bound inextricably to a German *Land*, according to the famous agreement from the Peace of Augsburg, *cuius regio, eius religio* (literally, 'whose region, his religion'). That the *Landeskirchen* were independent also meant that they were often not clearly united.

The second aspect, democracy, stems partially from Martin Luther's concept of a universal priesthood of believers. The Protestant Church is hierarchical in the sense that there are bishops, *Generalsuperintendenten*, *Superintendenten* and pastors, but this hierarchy is not based on command and obedience. Church leaders are elected and can be removed or demoted by the Synods. This democratic structure made it difficult for Church leaders to impose their will on the Church as a whole, especially if they were not united. Nevertheless, the Church leaders did not merely play a representative role; they sought to lead. The relationship between the Church leadership and the general membership was therefore one of tension. Occasionally the Church leaders would strike out on their own path without the majority of Church members behind them; at other times they would hesitate even when it seemed the majority of Church members were pushing them towards action.[2] Their at times precarious position within the Church weakened their influence and made it difficult for them to adopt a strong, uniform stance towards the State and the grass roots groups.

The Church gained more unity in the GDR when the eight East German churches broke away from the West German churches in 1969 to form their own Federation of Protestant Churches (*Bund der evangelischen Kirchen in der DDR*, or *Kirchenbund*). Thereafter they enjoyed a single Conference of Church Leaders (KKL) and *Kirchenbund* Synod, but the plurality, independence and democratic structure of the Church remained. The Federation was a loose one, and the eight East German churches remained fully autonomous actors, free to disagree with each other and the KKL if they so chose. The failure of the SED-State to grasp this Protestant mix of independence and democracy led to its development of a *Kirchenpolitik* which concentrated on pressuring and winning over Church leaders, without realising that those Church leaders did not have the power to 'discipline' and 'integrate' rogue elements within the Church.

Organisation of the State

The formulation and pursuance of the State's policy on the Church, or *Kirchenpolitik*, was determined by the organisational structure of the SED-State itself. Due to its central importance, *Kirchenpolitik* was handled by the General Secretary himself, assisted by the Minister for State Security, Erich Mielke, and the Politburo member responsible for Church Affairs, Paul Verner, who led the SED Working Group on Church Affairs. Yet while policy decisions were being made by the Party, actual negotiations with the Church, day-to-day affairs and meetings were handled by the State offices, usually by the State Secretary for Church Affairs, a post held from 1979-1988 by Klaus Gysi. Gysi's recollection of what Honecker told him upon his appointment as State Secretary for Church Affairs describes this confusing arrangement:

> The SED will refrain from talks with the churches, since it must be seen
> as an 'atheistic party against the Church'. Thus, negotiations must be led
> by the State, which is understood to be non-partisan, namely by the State
> Secretary for Church Affairs. But decisions on Church policies are to be
> made exclusively 'in the party' and indeed by himself, Erich Honecker,

so that the confrontation between Church and State predicted by the western press would not take place.[3]

In this arrangement, the State Secretary for Church Affairs – a weak body – handled most of the interaction with the Church, while those actually making policy (Honecker, Mielke, Verner, and Margot Honecker in the highly contentious field of education) rarely met with Church leaders. This deficit in the interaction between Church and State made the SED leadership especially dependent on the reports they were receiving from groups such as the SED Working Group on Church Affairs.

An examination of these important reports highlights the problematic nature of such an organisational structure. When compared with the documents of the *Kirchenbund* Synod meetings themselves, it is clear that they frequently downplayed or even fully ignored serious criticism of State policy by Synod members in order to cast the meetings in a positive light. Horst Dohle, who himself worked for the State apparatus, writes that this happened either 'in order to avoid excited or angry decisions, or to confirm the predominant picture among the recipients of the report of harmonious societal development'.[4] Serious demands on questions of education and freedom to travel abroad were euphemised in the reports as 'requests and wishes' (*Bitten und Wünsche*), statements made by Church leaders were taken out of context and misused, and there was the perennial, highly dubious claim that Church leaders would do nothing to risk what they had achieved thus far.[5] Commenting on an SED Working Group report to the Politburo of 7 January 1986 Dohle notes wryly: 'This "Information Report" stands out above all in the fact that it is not one, i.e. it does not in the slightest reflect the actual situation of Church politics. It was clearly aimed at reassuring the SED leadership'.[6] Thus these inaccurate reports pleased those in power, most importantly Honecker, who was eager to avoid open confrontation with the Church, and his pleasure on reading them inadvertently encouraged the continuation of such behaviour.

The 1987 *Kirchenbund* Synod in Görlitz provides an example of this. This Synod meeting ignited a sensation due to a proposal by Provost Heino Falcke that the Church voice a firm rejection of the State's policy of delimitation (*Abgrenzung*). On the first day of the Synod meeting the SED Working Group wrote that 'reactionary forces' had prepared a proposal to be presented by Falcke, but that, remarkably, 'the concrete contents are not yet known to us' – despite the fact that the proposal had been in circulation for half a year.[7] As soon as the contents of the proposal became known during the Synod, Politburo member Jarowsinksy, who by this time headed the SED Working Group, dispatched a report to Honecker in which he detailed the aggressive actions of 'politically negative forces' such as Falcke. But when Honecker flew into a rage upon reading this report, claiming that oppositional forces were attempting 'to attain through the Synod members what could not be attained through the bishops',[8] Jarowinsky quickly responded with a more subdued report, in which he noted how 'analysis and internal reports' revealed a 'more differentiated picture' as well as 'important background facts', which had not been clear before.[9]

These factors help to explain why the State's *Kirchenpolitik*, which targeted Church leaders in the hopes that they would then discipline their rank-and-file, was a misguided failure. In her study of the GDR, *Anatomy of a Dictatorship*, Mary Fulbrook writes:

> The SED, for its part, sought to make use of the Church hierarchy as an extended arm of the state. The main miscalculation on the part of the SED here, however, was to assume that the Church operated according to the same hierarchy of command – in other words, that it was essentially characterized by the same democratic centralist structures – as the SED itself. To the SED's dismay, it discovered too late that it could not rely on the leadership of the Church to contain unruly spirits below; that 'turbulent priests' had greater leeway in the Church than did their secular counterparts under the iron hand of communist party discipline. The attempt to use the apparently compliant Church was to backfire very badly in the longer term.[10]

It was the 1987 Görlitz Synod which eventually forced the SED to re-evaluate and abandon its *Kirchenpolitik*, leading to the raid on the Environmental Library of Berlin's *Zionskirche* in November 1987 and several subsequent acts of open State repression.

Just as the mode of interaction between Church and State hindered the State's pursuit of its *Kirchenpolitik*, it also hindered the Church leadership. Unable to communicate directly to those making policy, such as Erich Honecker or Margot Honecker in the field of education, the Church leaders had to rely on the State Secretary for Church Affairs for much of their information. Their own misunderstanding of the strictly hierarchical SED-State may have hindered them from realising that the State Secretary himself enjoyed no power at all. Several of them seem to have harboured the vain hope that, through moderation on the Church side, moderate elements within the State might be strengthened. Once the State abandoned its ineffective *Kirchenpolitik*, this left them with no clear path to pursue.

Dichotomies

Along with the broad issues of Church-State interaction discussed above, theological and ideological considerations also affected the actions and views of the Church leadership. On the theological level, two chief internal conflicts, themselves paradoxes, are apparent.

The first pertains to two opposing yet complementary functions of Christianity, presented by Harald Wagner as the integrative/stabilising function and the liberating function.[11] Throughout the history of Christianity, Wagner argues, the Church has tended to emphasise the integrative/stabilising function over the liberating function, but it has recognised the importance of both. Thus the Church in the GDR sought to create a stable, united community, restricting chaos and promoting order and peace – sometimes through vocal support of the SED-State and its policies – all in full accordance with Luther's 'Two Kingdoms' doctrine. At the same time, however, it called on parishioners to engage themselves actively for the betterment of society. The conflict between these two functions sheds light on the Church's ambivalent, or divided, stance towards the grass roots groups. The integrative/stabilising function of the Church may have led Church functionaries to exclude, isolate or silence more vocal members of the Church in the interest of making peace with the State. But even if their actions benefited the State, one must not mistakenly conclude that they were therefore working *for* the State. On the contrary, they were operating for what they thought were the best interests of the Church based on their conceptions.

A second internal conflict involved pastoral duties versus political duties. Pastors sometimes tried to escape the responsibility of their political duties by confining themselves to purely pastoral activities. Political activism – such as drawing attention to election fraud, discrimination against Christians, or the issue of military education – was viewed by some as irresponsible, because it threatened the ability of the Church to fulfil its pastoral role, including its important social work. The strategy of the State focused on pressuring the Church to restrict itself entirely to its pastoral duties, and denying that the Church had any political duties.

That these internal tensions resulted in conflicting statements even within a single *Landeskirche* over a single issue can be seen from another example taken from the 1987 *Kirchenbund* Synod in Görlitz. On that occasion, Bishop Werner Leich opposed Falcke's proposal for a Church rejection of *Abgrenzung* by introducing the concept of 'what is reasonable' (*Zumutbarkeit*) in the eyes of the State.[12] Leich said, 'We must use the concept of what is reasonable as a critical measure in dealing with the proposal or submission before us.'[13] But in January 1989 a letter from the *Arbeitskreis Solidarische Kirche* in Leich's own Landeskirche of Thuringia rejected this mentality, stating, 'It cannot be the task of the Church of Jesus Christ – even and especially in difficult conflict situations – to adopt the legalistic argumentation of the ruling State organs'.[14]

It must be realised that in both these internal conflicts, the two sides not only stand in opposition to each other, but also complement each other, combining to form a complex whole. Nevertheless, they reveal deep inner tensions which divided Church leaders and members, and thereby provided the means by which the MfS could effect its *Differenzierungsprozess*.

Views toward Socialism

It is evident through their actions and words, both before and after 1989, that the vast majority of Church leaders believed in some form of socialism. This was true even for those such as Falcke who were labelled by the State as 'hostile-negative' elements because they fought for an improvable socialism. But their understanding of 'socialism' was not the rigid Marxism-Leninism of the SED; it was instead equated with the positive traits of equality, human development, peace, and brotherhood, in sharp contrast to the crass materialism of the West. Pastor Friedrich Schorlemmer writes critically: 'There were Christians who saw in socialism the incarnation of everything that was better. They would have needed an optician to see clearly politically'.[15] Indeed, there were many along the lines of Manfred Stolpe who appeared to desire nothing more than a stable and content SED-State, but alongside stood individuals like Bishop Forck, Heino Falcke and Rainer Eppelmann who refused to be content with the current state of socialism in the GDR and were duly labelled 'enemies of the State'.

The internal dichotomies within the Church have already been mentioned as a means by which bishops and pastors might have been divided in their stance toward the SED-State. Along with several other factors which might be enumerated, however, such as differences in personal experience and individual character, a word might be said about the generational factor. It is possible to divide the Church pastors and leaders into three generations. First, there were the older bishops, such as Albrecht Schönherr and Gottfried Forck, born in 1911 and 1923 respectively. Both had grown up in the Weimar Republic and had fought in World War II. They were men of strong integrity and courage, and they enjoyed the respect of their colleagues and followers. Second, there was the middle generation, men such as Bishop Christoph Demke and Manfred Stolpe, born in 1935 and

1936 respectively. They belonged to a generation whose youth had been characterised by war, then defeat and occupation. Many of them, such as Demke, had lost their fathers in the war. Speaking of her father's generation, Demke's daughter said: 'They tend to be lonely people and lack some of the confident moral grounding of the older generation'.[16]

Finally, there was the third and youngest generation – the generation of Rainer Eppelmann and his colleagues. Here were young Christians who had never known any system other than the GDR brand of socialism and who, unlike the older generations, had not had the chance to leave the GDR before the building of the Berlin Wall. They never chose to live in the GDR, they did not help build it, nor did they feel directly responsible (through the guilt of war) for its existence in the first place. Generally not in leadership positions, they were not constrained by the game of compromise and negotiation, and they felt an anger towards the system that kept them inside yet robbed them of a normal career or education simply because of their religion.[17] Not ignoring other considerations, the generational factor may help to explain why individuals like Demke and Stolpe could not conceive of another political or social system and believed that co-operation with the State was the only possible road, whereas younger individuals such as Eppelmann were much more open to confrontation.

Conclusion

After long and inconclusive conflict between Church and State, the agreement of 6 March 1978 solidified an uneasy partnership that was to last until late 1987 and the Görlitz *Kirchenbund* Synod. During that time the organisational structures of Church and State shaped the way these two institutions interacted, and it might be said that their peaceful co-existence led to a gradual co-acceptance and growing together. Thus for almost a decade the Church leaders increasingly defined their role with regard to the SED-State. As that State's power began to crumble, the Church leaders found that their own role diminished as well, so much so that one might claim that the collapse of the SED-State was a hard blow to many of the Church leaders. Everything they had been working on and developing since 1978 – and for some of them, much longer – now lay in rubble. In a meeting in December 1988 with local Dresden SED functionaries, Bishop Hempel was asked whether he still held to the 6 March 1978 understanding. His reply is illuminating: 'Therein lies a part of my life's work. I fear however that this course cannot continue for much longer'.[18]

The effort on both Church and State sides to maintain the relationship which had lasted almost a decade since March 1978 is understandable, and the Church leaders, who could hardly have foreseen the demise of the GDR any more than anyone else at the time, should not be unsympathetically blamed for their cautious stance. Nevertheless, an understanding of their organisational position both within the Church and with relation to the State helps to explain their lack of initiative in the final months of the GDR's existence.[19] With the collapse of the GDR the Church leaders lost their role in society as the voice and protector of the people – the counterweight to the State – and they have been struggling to find a new role for themselves ever since.

NOTES

[1] This acceptance of socialism coincides with a growing acceptance of the 'Church in Socialism' formula promulgated in 1971 'to proclaim and to live the Gospel in a socialist environment' (Bericht des Themenausschusses der Bundessynode 1971). Detlef Pollack writes, '"Church in Socialism" was without a doubt a formula of loyalty[...] The Church found itself ready to conform in order to achieve an increase in its autonomy and ability to act.' Detlef Pollack, 'Der Umbruch in der DDR. Eine Protestantische Revolution? Der Beitrag der Evangelischen Kirchen und der politisch alternativen Gruppen zur Wende 1989' in Trutz Rendtorff, ed., *Protestantische Revolution? Kirche und Theologie in der DDR: Ekklesiologische Voraussetzungen, politischer Kontext, theologisch und historische Kriterien* (Göttingen, 1993), p. 53f.

[2] Thus, after the introduction of the *Jugendweihe*, a communist youth ceremony, Church leaders were forced to back down when they saw that the vast majority of their membership were participating despite the Church leaders' vocal opposition.

[3] Quoted in Frederic Hartweg, ed., *SED und Kirche. Eine Dokumentation ihrer Beziehungen. Band 2: SED 1968-1989* (Neukirchen-Vluyn, 1995), p. 5f.

[4] Ibid. 489.

[5] 'Information der Arbeitsgruppe Kirchenfragen im ZK an Paul Verner vom 5.9.1984 über die Synode des BEK vom 21.-25.9.1984' in ibid. p. 517.

[6] Ibid. 492. Dohle refers here to the report included in 'Beschluß des Politbüros des ZK der SED vom 7.1.1986 zu aktuellen Fragen der Politik gegenüber den Evangelischen Kirchen' (Hartweg, op. cit., pp. 524-530). Dohle also writes, 'At that time Klaus Gysi also considered breaking open the ideological crust and ossification in the *Kirchenpolitik* and doing away with the primitive discussions of the supposed limits of the Church's work or its misuse through a discussion and policy that built on the positive chances and possibilities of a Church in society' (Hartweg, op. cit., p. 489). However, Gysi lacked the authority to make any significant changes, and thus his opinion amounted to little.

[7] Gerhard Besier, *Der SED-Staat und die Kirche 1983-1991. Höhenflug und Absturz* (Berlin, 1995), p. 230.

[8] Quoted in Anke Silomon, *Synode und SED-Staat. Die Synode des Bundes der Evangelischen Kirchen in der DDR in Görlitz vom 18. bis 22. September 1987* (Göttingen, 1997), p. 180.

[9] Letter of 29 September 1987 in Hartweg, op. cit., p. 540.

[10] Mary Fulbrook, *Anatomy of a Dictatorship. Inside the GDR: 1949-1989* (New York, 1997), p. 116.

[11] Harold Wagner, 'Friedensgebete – Symbol der Befreiung', in: Christian Dietrich and Uwe Schwabe, eds., *Freunde und Feinde. Dokumente zu den Friedensgebeten in Leipzig zwischen 1981 und dem 9. Oktober 1989* (Leipzig, 1994), p. 21.

[12] Though this would have been the first time most heard Leich using this term, he had actually used it earlier in a meeting of the KKL on 4/5 September 1987 regarding the Olof Palme Peace March, when he said: 'Church representatives must learn where the limits of reasonableness lie for our State partners'. Protocol of the 113th meeting of the KKL on 4/5 September 1987 in Berlin. Evangelisches Zentralarchiv (Berlin) 101/93/73.

[13] Gerhard Rein, *Die protestantische Revolution 1987-1990. Ein deutsches Lesebuch* (Berlin, 1990), 31. For this statement, Leich was even accused of acting like the Reichsbischof in the Third Reich. See Besier, op. cit., p. 233.

[14] Quoted in Wagner, op. cit., p. 27.

[15] Friedrich Schorlemmer, 'Kirche, Opposition und Umbruch. Ein persönlicher Rückblick' in Gert Kaiser and Ewald Frie, eds., *Christen, Staat und Gesellschaft in der DDR* (Frankfurt, 1996), p. 235.

[16] Interview with Elena Demke on 18 April 1998 in Berlin.

[17] Mary Fulbrook notes that by denying Christians the opportunities of higher education and good careers, the regime inadvertently helped to create a group of frustrated dissidents within the Church. Fulbrook, op. cit., p. 89f.

[18] Quoted in Besier, op. cit., p. 354.

[19] The Church leaders played a critical role during these months, facilitating the peaceful nature of the 'revolution', but their role was much more reactive than active.

Michael Ploetz

THE EAST GERMAN PEACE COUNCIL IN THE PEACE STRUGGLE OF THE EARLY 1980s

This article discusses the important, yet hardly recognised, role of the Peace Council of the GDR in the communist 'peace struggle' against Western armament programmes and NATO. The Peace Council, an executive bureaucracy of the SED which co-operated closely with the MfS, attempted to influence Western debates on security policies, using inter alia its extensive contacts with groups such as the British Campaign for Nuclear Disarmament. Using archival evidence, this paper studies the intrinsic nature of the Peace Council, its use as an instrument of influence on Western protest movements and its role as a propagandistic supplement to the military build-up of the Brezhnev era.

In December 1979, NATO adopted the two-track decision that offered the USSR negotiations on Intermediate Range Nuclear Forces but threatened to deploy new Eurostrategic missiles if no arms control agreement was reached by the end of 1983. After two decades of military build-up, however, Brezhnev's Politburo was determined to thwart the deployment of the new American missiles by a 'peace struggle' rather than by a mutually acceptable arms control agreement.[1] Moreover, a Soviet military textbook described the struggle for peace as an integral element of a revolutionary strategy:

> It is one of the most important tasks of the communist and workers' parties in the capitalist countries to win over the majority of the working people and to create a broad front of anti-imperialist forces. The struggle of the communist and workers' parties for the realisation of general democratic slogans and for peace contributes to the formation of a political mass army for the Socialist revolution. The general democratic struggle does not postpone the Socialist revolution but brings it closer.[2]

The peace struggle was thus preordained to alienate many of those Western Europeans who, although opposed to NATO's two-track decision, were equally unwilling to subordinate themselves to the schemes of Marxism-Leninism. In the Western peace movements, the questions were bitterly disputed whether anti-nuclear protests should include the Soviet SS-20 missile, or how the independent peace movement in East Germany should be dealt with. Yet these feuds were never a purely Western affair. The Communist World Peace Council (WPC) and its sub-organisations in the Socialist states waged both an open and a covert campaign to keep control of the Western peace movements. Since the Peace Council of the GDR (henceforth: the Peace Council) maintained a world-wide network of contacts and closely co-operated with the dependencies of the West German Communist Party (DKP), it was well placed to interfere in the politics of Western pacifism. Ironically, the Marxist-Leninist campaign against the pacifist critics of the 'Socialist Camp' was most severely hampered by the mindless orthodoxy of the Soviets. After Gorbachev's ascension to power, however, things became even worse from the perspective of the Peace Council, since the new Soviet leadership felt strongly attracted by the sincere pacifism of what they called 'divisive elements'.

The Peace Council

The Peace Council was one of those front organisations which the Marxist-Leninists traditionally employed to rally broad coalitions around a minimal consensus. In 1980, the so-called 'Krefeld Appeal' became a last triumph for this strategy. Although decisive in mobilising the West German public against the two-track decision,[3] this petition had been launched at the WPC's 'Peoples' Parliament in Sofia', in September 1980. In West Germany, the campaign was conducted by a front organisation of the DKP with close organisational ties to the Peace Council.[4]

Despite all protestations about its political independence,[5] the Peace Council was an executive bureaucracy of the SED.[6] The Peace Council closely co-operated with the Ministry for State Security (MfS; Stasi); it supplied the MfS with detailed reports on all its Western contacts,[7] and with photocopies of all the letters it received, including copies of both sides of the envelope.[8] As a research facility on Western pacifism,[9] the Peace Council provided detailed notes on the personality of its Western 'friends' for the MfS.[10] Both organisations co-ordinated the surveillance of the Peace Council's Western visitors.[11] Nevertheless, the Stasi-informers in its staff were also responsible for monitoring the activities of the Peace Council and the behaviour of its functionaries.[12]

Conceptually, the Peace Council was guided by the Leninist dogma of imperialism's unalterable aggressiveness. It believed in a strictly dualistic world in which the forces of peace were struggling against the forces of war and permanent peace would only come after the global eradication of capitalism.[13] To reach this goal, the Peace Council tried to influence the political debates in the West by 'unmasking' 'anti-communism and anti-Sovietism' and by refuting 'the propaganda lie [...] about an alleged threat from the East.'[14] The monopoly on peace which the Marxist-Leninists claimed for themselves, however, dialectically transformed all of their opponents into enemies of peace:

> In the GDR, a big unified peace movement fights in complete agreement
> with the foreign policies of the Socialist state. Any 'opposition' against
> it would not only be disturbing but objectively also be hostile towards
> peace.[15]

When, from 1979 onwards, East German citizens increasingly voiced their concerns about the military policies of their state in what was to become an independent peace movement, the Marxist-Leninists responded by reasserting their monopoly on peace: 'Of course, a movement "independent" of the GDR-Peace-State and of its peace policy can only be a movement against peace, the state, and its policy.'[16] Consequently, independent peace campaigners were treated as criminals and Western protests about their harassment were dismissed as malevolent propaganda:

> Spreading the lie that the socialist countries suppress, arrest, or harass
> citizens for their commitment to peace is a particularly unbridled
> defamation of socialism [...].

The conviction of some individuals who have committed crimes in the socialist countries under the flag of peace, is taken [...] as an occasion to direct the peace forces in the NATO-states into an anti-socialist position of confrontation [...].[17]

Combating 'divisive elements and enemy strongholds' in the Peace Movement

In July 1982, the campaign for European Nuclear Disarmament (END) invited a number of groups to a conference in Brussels. Among the participants were the Dutch Interchurch Peace Council (IKV), West Germany's Green Party, the Italian Communist Party, and the Bertrand Russell Peace Foundation. These groups held both military blocs equally responsible for the arms race. Therefore, they were determined to repel the influence of the WPC on the Western peace movements. Particularly the British peace campaigner E.P. Thompson opposed the strategy of the WPC to turn the peace movement exclusively against NATO.[18] Since the WPC had never criticised the USSR, Thompson feared that its influence might easily discredit the entire struggle against nuclear arms. In order to gain political respectability, Thompson recommended that Western pacifists should co-operate with East European dissidents.[19]

The second END-Convention took place in West Berlin in May 1983. Initially, the Soviets had hoped that the massive participation of communist groups might change the 'correlation of forces' at this convention. To enforce the participation of the WPC members as co-sponsors, the Soviet Peace Committee threatened to use its influence within the peace movement to make the convention a failure. Since the organisers of the END-Convention were determined to forestall a hostile take-over, they invited the Marxist-Leninist Peace Committees as observers only. G.A. Zhukov, the President of the Soviet Peace Committee, responded with an open letter calling for a boycott of the END-Convention.[20] In his circular, Zhukov 'unmasked' the 'conception of "equal responsibility"' as a means 'to disorient, weaken, and undermine the peace movement'. By asserting that the organisers of the END-Convention tried 'to drag the members of the peace movement into a downright cold war against the public of socialist countries',[21] however, it was actually Zhukov who issued a declaration of war. The results of his letter were rather mixed. Zhukov's hyperbole prompted the Dutch Communists to distance themselves from Moscow.[22] Nonetheless, one of the organisers of the END-Convention was quite impressed by the wave of cancellations of attendance that followed Zhukov's letter.[23]

The SED and the Peace Council were also determined to make the END-Convention a failure. While the Peace Council mobilised its allies in West Germany[24] and Europe,[25] the SED co-ordinated its activities with the DKP and the Socialist Unity Party of West Berlin.[26] Although the SED shared Zhukov's strategic aim of spoiling the END-Convention, it disliked the heavy-handed tactics of Zhukov and Romesh Chandra, the Indian President of the WPC.[27] In March 1983, Hermann Axen, the foreign policy architect of the SED, insisted that the campaign against 'the divisive undertaking in West Berlin' should be conducted in such a way that the 'true adherents of peace' were separated from the 'divisive forces'.[28] In regard to the IKV, the SED clearly favoured a policy of 'differentiation' to 'isolate the hostile forces around [the General-Secretary Mient] Faber' and to reanimate the 'progressive potential' of this organisation.[29] Zhukov's instincts, however, rebelled against subtle approaches like this. In 1984, he reiterated that 'all movements co-operating with Faber belong to the enemy camp and must be treated accordingly'.[30]

In order to make themselves heard in West Berlin, the Marxist-Leninist absentees planned to recruit independent personalities like Petra Kelly and Gert Bastian as their spokespersons.[31] Yet such schemes had to be shelved when Kelly, Bastian, and three other Greens used the occasion of the END-Convention to stage a small peace demonstration in East Berlin. Unsurprisingly, they were immediately arrested and deported to West Berlin. The Social Democrats who participated in the conference strongly disapproved of this demonstration, since it would negatively affect the peace groups in the GDR. Yet two East German peace campaigners who had been recently expelled from their country lent their full support to the Greens. Peter Rösch emphatically called for more contacts between Eastern and Western pacifists. He also stressed that the SED had to be forced to respect human rights.[32]

Since the members of END had realised that the status quo in Europe was the political cause of the arms race, they combined their struggle against nuclear arms with calls for a 'reunification of Europe' and the 'liberation of Europe from the superpowers'.[33] People like Mary Kaldor of END wanted the peace movement to organise 'resistance from below transcending the blocs'. In West Berlin, she explained that a policy of détente pursued by the Western governments would not automatically lead to a liberalisation of the communist countries. Therefore, the peace movement had to seize détente as an opportunity to influence social development in the East.[34] By September 1982, END had already established working contacts to East German pacifists.[35] Since the MfS knew that it would be impossible to prevent participants of the END-Convention from entering East Berlin, the MfS, the Peace Council and pro-Communist Christian peace activists from West Berlin planned to organise doctored meetings between Western pacifists and Marxist-Leninist loyalists from among the East German Churches.[36] Eventually, however, it was END that managed to mislead the Stasi. When, on 11 May 1983, a large group of Western pacifists crossed the border and met with independent peace campaigners in Ulrike and Gerd Poppe's flat, the MfS was taken by surprise.[37] Erich Mielke's seemingly omniscient Ministry had been successfully misled about both the date and the place of the meeting.[38] Ulrike Poppe recently recalled this event: 'For the GDR-misfits, this became a completely unbelievable situation: the World met in the back yard rooms of this otherwise so hermetically sealed-off country'.[39]

After all attempts had failed to thwart the END-Convention, the WPC launched a series of conferences to regain the initiative on the peace front. Nonetheless, the narrow-mindedness of its leading functionaries invariably turned these meetings into public relations disasters. In Prague, where the WPC held an international rally in June 1983, the Greens walked out in protest after the police had dispersed a meeting between them and the civil rights movement, Charter 77. The bad impression of this rally was further reinforced by a police action against an unlicensed peace demonstration.[40] In January 1984, the extraordinary conference of the WPC's Presidential Committee also failed to create new bonds between the WPC and the Western peace movements. Instead, the militancy of Chandra and Zhukov led 'to unnecessary divergence with the representatives of different capitalist countries'. Additionally, this conference was overshadowed by the disunity of the communist movement. The French 'comrade Yves Cholière' rejected the Soviet demand for a no-first-use pledge by all nuclear powers. According to him, the small scale of the French deterrent in itself forestalled any first-use. Cholière also refused to blame only Reagan for the prevailing tensions. [41]

At a broadly attended peace conference in Athens in February 1984, the Dutch communist Nico Schouten criticised the Soviet counter-deployment of short-range missiles, which had immediately followed the onset of NATO's deployments. Schouten attacked the USSR for its 'doubtful concept' of 'military parity'. '[T]wo unsuccessful provocation attempts' were directed against the GDR: the IKV collected signatures for a letter demanding the release of imprisoned East German 'peace fighters'; another letter was circulated in which East German citizens voiced their concerns about 'the criminalisation of peace forces' in their country.[42] After this conference, the MfS meticulously checked to whom the signatures under the petition to Honecker belonged.[43]

Alarmed by its growing isolation, the WPC adopted a new 'offensive tactic'. In May 1984, the Soviet Peace Committee suddenly decided to attend the third END-Convention in Perugia (Italy) on the grounds that 'one must not entrust the progressive movements of the capitalist countries alone with the struggle against such a grave opponent'.[44] Inside the highly heterogeneous 'convention movement', the full participation of the Communist Peace Committees had become a hotly debated issue. The West German Social Democrats Jo Leinen and Gert Weißkirchen, in particular, tried to secure 'a maximum of equal participation' for the Marxist-Leninists. While the Socialist states strove for full participation, they refused to grant travel permits to the independent peace campaigners from their own countries. When Weißkirchen pleaded with the East Germans to send at least some 'semi-independents', like the writer Christa Wolf, he only got the usual rebuff: 'Such suggestions for the trade in human beings were vehemently rejected by us [the Peace Council]'.[45] In Perugia, the participating Marxists-Leninists were nevertheless confronted with their opponents: '[f]ormer citizens of the socialist states' spoke for 'counter-revolutionary groupings' like Solidarity, the Polish civil rights groups KOR, and Charter 77.[46] In order to avoid a similar confrontation, the Peace Council had stayed at home.[47]

After Perugia, however, the conflicts inside the 'convention movement' intensified. Acting as the principal opponent of Faber, Jo Leinen advocated that one should either let the Marxist-Leninist Peace Committees participate fully or invite no Eastern Europeans at all. The Polish and Hungarian Peace Committees became quite confident that, 'with the help of the Social Democrats', it would become possible to restrict 'the leeway of the divisive elements' and to exert 'a positive influence' on the convention movement.[48] Further inroads on the convention movement were made by informal collaborators. The MfS, for instance, had a source with direct access to the leadership of END.[49]

In 1985, the WPC returned to its boycotting policy. The SED, in particular, feared that it might look like a political recognition of the independent peace movement if its exiled members were appearing on the same stage as the Peace Council.[50] The absence of the Marxist-Leninist Peace Committees did not spoil the fourth END-Convention in Amsterdam. With the signing of a personal peace treaty between Faber and the absent Rainer Eppelmann, the independents of both blocs symbolically codified their unity. Petra Kelly opened her speech with a 'peace poem' by the peace campaigner Bärbel Bohley, whom she called 'her "sister in East Germany"'. Letters by Eastern European dissidents were read out and Vaclav Havel addressed the conference on a videotape.[51] By and large, the 'convention movement' had indeed succeeded in creating a pan-European peace movement transcending both blocs. By adhering to their own moral standards, furthermore, the 'convention movement' acquired a political stature that was finally recognised by the new Soviet leadership. In 1988, the Soviets invited Faber and Kaldor to observe the dismantling of SS-20s – the very missiles whose massive deployment had once triggered the two-track decision.[52] To the completely unreformed SED, this invitation was just another harbinger of its subsequent downfall.

Conclusion

Due to the Manichaean character of Marxism-Leninism, orthodox communists could not really understand the pluralist character of Western societies. In 1985, Vadim Zagladin, a high-ranking CPSU functionary, gave an amazing demonstration of the resulting inability to comprehend the political discourse in the West. Zagladin found it quite noteworthy that the USA, too, were concerned about the superpower theory. This discovery became only explicable to him when he suddenly realised that this theory automatically ascribed half the guilt for the arms race to the USA. Still not entirely reassured by this new insight, Zagladin urged his DKP interlocutors to confirm that the superpower theory was only adhered to by some 'élitist circles' whereas 'those at the grass roots would instinctively take the correct position'.[53]

This inability to understand Western plurality was seriously hampering the Marxist-Leninist peace struggle. On the operative level, the Marxist-Leninist dichotomy resulted in a strategy of relentless enmity that could only differentiate between friend and foe. Whether Marxist-Leninists considered another group hostile or not was never a matter of the self-perception or declared aims of such a group. Enemies were all those who criticised Marxism-Leninism. Since the Marxist-Leninists themselves were dedicated conspirators, they tended to believe that all their critics were agents of the enemy. Amnesty International, for instance, was categorised as an 'Imperialist propaganda agency' and 'an anti-Communist and neo-colonialist instrument of subversion'.[54] A similar reasoning governed the Marxist-Leninist approach towards the 'convention movement'. Although admittedly no evidence indicated their affiliation to Western intelligence services,[55] the WPC habitually described dedicated pacifists like Faber and Kaldor as 'paid agents of the enemy and professional troublemakers'.[56] In 1985, Mielke concluded against all available evidence that Petra Kelly was an agent of the CIA.[57] To the Marxist-Leninists, the activities of the 'convention movement' were nothing but subversive diversions 'to divert the peace movement from the direction of its main thrust [*Hauptstoßrichtung*]'.[58] Apparently unable to regard the 'convention movement' as a manifestation of understandable fears, the SED classified it instead as a fifth column in a 'general attack against the peace movement' – 'a complex, co-ordinated, and centrally controlled action of all available ideological-propagandistic, psychological, intelligence, and subversive means, methods, and forces'.[59]

It was actually the self-styled Marxist-Leninist monopoly on peace that did most to disunite the peace movement. In 1984, for instance, the pro-Communist majority at the 'action conference' of the West German peace movement adopted a resolution which 'recognised' that the deployment of Soviet short-range missiles 'constituted an answer to the American deployments'. The opposition of the Greens was recklessly pushed aside.[60] The Pyrrhic character of such victories became apparent after the onset of the missile deployments had stripped the peace movement of its unifying purpose. In 1984, Kelly and

Bastian left the committee organising the 'Krefeld Appeal' in protest against its persistent unwillingness to show any solidarity with East Germany's independent peace groups.[61] Yet the inability of the Marxist-Leninists to make any compromises not only divided the peace movement but also accelerated the disintegration of the 'Communist World Movement'.[62] In an ironic twist of history, the peace struggle thus helped to bring about the downfall of Communism.

NOTES

[1] Michail Gorbatschow, *Erinnerungen* (Berlin, 1995), p. 620f.

[2] A.S. Milowidow et al., *Krieg und Armee* (Berlin, 1979), p. 142.

[3] Clive Rose, *Campaigns Against Western Defence: NATO's Adversaries and Critics* (London, 1985), p.167f.

[4] Bundesarchiv-Zwischenarchiv-Dahlwitz-Hoppegarten (henceforth: BA-ZA-DH), DZ9.39.193., 'Bericht über den Studienaufenthalt einer Delegation der bildungspolitischen Kommission beim Bundesvorstand der Deutschen Friedens-Union vom 24. bis 30. Oktober 1980 [...].' p. 2.

[5] BA-ZA-DH, DZ9.K.295.1578., 'Zur '"unabhängigen Friedensbewegung"' pp. 4-8.

[6] Stiftung Archiv der Parteien und Massenorganisationen der DDR im Bundesarchiv (henceforth: SAPMO-BA), DY30/IV2/2.037/20, p. 32; SAPMO-BA, DY30/JIV2/2/1785, p. 10.

[7] Der Bundesbeauftragte für die Unterlagen des Staatssicherheitsdienstes der ehemaligen Deutschen Demokratischen Republik (henceforth: BStU), ZA, MfS-HA XX, Nr.853, p. 4-25; BStU, ZA, MfS-HA XX Nr.854.

[8] BStU, ZA, MfS-HA XX Nr.855, pp. 261-280.

[9] Ibid., pp. 22-25.

[10] Ibid., pp. 162-172.

[11] BStU, ZA, MfS-HA XX Nr.853, p.224; BStU, ZA, MfS-HA XX Nr.855, p. 29.

[12] BStU, ZA, MfS-HA XX Nr.855, p. 86.

[13] Waltraud Böhme et al., *Kleines Politisches Wörterbuch* (3rd edition, Berlin: Dietz Verlag, 1978), pp. 245-255.

[14] BA-ZA-DH, DZ9.262.1329., 'Information über die Tätigkeit der Arbeitsgruppe BRD des Friedensrates der DDR für das Jahr 1978', p. 1.

[15] BA-ZA-DH, DZ9.12.60., 'Empfang einer Delegation des Bundesvorstandes der Deutschen Friedensunion vom 29.11. bis 2.12.1982 [...]', p. 1.

[16] BA-ZA-DH, DZ9.K.295.1578., 'Zur "unabhängigen Friedensbewegung"', p. 4.

[17] BA-ZA-DH, DZ9.K.295.1578., '[...] Strategie und Taktik des Kampfes feindlicher Stützpunkte und spalterischer Kräfte gegen die Friedensbewegung', May 1985, p. 4.

[18] Rose, *Campaigns*, pp. 150-155.

[19] BStU, ZA, MfS ZAIG 7164c, p. 37.

[20] Rose, *Campaigns*, p.152

[21] BA-ZA-DH, DZ9.455.2378., 'Abschrift des Briefes des Sowjetischen Komitees zum Schutz des Friedens an die Friedensbewegung in allen Ländern', pp. 3f., 6.

[22] BA-ZA-DH, DZ9.14.69, 'Bericht über den Aufenthalt einer Delegation der niederländischen Bewegung "Stopp der Neutronenbombe – Stopp dem Kernwaffenwettrüsten" vom 21.-26.3.1983 [...]', p. 3f.

[23] BStU, ZA, ZAIG MfS 7164c, p. 68f.

[24] BA-ZA-DH, DZ9.14.69, 'Information über den Aufenthalt der Delegation der Bundesgeschäftsstelle der Deutschen Friedensgesellschaft/VK vom 17.-20. Januar 1983 [...]', p. 2.

[25] BA-ZA-DH, DZ9.12.60, 'Information über die Gespräche mit dem Generalsekretär des Finnischen Friedenskämpferverbandes Dr. Johannes Pakaslahti, [...] 3.9.-8.9. 1982 [...]', pp. 1ff.

[26] BStU, ZA, ZAIG MfS 7164c, pp. 97-109.

[27] Ibid., pp.99-100; BA-ZA-DH, DZ9.14.69, 'Bericht über bilaterale Arbeitsgespräche mit Vertretern des Polnischen Friedenskomitees am 16. und 17. März 1983 [...]', p. 3f.

[28] SAPMO-BA, DY30/IV2/2.035/24, p. 53f.

[29] BA-ZA-DH, DZ9.K.295.1578, '[...] Strategie und Taktik des Kampfes feindlicher Stützpunkte und spalterischer Kräfte gegen die Friedensbewegung', p. 6.

[30] BA-ZA-DH, DZ9.55.275, 'Information über die Konferenz der Bewegungen Europas und Nordamerikas für Frieden, Abrüstung und gegen Krieg, 5. bis 7. Oktober 1984, in Espoo Finnland', p. 3.

[31] BStU, ZA, ZAIG MfS 7164c, p. 102.

[32] BStU, ZA, MfS ZAIG 7164b, pp. 251-254, 261f.

[33] BA-ZA-DH, DZ9.K.295.1578, '[...] Strategie und Taktik des Kampfes feindlicher Stützpunkte und spalterischer Kräfte gegen die Friedensbewegung', May 1985, p. 12f.

[34] BStU, ZA, MfS ZAIG 7164b, p. 160.

[35] BStU, ZA, MfS ZAIG 7164c, p. 37.

[36] Ibid., p. 33.

[37] BStU, ZA, MfS ZAIG 7164b, p. 163f.

[38] Ibid., pp. 144; BStU, ZA, MfS ZAIG 7164c, p. 76.

[39] Ulrike Poppe, '"Der Weg ist das Ziel". Zum Selbstverständnis und der politischen Rolle oppositioneller Gruppen der achtziger Jahre.' in: Ulrike Poppe et al. (eds.), Zwischen Selbstbehauptung und Anpassung: Formen des Widerstandes und der Opposition in der DDR (Berlin, 1995), p. 247f.

[40] Vladimir Kusin, 'World Peace Assembly in Prague Backfires', in: Vojtech Mastney (ed.), Soviet/East European Survey, 1983-1984: Selected Research and Analysis from Radio Free Europe/Radio Liberty (Durham, 1985), p.61f.

[41] BA-ZA-DH, DZ9.55.273, 'Information über die Tagung des Präsidiums des Weltfriedensrates vom 21. bis 24.1.1984 in Berlin (West)', pp. 2-6.

[42] BA-ZA-DH, DZ9.55.273, 'Anlage: 2 zum Originalprotokoll Nr.: 4/84, 13.02.1984', p.6f.

[43] BStU, ZA, MfS ZAIG 7164b, pp. 31-39.

[44] BA-ZA-DH, DZ9.55.273, 'Anlage: 5 zum Originalprotokoll 12/84, 24.05.1984', p. 1f.

[45] BA-ZA-DH, DZ9.55.273, 'Anlage: 4 zum Originalprotokoll Nr.12/84, 22.05.1984', pp. 1, 6-7.

[46] BA-ZA-DH, DZ9.K.295.1578, 'Interne Studie zur Strategie und Taktik des Kampfes feindlicher Stützpunkte und spalterischer Kräfte gegen die Friedensbewegung', May 1985, p. 27.

[47] BStU, ZA MfS-HA XX/AKG/II 108, pp. 54f.

[48] BA-ZA-DH, DZ9.55.275, 'Anlage: 7 zum Orginalprotokoll Nr.27/84, 29.10.1984', p. 4.

[49] BStU, ZA, MfS-HA XX/AKG/II 108, pp. 14ff.

[50] BStU, ZA, MfS-HA XX/AKG/II 108, pp. 54f.

[51] Ibid., pp. 250-257.

[52] BStU, ZA, MfS-ZMA XX/1814, p. 31.

[53] SAPMO-BA, DY30/JIV2/10.02/17, 'DKP Information: In der Zeit vom 26.-29. April weilte Karl-Heinz Schröder,[...] und Wilhelm Sprenger, [...] zu einem Informationsbesuch [...] beim Zentralkomitee der Kommunistischen Partei der Sowjetunion in Moskau', pp.7, 13.

[54] BStU, ZA, MfS ZAIG 5161, p. 123.

[55] BA-ZA-DH, DZ9.K.295.1578, '[...] Strategie und Taktik des Kampfes feindlicher Stützpunkte und spalterischer Kräfte gegen die Friedensbewegung', May 1985, p. 36.

[56] BA-ZA-DH, DZ9.55.273, 'Anlage: 3 zum Originalprotokoll Nr.2/84, 16.01.1984', p. 5.

[57] BStU, ZA, MfS ZAIG 5178, p. 56.

[58] BA-ZA-DH, DZ9.K.295.1578, '[...] Strategie und Taktik des Kampfes feindlicher Stützpunkte und spalterischer Kräfte gegen die Friedensbewegung', May 1985, p. 12f.

[59] Ibid., p. 1.

[60] SAPMO-BA, DY30/JIV2/10.04/11, 'Zur Entwicklung der Massenbewegung für Frieden und Abrüstung in der BRD [...]' 25/06/1984, pp. 13, 5.

[61] BA-ZA-DH, DZ9.55.237, 'Anlage: 1 zum Originalprotokoll Nr.2/84.' 17/01/1984.

[62] SAPMO-BA, DY30/IV2/2.035/12, 'Neue Probleme der kommunistischen Weltbewegung [...].' 23/10/1985, pp. 50-63.

SECTION FOUR

INSTITUTIONS AND PARTIES

Peter Barker

INTRODUCTION

The three papers in this section are concerned with the transition of parties and institutions from the GDR into a unified Germany: the first by Daniel Hough considers the position of the only political party with an overwhelmingly eastern identity, the PDS, eight years after unification; Julian Rhys examines the surprising survival of the the FDJ as a separate youth organisation; Thorsten Lauterbach's paper is concerned with the demise of an institution, the GDR legal system, and its replacement by West German constitutional and judicial structures.

The PDS, the successor party of the SED, represents one of the most successful instances of the survival of GDR institutions in a united Germany, comparable only with the continued popularity of the socialist confirmation ceremony, the *Jugendweihe*. The federal and Land elections of 1998 only confirmed the solid basis of its recovery from its low point in 1990 and 1991. In the federal election on 27 September 1998 it increased its votes by over half a million, largely due to an increase in support in Saxony and Thuringia, thus confounding the view of a number of observers that it had reached the high point of its possible reservoir of voters. It also narrowly crossed the five-percent hurdle gaining 5.1%, and thereby achieving the status of a *Fraktion* in the *Bundestag*. In the Land election in Mecklenburg-Vorpommern on the same day, it also increased its vote to nearly 25% and now has three ministers in a new SPD/PDS coalition government. So, only nine years after the collapse of the SED, the PDS has successfully negotiated itself back into a position where it has a direct involvement in the exercise of governmental power, albeit only at Land level. Hough stresses in his paper that despite the continuities that can be traced back to the SED the PDS of today cannot be equated with the SED, arguing that despite its criticism of capitalism it has made substantial steps towards accepting the rules of the democratic game. The 1998 election, however, did confirm its position as a party which primarily represents eastern interests; it again failed to make any substantial impact in the western Länder, increasing its vote there by only 0.2% to 1.1%. Hough argues that the PDS should accept its role as a regional party and build on its present position of relative strength there. Recent events surrounding the latest *Parteitag* in January 1999 suggest that this might prove difficult: the party's main reformist thinker, André Brie, refused to stand again for the executive committee and criticised many in the party for preferring to turn inwards and ignore the chance the election result has given the PDS to turn itself into a real alternative on the left to the SPD and the Greens, both of which are moving further into the central ground.

The comparison with the FDJ (fdj since January 1990) is an interesting one; this was an organisation which was totally dependent on the SED's monopoly of power in the GDR, and when that power crumbled, any justification for its existence disappeared. Apart from its role in the GDR as a transmitter of ideology to young people, it provided the essential stepping stone for those anxious to make their way to university and then on into the upper echelons of power in the GDR. Once the SED was no longer a *Staatspartei*, the FDJ became redundant. It has survived, but unlike the PDS, according to Rhys, it is, in its lower-case form, a purely backwards-looking organisation with a tiny membership. It has allied itself with the PDS, but the reformist leadership of the PDS is uncomfortable with a group which seems only nostalgic for the GDR, while the PDS's agenda has to be dominated by the preoccupations of the present.

The transformation of the legal system of the GDR presents a different set of questions. Lauterbach demonstrates the different philosophies behind the two legal systems. The legal system of the GDR was an extension of state power and therefore could not continue to exercise that function when that power collapsed. Lauterbach maintains that the majority of GDR lawyers survived unification, and that even 50% of judges have managed the transition into the all-German legal system, despite the question of the role that judges played in suppressing opposition providing a sharp focus for *Geschichtsaufarbeitung* in the post-unification period. The recent trial of the judges involved in the sentences pronounced against Robert Havemann in the late 1970s, in which the judges were finally acquitted, provides one of the clearest examples of the difficulties faced by a democratic legal system in judging a legal system using different principles and practices. Lauterbach concentrates also on the perceived failure of the West German legal system to 'deliver justice'; a criticism made in particular by the citizens groups from the GDR. He also sees the opportunities presented during the period after unification to simplify the excessively over-complicated German legal system as having been largely missed, another point which has reinforced the eastern deficit of trust in democratic institutions, exemplified above all in the lengthy processes involved in cases of dispute over property rights.

These three papers therefore provide clearly contrasting case studies of institutions from the GDR in transition. That period of transition is by no means over, and particularly in the case of the political parties it is going to be interesting to see whether the PDS will have a long-lasting effect on the shape of the political system, especially at Land level where it is now firmly established as the third force after the SPD and the CDU.

Daniel Hough

SED TO PDS – A CASE OF CONTINUITY THROUGH CHANGE?

Within months of the Berlin Wall being breached, the SED moved to adopt a new party name (the PDS), a new party constitution and new ideological directions. Since this chaotic early development, the PDS, the direct successors of the SED dictatorship, has established itself as a genuine and sustainable actor in Neufünfland. The PDS has done this by incorporating carefully conducted changes in structure, ideology and personnel with strong elements of continuity inherited from its predecessor. The reforming leadership of the party has presided over a skilful re-interpretation of the party as an articulator of eastern German interests.

Introduction

This paper sets out with the aim of illustrating how the once all powerful *Sozialistische Einheitspartei Deutschlands* (Socialist Unity Party – SED) developed from a *Staatspartei*, the type of which governed in all of the Soviet Union's former eastern European satellite states, into a regional, left-wing 'protest' party, that has been able to both stabilise itself, and subsequently flourish, on the territory of the former GDR. The questions that this raises about both German politics and German society are multi-faceted and loaded with subjective undertones. Hence assessing the position of the PDS is a far from straightforward task. The main issues that this paper will attempt to address concern two broad areas. Firstly, has the stabilisation of the PDS's position been accomplished as a result of deep-seated, inner-party reform and development, with the aim of forging a role for itself in the new and unified Berlin Republic? Or is the PDS merely an expression of a failed and discredited socialist experiment? Secondly, but interrelated, has the (at least superficial) move away from its anti-democratic, authoritarian past provided a genuine stimulus to act *within* the system, in an attempt to influence and affect the perceived injustices evident in the BRD today? Or is this political pragmatism, as some writers suggest,[1] more of a darker charade, or tactical ploy, hazing over genuine extremist and anti-democratic ideals?

From the SED to the PDS

The fall of the Berlin Wall on 9 November 1989 signalled the beginning of the end for the Socialist Unity Party of East Germany, as the processes and developments triggered, inter alia, by the appointment of Mikhail Gorbachev as General Secretary of the Communist Party of the Soviet Union undermined the absolute position of power that the party had held since the GDR's inception in 1949, eventually culminating on 3 October 1990 in the reunification of the two Germanies. After initially attempting to take up a position on the left of the political spectrum, as a counterweight to the Conservative coalition led by Helmut Kohl, the SED, in the face of plummeting support and internal crisis, faced the inevitable fact that it was going to have to be disbanded. Hence, on 17 December 1989 the party moved to adopt a new, transitional, name - the SED/PDS.[2]

Following the formation of the SED/PDS, Gregor Gysi, a witty Berlin lawyer who had had no position in the old hierarchy of the SED, quickly (within a matter of weeks) became party leader. He championed the dropping of the name SED altogether, signalling a clear and definitive break with the past. Hence the name SED was dropped, and the PDS was born. Despite this rapid development, however, it is clear that without the connections and networks inherited from the SED, the PDS would never have survived the initial 'transitional' phrase after unification.[3] The heritage of the party remains unambiguous: the acquisition of the SED's assets and possessions, a financial temptation that proved too great to resist, left no one in any doubt as to the PDS's point of origin. Internal reforms could not prevent the party from, between mid-1989 and December 1991, losing over two million members with only the former SED cadre remaining loyal to the party.[4] The denunciation of democratic centralism, which in the GDR had led not only to the inflexibility of decision-making but also to the concentration of power in the party leadership, and, as was agreed at the so-called 'debate of the round-table', the rejection of any form of secret police, were insufficient to help the party regain some of its destroyed credibility. Both legally and constitutionally, the party moved to become the *Nachfolgepartei* of the SED – a fact that opponents and supporters of the PDS alike do not dispute.

In the years immediately following unification, both political commentators and politicians consequently wrote off the party as an anachronism of a bygone age that, over the course of time, would disappear from the party political map.[5] And it does appear a reasonable assumption that, if eastern Germany had blossomed into the 'flourishing economic landscape' that Federal Chancellor Helmut Kohl had promised, then it is likely that the PDS might well have drifted, as the cadre gradually died off, into non-existence. Yet, by the end of 1991, and certainly thereafter, the fallout from unification was beginning to disillusion many eastern Germans, and new electoral potential was developing. The perceived arrogance of western politicians, the apparent annexation (although initially approved) of eastern Germany and the blatant disregard for most things 'East German' led many to feel like strangers in their own land.[6]

The PDS developed a role for itself as the articulator of dissatisfied sections of the eastern German electorate. Those who perceived themselves as being subjectively worse off, or uneasy with the social and economic fallout from unification, consequently expressed themselves politically, in increasing numbers, with a vote for the PDS. The enduring material and psychological differences between eastern and western Germany have therefore ensured that the PDS has been able to develop and expand on its steady bedrock of former functionary support.

Continuities between the PDS and the SED

The PDS, despite its protestations to the contrary, is still no 'ordinary' political party. Both its history and heritage ensure that it occupies a special position on, at best, the fringes of 'normal' political life. In order to address these complex issues, however, one must appreciate the complexity of the phenomena with which people are forced to deal. It is apparent that for its opponents and supporters alike, the PDS represents an element of continuity within the 'new' party system. The bedrock vote of the old party functionaries and those who are seen as the 'psychological' losers of unification have helped form the first segment of the PDS's electorate. While the sub-cultural milieu within which the PDS excels has broadened to include the votes of those protesting against the injustices and broken promises of the transformation process, the element of continuity that the PDS provides for those who saw the end of the GDR in more negative terms is clearly apparent. It came as no surprise that the PDS was able to mobilise this vote in the immediate post-1989 elections. What is more surprising are the increases that have been built on top of this in the years since.

The element of pre-1989 continuity that the PDS provides is therefore clearly a strong factor in helping it achieve parliamentary representation. It is highly likely that without it the party would not be represented at the Federal, or even Land, level today – a fact all too obvious to both party leadership and party activists. For many party members, and a considerable number of PDS voters, the link that the PDS provides to pre-1989 days is indisputable, and this prevents a genuine coming to terms with the past, and subsequently an orientation towards the future, from taking place.

Although the PDS leadership of today (centred primarily around Gregor Gysi, Lothar Bisky, Dietmar Bartsch and, until he stepped down from the party *Vorstand* in January 1999, André Brie) were not principal actors within the SED hierarchy, it is obvious that they, along with the vast majority of PDS members, were once members of the SED, and that much of the ideological rhetoric still evident within the party is based on that premise.

Programmatically, communist rhetoric and beliefs are by no means non-existent in the PDS. The existence of the Communist Platform (KPF), around which outspoken critics of the capitalist societal system like Sarah Wagenknecht and Michael Benjamin, as well as the Marxist Forum and various other extreme left groups (e.g. the AG Junge GenossInnen - the 'youth wing' of the party) illustrate that within the PDS there exists what can be best described as a strong current of communist support. Although Communists have been deprived of leadership positions since the 1995 Schwerin conference and they are, in reality, small in number (estimates of KPF membership range from 1000 to 5000), the election of Benjamin at the Berlin party conference of 1999 to the party executive has produced renewed talk about the influence of Communists within the PDS. Communist rhetoric does receive popular support among the 'basis' and it is inconceivable that, despite the considerable pressure on the leadership to cleanse the party of the KPF, any leader should wish to antagonise such a large portion of the party membership.

The existence of such groups is often taken as clear evidence that a reconciliation with the past has not been carried out, and only when the PDS undertakes such a thorough self-evaluation, as even members of the KPF admit,[7] will the party be able to decouple itself from its SED heritage. Expelling the KPF alone would not, in itself, resolve this problem, as, for as long as the party refuses to go beyond symbolic gestures and declarations (like those condemning Stalinism) and fails to conduct its own process of *Vergangenheitsbewältigung*, then it will render itself *politikunfähig*. To demonstrate that the party has truly changed, a clear evaluation of what exactly was wrong with the GDR, why, and what this means for the future of socialism will be necessary.

There are, therefore, discernible continuities with the SED, particularly with regard to the party's ideological underpinnings, while at the same time considerable pragmatic change has been undertaken, clearly differentiating and distinguishing the PDS from its predecessor.

'New' PDS?

It is all too easy to emphasise the continuity factor when discussing the longevity of the PDS. What is often undervalued and under-discussed is that in order to be able to merit a place in the 'new' party system, the party has also had to undertake considerable pragmatic change, particularly in areas of policy formulation, party structure and general *Weltanschauung*. Subsequently, the PDS has developed into a post-communist party, of the type much in evidence across central and eastern Europe, while simultaneously representing its eastern German clientele, much as the other 'regional' parties in western Europe do. The result of this is a complex, often schizophrenic, party, that competes ably and effectively with the other 'western' parties for votes and influence within the five eastern Länder and Berlin, as well as at the federal level.

Despite the inability and/or unwillingness of the party's leadership to completely distance itself from its SED past, it is indisputable that the PDS has moved irrevocably away from the *Staatspartei* structure of pre-1989. No votes are contrived (or at least no more than any other party attempts to impose its will on its members) and any member is free to stand for election to any office. Furthermore, the resignation of leading lights like André Brie illustrates that the party 'basis' does not always act as the leadership expects or hopes it will. The election of western German media professional Dieter Dehm to the position of vice president at the 1999 Berlin conference, having only been a member of the party for four months and whose candidature received only lukewarm support from the leadership, provides further evidence of this. In this sense the democratic changes, the pluralist interest articulation and the healthy debates that have come to characterise conferences since 1989 represent a clear and distinct metamorphosis from SED times.

The all-encompassing Marxist-Leninist ideology of the SED has been replaced and the PDS now attempts to portray itself more as a broad church of leftward leaning opinion, having denied the importance of the leading role of the working class and chosen to adopt less ideologically extreme positions. Anyone who wishes to oppose capitalism and the societal relationships that it fosters is welcome within the party, and although definitive statements of what the party hopes to achieve (particularly the party's rather flimsy semi-definition of socialism) are lacking, it is clear that the PDS has moved towards being a broad left-wing alternative to the SPD. It accepts the democratic 'rules of the game', and attempts to offer a clear alternative to what it sees as an unjust capitalist system.[8] Regardless as to the coherence of this alternative, the party has clearly adapted to the system, and now adheres to the rules of the political game like any other party.

The attitudes of the major parties towards the PDS, particularly at the local level, are changing. This was illustrated by the creation of the first PDS-supported SPD/B90/Green government in Saxony-Anhalt in 1994 and was further demonstrated by the continuation of this 'Magdeburg Model' (minus the B90/Green Party) after the Land election of April 1998. This progression reached its (current) highpoint with the formation of the first SPD/PDS coalition in Mecklenburg-West Pomerania in October 1998. Proposals like the 'Erfurt Declaration' of January 1997, calling for an effective left-of-centre alliance to oust the centre-right ruling coalition further illustrate not only *how* the PDS has developed, but also how *perceptions* of the party have changed. Despite the fact that only one office-holding SPD politician, Richard Dewes from Thuringia, signed the declaration, it is clear that such a document, and the participation of the PDS in governmental activity in Saxony Anhalt and in a coalition in Mecklenburg-West Pomerania, can be seen as clear evidence of progress. Only a few years ago such developments would have been completely unthinkable.

The PDS is no longer a wholly irrelevant political actor, as is illustrated by its energetic and wide-ranging activity within the institutional structures of the new *Länder*. In eastern Germany the PDS has formed a positive association with the electorate, often being perceived as caring for the interests of the 'small man', and if the changes that have been undertaken thus far are to continue bearing fruit, then it is this author's contention that it is as a *Volkspartei* in the East where the future of the party will be.

The PDS as a regional actor

It is clear that in order to survive over and beyond the period of the 'transformation process', the PDS needs to continue fashioning a role for itself within the Berlin Republic. At present the PDS articulates the opinions and interests of disgruntled and disaffected eastern Germans, who subjectively perceive themselves as 'disadvantaged' (often socially and psychologically, as opposed to materially) on account of the radical economic, political and social transformation that the territory of the former GDR has undergone since 1989. Much of this support centres around the former *Dienstklasse*[9] of the GDR – but it is noticeable that in recent elections this base of support has both broadened and stabilised, consequently leading to the party's stabilisation within the eastern German party political landscape[10]. The 1998 state and federal elections have shown that the PDS attracts votes from eastern Germans of all ages, with younger electors supporting the party in roughly the same proportion as older voters. The state and federal elections of 1998 have subsequently illustrated that the PDS has established itself as an eastern German *Volkspartei*.[11]

Table 1
The PDS share of the vote at the 1998 federal election by sex and by age-group

Category	The PDS percentage share of the total votes cast by sex and by age group
Male	19
Female	21
18-24	20
25-34	19
35-44	20
45-59	19
60+	19

Source: Matthias Jung & Dieter Roth (1998).[12]

It is as a result of this that one potentially appealing strategic approach is available to the PDS – that of becoming a key regional actor in the new *Bundesländer*, a strategic approach which is actually currently dismissed by the party out of hand. The party is already an articulate representative of eastern German interests – and the prospect of further developing into a party that represents not just the subjectively worse off and the mass of protesters, but instead all eastern Germans, is a viable theoretical alternative. Growing eastern German consciousness, while not representing calls for a return to the GDR or to radical socialist ideals, offers the PDS the opportunity to act in a manner equal to the Bavarian CSU, as a regional voice. Much has been made of the rise of so-called *Ostalgie* (a play on words, conflating the words for 'East' and 'Nostalgia'), linking the *Ernüchterungsprozeß* among East Germans who, instead of the much promised higher standards of living and peaceful prosperity, face the multi-faceted and complex problems of high unemployment, social insecurities amidst the cold winds of exploitative capitalism. While it is easy to overplay the importance of such emotions (it is clear that very few eastern Germans would actually wish to return to the GDR), the vast majority are articulating feelings of bitterness and dissatisfaction at the apparent take-over of their country.[13]

This has helped contribute towards the growing societal cleavage between East and West and, coupled with the effective representation that the party possesses at all levels in the new Länder, offers the PDS the rudiments of an approach that could see them develop into a regional party much along the lines of other such parties across differing western European polities. But in order to do this the party will have to conduct a radical self-examination, and move further, particularly with regard to the party's origins and history, than the considerable distance that the PDS has travelled to date.

A suitable theoretical approach to doing this would be to pursue an idea originally articulated by a PDS member of the Saxony Landtag, Christine Ostrowski,[14] and a member of Dresden city council, Ronald Weckesser, who stressed the importance of the PDS exerting influence on the SPD as a left-wing, eastern German regional party.[15] The formation of a 'big idea', in the shape of the themes discussed above, would be integral to this, leading to the PDS developing a clear and distinctive role as an articulator of eastern German issues. The 'Rostocker Manifest', published at the Rostock conference of April 1998, illustrated such a willingness to act as a genuine articulator of eastern German sentiment. The calls for the establishment of a 'non-profit' sector and a so-called 'Pilot Projekt Ost', aimed specifically at rejuvenating the eastern economy and creating much needed jobs, set the PDS apart from the other 'western based' political parties.[16] Such a strategy does not necessarily mean the abandonment of the party's left-wing principles, nor a necessary development into a pure social democratic party, but rather the establishment of the PDS as a broad church of reforming, leftward leaning, eastern German opinion.

Other regional movements illustrate the diversity evident across successful European regional parties.[17] Plaid Cymru, for example, furthers Welsh cultural issues from a left-of-centre basis,[18] while the Scottish National Party (SNP) has promoted calls for greater Scottish powers within the Union of Great Britain and Northern Ireland, with the ultimate aim of Scottish independence.[19] This is once again achieved from a broadly left-of-centre platform. The various regional parties in the Basque Country forward clear nationalist policies, based primarily on historical claims to statehood.[20] The Lega Nord in Italy has capitalised on systemic breakdown and focuses on the straightforward economic benefits that a northern Italian state would enjoy, and hence has stressed separationist policies.[21] In Germany, meanwhile, the CSU has also successfully adapted itself to a role as the voice of Bavarian interests. Although eastern Germany has a very different social, political and economic structure, it is this author's contention that if the PDS is to effectively build itself into the political system, then it will be in a similar function to that of the CSU in Bavaria.

Despite the clear distinctiveness of eastern regional identities like those in Pomerania or Saxony, social, political, but primarily economic events, have led to the development of a superficial eastern German identity. While German regional identities are based more on historical factors, much akin to those in, for example, Bavaria or Swabia in the West, the development of a *Trotzidentität* has manifested itself in the new Länder. The manifestation of such an identity is attributable both to the socialisation process experienced by citizens in the GDR as well as the ongoing economic, social and political transformation process undertaken since 1989, offering the PDS capital to articulate self-perceived eastern German interests. The neo-liberal policies of Helmut Kohl's former government, coupled with the much vaunted drift rightwards of the SPD and the B90/Greens, leaves the PDS (with the exception of extremist parties like the DVU) as the only party effectively speaking out against economic policies that are widely perceived in the East as having led to the social and economic turmoil now widely evident.

As a result of the party's historical legacy, and the negative perceptions of socialism in the West, the PDS currently finds itself appealing to an eastern electorate on the twin grounds of collective experience (i.e. that of, despite the many negative pre-1989 experiences, being guaranteed a job and the importance subsequently attached to being in work, receiving adequate social provision and so on), and the formation of a clear societal cleavage along the line of the former inner-German border.

Many eastern Germans, despite having voted for voluntary annexation to the FRG in 1990, are deeply suspicious of the societal system within which they now live. The 'western' parties have not convinced many eastern Germans that their interests are to be furthered by voting for them, as large-scale mistrust in current institutions illustrates. While the 'system', having developed over forty years in the Federal Republic, struggles to adapt to the differing environment of the former GDR and continues to fail eastern Germans, a path is open for a regional representative to establish itself.

Adopting such a strategy, however, would involve a change that the party is, as yet, unable to contemplate, let alone undertake. The party remains committed to exercising fundamental societal change as an all-German force to the left of the SPD. Reform-minded thinkers like the Dresdner Christine Ostrowski have been subjected to extreme criticism after suggesting such a radical change in direction. Yet, bearing in mind the implausibility of the PDS developing into a Germany-wide socialist organisation, it is clear that only by continuing to change will the party be able to forge a nationally relevant role for itself.

Conclusion

This paper has argued that the PDS has gone through a process of remarkable change, within the broad limits it has set for itself. Gregor Gysi and the 'reformers' within the party clearly recognise that the party base is currently limited by the PDS's history and development, and despite rapid inner party democratisation and an uneasy realignment with the pillars of the social-market economy, underlying continuities with the SED remain.

For the membership of the PDS, as well as those who vote for it, the PDS acts as a strong element of continuity in a world that, over the past nine years, has changed beyond all recognition. This is not a demonstration of any form of collective amnesia, but rather a simple human reaction to times of uncertainty and discontent. The PDS has fostered its image to such an extent that it is able to play on the selective memory of many, and as a result benefits from the many transformation problems still evident within the new Länder, like, for example, high unemployment, lack of social and job security, or integration problems with westerners. Yet the party leadership continues to have to perform a delicate balancing act, matching the necessities of programmatic change in a competitive party political system, with the conservative instincts of much of the party membership and of segments of the electorate.

That the PDS provides a home for ex-SED functionaries is not disputed. That the party finds it difficult to come to terms with its uneasy past is also no surprise. But even after the skilful mobilisation of (particularly young) protest voters is taken into account, it remains clear that if the party is to survive in the long-term, further policy change and psychological development will be necessary. Ideally, the leadership and 'basis' would like to feel in a strong enough position to drop the ideological baggage inherent in being a descendent of the SED, while developing into an all-German socialist party. Closer analysis of the PDS's party programme and its various electoral statements indicates that this is what the party is attempting to do. With the rightward drift of the SPD and the current 'realo' nature of the Greens there is clearly room on the ideological left that such a party could fill, but the likelihood of the PDS being that vehicle remains minimal.

The failed expansion westwards, and particularly the weak showing in the Bremen Land election of 1995, illustrates that the western electorate sees no place for what they perceive as a pure SED *Nachfolgepartei*. Even if it were to develop a coherent and streamlined programme, the western electorate is unlikely to warm to what it sees as the remnants of a failed and bankrupt regime. Hence the PDS should not shy away from positioning itself as a regional movement, eventually stretching out to eastern Germans from all social strata. The development of clear psychological differences between those in the East and those in the West could form the basis for the success of just such a movement, and by building on the already comprehensive eastern party structure in place, the PDS could continue to fashion a longer-term role for itself. This is the principal way in which the PDS will be able to exert influence on a German political system that the PDS so badly believes needs reforming.

NOTES

[1] See Patrick Moreau, *Anatomie einer postkommunistischen Partei* (Bonn/Berlin, 1992); Patrick Moreau and Jürgen Lang. *Was will die PDS?* (Frankfurt am Main, 1994); Patrick Moreau and Jürgen Lang, *Linksextremismus. Eine unterschätzte Gefahr* (Bonn, 1996); Patrick Moreau, *Profil einer antidemokratischen Partei* (Munich, 1998).

[2] For a detailed analysis of the PDS's development out of the SED, see Peter Barker: From the SED to the PDS: Continuity or Renewal?, in Peter Barker (ed.), *The Party of Democratic Socialism in Germany: Modern Post-Communism or Nostalgic Populism?* German Monitor 42 (Amsterdam, 1998), pp. 1-17.

[3] See Gero Neugebauer, 'Hat die PDS bundesweit im Parteiensystem eine Chance?': in Michael Brie, Martin Herzig and Thomas Koch (eds.), *Die PDS. Empirische Befunde und Kontroverse Analysen* (Cologne, 1995), pp. 39-57.

[4] In October 1989 the SED officially had 2.3 million members, but by the end of 1991 the PDS's membership had plummeted to 172,000. Following these initial losses, the membership of the party has stabilised somewhat, and membership numbers have been falling at a much more gradual rate. At the end of 1997 the PDS was still able to register just over 100,000 paid-up members. See Patrick Moreau (1998), op. cit. p. 97.

[5] See Manfred Gerner, *Partei ohne Zukunft? Von der SED zur PDS* (Munich, 1994).

[6] See Peter Pulzer, 'Political Ideology', in Gordon Smith, William E. Paterson, Peter H. Merkl and Stephen Padgett (eds.), *Developments in German Politics* (Durham, 1993), p. 303-326 (p. 325).

[7] Michael Benjamin 'DDR-Identität und PDS', in: Lothar Bisky, Jochen Czerny et al. (eds.), *Die PDS – Herkunft und Selbstverständnis* (Berlin, 1996), p. 230.

[8] The PDS has continued to align itself with all the fundamental requirements of the constitution, and the party's programme and policy documents do not seek to overthrow the democratic structures on which the FRG has been built. A number of commentators focus considerable attention on the alleged 'anti-constitutional' activities of the KPF (*Kommunistische Plattform*), neglecting the fact that the party has clearly renounced all claim to societal transformation by any other means than through the democratic process. See Patrick Moreau (1998).

[9] The term *Dienstklasse* can be traced back to Heike Solga and her work on the class structures in East German society. She coined the term to refer to the privileged, highly-qualified and socially secure functional elites who occupied leading positions within the economy, administration, science, the media, the military or other organs of societal control. See Heike Solga, 'Die Etablierung einer Klassengesellschaft in der DDR: Anspruch und Wirklichkeit des Postulats sozialer Gleichheit', in: J. Huinink/K. U. Mayer et al. (eds.), *Kollektiv und Eigensinn. Lebensverläufe in der DDR und danach* (Berlin, 1995), pp. 45-89.

[10] For a comprehensive analysis of the PDS's electorate at the 1994 Federal election see Jürgen W. Falter and Markus Klein, 'Die Wähler der PDS bei der Bundestagswahl 1994. Zwischen Ideologie, Nostalgie und Protest', in *Aus Politik und Zeitgeschichte*, B51-52/94, pp. 22-34. For further discussion see also Patrick Moreau and Jürgen P. Lang 'Aufbruch zu neuen Ufern? Zustand und Perspektiven der PDS', in *Aus Politik und Zeitgeschichte*, B6/96, pp. 54-61. Ilse Spittman, 'PDS – Anwalt der Ostdeutschen', in *Deutschland Archiv*, July 1994, pp. 673-674. Joanna Mckay, 'The Wall in the Ballot Box', in *German Politics*, 2/5 (1996), pp. 276-291.

[11] See Daniel Hough and Stuart Graham: 'The end of an era: The Federal and State Elections of 1998 in Germany', in *Regional and Federal Studies* (1999) (forthcoming).

[12] Matthias Jung and Dieter Roth: 'Wer zu spät geht, den bestraft der Wähler', in *Aus Politik und Zeitgeschichte*, B52/98, p. 14.

[13] See Wolfgang Dümcke and Fritz Vilmar (ed.), *Kolonialisierung der DDR* (Münster, 1995), pp. 116-207.

[14] Christine Ostrowski is now an MP in the Federal Parliament, having been elected from place six on the PDS Landesliste in Saxony.

[15] See *Neues Deutschland*, 8 May 1996, p. 3.

[16] See Christa Luft et al., *Rostocker Manifest. Für einen zukunftsfähigen Osten in einer gerechten Republik* (Berlin, 1998).

[17] See Michael Keating, *State and Regional Nationalism – Territorial Politics and the European State* (London, 1988).

[18] See C. Ragin, 'Ethnic Political Mobilisation: The Welsh Case', in *American Sociological Review*, 44 (1979), pp. 619-634.

[19] See Michael Keating, *Nations against the State* (New York, 1996).

[20] See Daniele Conversi, *The Basques, The Catalans and Spain* (London, 1997). Davydd J. Greenwood, 'Continuity in Change: Spanish Basque Ethnicity as a Historical Process', in R. J. Johnston, David B. Knight and Eleonore Kofman (eds.), *Nationalism, Self-Determination and Political Geography* (London, 1988).

[21] See Tom Gallacher 'Regional Nationalism and Party System Change: Italy's Northern League', in *West European Politics*, 4/16 (1993); Martin J. Bull and James L. Newell, 'Italian Politics and the 1992 Elections: 'From "Stable Instability" to Instability and Change', in *Parliamentary Affairs*, 46 (1993); James Newell and Martin Bull, 'The Italian Election of 1996', in *Parliamentary Affairs*, 4/49 (1996).

Julian Rhys

'WAS DENN, ES GIBT EUCH NOCH?' THE *FREIE DEUTSCHE JUGEND* IN THE 1990s

Despite the very swift dismantling of East Germany at the turn of the decade, the Freie Deutsche Jugend, *the youth wing of the SED, continues to exist as a symbolic reminder of the GDR. Though no longer a major political actor, as was the case before 1989, the FDJ has retained and still expresses its ideological inheritance. The collapse of the FDJ and the organisation's current commitment to that inheritance are examined here, concluding that the long-term future of the FDJ is uncertain.*

When a system collapses and is rapidly replaced by a new one there are usually points of contact between what existed before and its replacement. Communism, as understood to mean the former system of economic and social organisation in central and eastern Europe, has gone, but an example of such a point of contact with the past is provided by the case of the *Freie Deutsche Jugend* which, unlike the *Sozialistische Einheitspartei Deutschlands*, the *Freie Deutsche Gewerkschaftsbund* or the *Ernst Thälmann Pioniere*, is still to be found in post-unification Germany. The events surrounding the decline of the FDJ in late 1989 will be examined here as will its activities and ideological continuation during the 1990s.

The FDJ before the *Wende*

It was a feature of several Iron Curtain societies that the parties in power attempted to influence the political beliefs of the population through repetition of standard communist thought. This was especially so with young people. In the USSR the *Kommunistitscheski Sojus Molodjoschi* (Communist Youth Association) existed to steer them towards a state-approved political orientation and the German Democratic Republic's equivalent to this was the FDJ set up by Erich Honecker on 7 March 1946.

The FDJ, open to fourteen- to twenty-five-year-olds, served the purposes of the SED by acting as a transmitter of its ideology, recruiting and preparing committed young people for careers in the party and acting as a device of control over them. The organisation was found in schools, universities, factories, barracks and agricultural cooperatives and it also had a representation in the People's Chamber. The FDJ in the western-controlled parts of Germany was not permitted to exist formally until 1947 and was banned on 26 June 1951.

The FDJ changed from being a semi-independent organisation to becoming the 'reserve' of the SED fairly rapidly. Although the party leadership declared in October 1946 that it had no desire to see the transition of the FDJ into a socialist youth organisation, as this would hinder the creation of a unified forum, it nevertheless observed during that month an 'inseparable unity between the party and youth.'[1] In its message of congratulation to the SED at its third congress in July 1950 the FDJ Central Council openly recognised the leading role of the working class and its party in East Germany.[2]

The organisation engaged in many activities to help the GDR including harvesting, housing renovation, scrap metal and waste paper collection. In addition to the political role of the FDJ it offered a whole variety of social activities for young people and herein lay its principal attraction for GDR youth.

Being in the FDJ was not, in many cases, an expression of one's political beliefs. Taking out membership was an utterly unremarkable act; it was refusing to join the organisation which attracted attention, especially if the child had reached the age of fourteen and was a *Thälmann Pionier*.[3] Committed FDJ functionaries understood this as a rejection of the GDR political system. Parents let their children join the FDJ in order to avoid the drawbacks associated with non-membership. The non-member, for example, would probably have found it difficult to secure a place at university, that is unless they studied theology.

The FDJ during the *Wende*

The 1960s and 70s were a comparatively quiet time for the FDJ. Discontent was usually concealed, relegated to the realms of the *Nischengesellschaft*, where one could reveal what one really thought when among friends or like-minded persons. Dissatisfaction with the GDR grew during the 1980s and, as Matthias Hoffmann[4] has pointed out, the FDJ came to be seen by East German youth more as a representative of the state and of the state's interest in the affairs of youth rather than acting as youth's representative in the GDR. Thus it was that the first principal demand of young East Germans in 1989 was the right to found their own movements.

The following report of 1989 shows how the FDJ was losing support amongst students at the Friedrich-Schiller University in Jena:

> [...] Zunehmend lässt sich eine Tendenz zur Distanzierung von der FDJ beobachten. Immer häufiger tritt die Frage auf, ob es nicht auch Organisationsformen für Jugendliche ausserhalb der FDJ geben müsste. [...] Besonders auffallend ist, daß ein Bedürfnis, sich ausserhalb der FDJ zusammenzuschliessen, nicht nur bei Studenten auftritt, die traditionell Probleme mit ihrer Integration in unserem sozialistischen Jugendverband haben, sondern zunehmend auch bei Genossen Studenten. [...] Viele Studenten warten darauf, daß irgendwann jemand 'von oben' irgendetwas ändert.[5]

On 17 October 1989 4000 Humboldt University students, encouraged by the developing nationwide protests, gathered to discuss the future of the FDJ. The history of the decline of the FDJ in late 1989 shows a rapid loss of control by the Central Council. Initially FDJ bosses resisted the idea of having various youth movements and suggested instead that the FDJ should be revitalised,[6] as a multiplicity of groups would dilute FDJ dominance. It later became clear that such a response was inadequate. The leadership assumed that GDR youth desired socialism but had a variety of approaches to it and that their dissatisfactions were with material provision, travel opportunities and a lack of a real voice in the FDJ. This analysis was incorrect. The word 'socialism' had become discredited among them. FDJ leaders agreed they would permit the existence of other groups which should come under the umbrella of the FDJ. The leadership, being closer to East German youth than the SED, were most probably aware of the very great, almost insoluble, problems with the condition of the FDJ at that time, but nevertheless attempted to maintain their position (the East German authorities were kept up to date on youth attitudes by reports from the Leipzig Youth Research Institute). In any case, the FDJ's room for manoeuvre was restricted because of the initially tough position of the SED. What young East Germans wanted, and were now demanding after years of silence, was the right to found their own groups which would reflect their own views, whether these views were socialist or not. The FDJ found itself responding to events rather than shaping them as developments at the Humboldt University were to show where an independent 'student council' *(Unabhängiger Studentenrat)* was founded on 17 November 1989[7] and by the end of that year similar councils were to be found at the universities of Halle, Jena, Leipzig and Rostock, the Hochschulen at Ilmenau and Weimar and at the Akademie Freiberg.

In January 1990, the FDJ held their Brandenburg Congress in order to identify the way ahead. One of the more important decisions was the change of lettering from 'FDJ' to 'fdj', i.e. the organisation was attempting to alter its identity without actually severing all links with its past (for clarity the original acronym will be used throughout the rest of this article). Hoffmann, commenting on the failure of the FDJ, has pointed out that its size rendered it largely unable to respond swiftly to members' specific interests. The exercising of democratic centralism led to some members believing that it was pointless to engage in the politics of the FDJ as policy was always determined from above. The SED's praise for the FDJ, irrespective of actual performance, led to apathy among some. The desire to raise young people to a 'socialist consciousness' excluded certain groups, e.g. Christians. Lastly, Hoffmann points out that the FDJ also disciplined its members, and some regarded this as not being its proper duty.[8] In addition to these problems which went back over many years the dubious financial dealings of top FDJ functionaries at the turn of the decade damaged members' confidence in the organisation considerably. During the somewhat chaotic period of late 1989 and early 1990 it came to light that large sums of money had been quietly invested in companies run by the FDJ. For example, on 20 October 1989 First Secretary Aurich put 1.5 million marks of FDJ funds into *Video Sound Service GmbH*. FDJ members were further disturbed by the leadership's desire suddenly to reactivate the firm *Jugendheim GmbH* which had lain dormant from 1956 to 1989. On 9 March 1990 Birgit Schröder, the new head of the organisation, put 50,000 marks of FDJ money into this *GmbH*.[9] Further changes occurred later which helped to give the illusion that *Jugendheim* was run by private business people. This misuse of power probably occurred because certain functionaries hoped to continue their work later on, possibly illegally, fearing that the ban of 1951 would be applied to the GDR. These activities of the FDJ were investigated by an independent commission which presented its findings to the Bundestag on 6 May 1996.[10]

Although in late 1989 the FDJ started to distance itself from the SED it then recognised the SED-PDS. Young people found it difficult to believe that the FDJ was now independent after forty-three years association with the SED. Functionaries joined the other youth groups that sprung up in November 1989 in an attempt to maintain their connections with young people. However, the social pressure, indeed requirement, to join the FDJ had gone and so members who had long since rejected it privately, simply wished to have nothing to do with it anymore.

At the elections of 18 March 1990 the FDJ, which described itself as anti-fascist, democratic and non-partisan,[11] did not put itself forward on its own since it realised that as a single entity it would stand little chance of electoral success. Therefore it teamed up with the *Alternative Jugendliste* (AJL) which was made up of various youth groups including the *Marxistische Jugendverband*, the *Arbeitsgemeinschaft Junger GenossInnen in der PDS* and the *Grüne Jugend*. This alliance was formed on 22 February 1990 and the PDS supported it. The result was disastrous: across the country the AJL got 14,573 votes or 0.13%.[12] The Bonn government decided that the ban on the FDJ in West Germany would remain in place but it would not be applied to the GDR.

The FDJ after the *Wende*

Through tenacity and drive the FDJ has survived the *Wende*, in much reduced form, and meets in the PDS *Karl Liebknecht Haus* in Berlin. Discussion centres mainly on the history of the FDJ; many of the people present at FDJ meetings are veterans of the organisation.[13] There are groups in Görlitz, Frankfurt am Main, Bremen, Nürnberg and Berlin[14] even though the ban on the FDJ in western Germany is still in place. This means that any successor to the FDJ would automatically be banned too. The FDJ is, however, determined to keep going. Without adequate funds, it remains to be seen just how this is to be done. Martina Holzinger, chair of the Berlin FDJ, sees the organisation as being unpopular in the eyes of the Bonn government. The FDJ thinks that if unemployment in eastern Germany worsens then citizens will increasingly turn to the PDS through which the FDJ might benefit.

The FDJ calls for the immediate dissolution of the office of *Bundesbeauftragter für Vereinigungsbedingte Sonderaufgaben* (BVS), the expropriation of the property of the warmongers of 1990 (*Kriegsbrandstifter*), the return of the GDR and its industry and compensation for the damage that has occurred in the former GDR since 1990, i.e. factory closure. A standard FDJ slogan is *Fabriken und Land wieder in unsere Hand* though the FDJ cannot be regarded as speaking for the mass of east Germans today as it claimed to do for GDR youth before 1989.

In order not to take votes away from the PDS, the FDJ does not put up candidates in elections itself. It is clearly against the CDU which it claims has 'annexed' the GDR and identifies the FDP as the party of the better off. However, it is curiously quiet on the SPD, the larger part of the present ruling coalition.

FDJ activities

On 11 April 1992, the FDJ held a soldarity meeting with representatives of the Cuban embassy. $3000 was raised for Cuba which, according to the FDJ, has been betrayed by the FRG as it has not honoured GDR / Cuban trade agreements despite this being part of the unification treaty. On 3 October 1993, the FDJ held an anti-unification demonstration. In 1995 the FDJ invited friends from the Czech Republic to Berlin for a 'Day against War' and remembered the German invasion of 1938. Leading up to the XIV World Festival of Youth and Students in the summer of 1997 in Cuba, the FDJ in Berlin hired a lorry and went round the city collecting paper and pencils for Cuban schoolchildren. In addition to this, the FDJ produces little leaflets for street distribution which read: 'Lieber sozialistische Experimente als grossdeutsche Katastrophen, Lieber raus auf die Strasse als heim ins Reich, Lieber raus aus der BRD als rein in den Krieg, Dank Euch, Ihr Sowjetsoldaten' (a reference to the Soviets giving permission for the FDJ to be founded in 1946), or simply 'Wir sagen NEIN zur BRD'.[15]

The continuation of the FDJ's pre-1989 ideology
In its literature the FDJ concentrates on what it terms 'German Nationalism' and makes much reference to Germany's Nazi past. It is right that the memory of the war should remain alive; however, to connect German aggression during war with west German investment in the new *Länder* after unification is unrealistic. The FDJ writes in one leaflet:

> Soldaten der Roten Armee schrieben dieses Wort Lidice [a reference to the German massacre of this Czech town on 10 June 1942] auf ihre Panzer und fuhren damit auf Berlin zu. Am 8. Mai 1945 pflanzten sie im befreiten Berlin die rote Fahne auf den Reichstag. Nie wieder Faschismus, nie wieder Krieg, darin waren sich alle vereinten Nationen einig. So weit darf es nie wiederkommen!
> Aber was ist heute, 50 Jahre danach, aus dieser Hoffnung geworden?
> Mit der Einverleibung der DDR sind die alten Kriegsverbrecher, die Monopole der Elektro- und Chemieindustrie, die Banken und Grossgrundbesitzer schon längst wieder in das erste ihnen durch den verlorenen Krieg abhanden gekommene Ostgebiet eingezogen.[16]

The FDJ pushes the argument that the GDR was taken over by the BRD. It views unification really as an act of 'imperialist' aggression albeit an invasion of the Deutschmark rather than military action. East Germans voted in March 1990 for a new system and against the existing one. Little time was lost in the summer of that year when the opportunity was presented to them to exchange Ostmarks for Deutschmarks. It may be that some older East Germans really do feel that the former GDR has been 'annexed' (to use an FDJ term) and sincerely believe that the unification process degenerated from being a discussion between partners with mutual respect to a complete take-over by West Germany, but this is less the case with young east Germans. Indeed, as Professor Ernst Hoffmann states when examining east German youth in the early 1990s:

> [...] die damalige Jugend kennt aus eigener Erfahrung die DDR und Länder des Sozialismus, insbesondere die FDJ, nur aus der letzten Zeit des sichtbar werdenden Niedergangs. Die Mehrheit der Jugend lehnte aufgrunddessen den Sozialismus ab und fühlte sich vom Westen angezogen.[17]

To employ the term *Anschluss* is an overreaction. An *Anschluss* occurred in 1938 when German troops marched into Austria. In 1990 elections were held to establish the legitimacy of unification. The FRG is a pluralist democracy: it maintains no regular army and the Bundestag deliberated greatly over the deployment of German troops in the former Yugoslavia. The GDR was a state which had little respect for its citizens. The SED was concerned with the control of the people: work was made available, irrespective of required manpower levels, so that each citizen was in his or her place, travel was restricted and the media controlled. In addition the *Ministerium für Staatssicherheit* monitored citizens' activities, sometimes taking action to prevent peaceful critical expression of SED policy. The FDJ, which in its literature ignores the Monday demonstrations, including the mass demonstration of some 500,000 people in Berlin Alexanderplatz on 4 November 1989, is prepared to claim that unification has been an *Anschluss*; a merger, certainly, but the application of the word *Anschluss* is inappropriate.

This is a continuation of FDJ ideology from before 1989, which holds that in the East there was a new start and a complete break from Nazism whereas in the West the old economic structures and the power of capitalists were largely restored. The FDJ continues the pre-1989 idea that the FRG was an aggressive state. The communists in East Germany made much of the fact, and justifiably so, that much resistance to the Nazis came from their ranks. The FDJ frequently refers in its literature to the country's Nazi past and so carries on an activity from GDR times reminding young Germans of just how disastrous the Nazi experience was. The organisation praises the GDR in the same way it did before 1989 and largely ignores the failures of that state. It urges young people to vote for the PDS, the SED's successor.

This ideological continuity is possible because the FDJ sees GDR socialism as an attempt, no matter how imperfect, to release the individual from uncertain employment and the cyclical nature of western economies which historically have experienced both growth and recession. The FDJ regards the multi-national corporation, absent from the GDR and able to move operations comparatively quickly internationally, as a dangerous concentration of power in a few hands with a resulting reduction of people's ability to direct their own futures. The FDJ today is not impressed by the 'need' to buy consumer products which it sees as an invention designed to boost sales. The GDR may have gone but greed has not and the FDJ sees the current German economic system as one that encourages greed and selfishness.

Many members of the FDJ are of pensionable age and find it difficult to change their views, ironic perhaps for a youth movement. Some are veterans of the organisation, whose first association with the FDJ goes back to the heady days of the 1940s. These men and women are simply too close emotionally to the organisation for them to accept anything more than just a minor change in ideological direction.

Conclusion

The FDJ/fdj, both before and after unification, never lived up to the three claims in its title: before 1989 it was certainly made up of German young people but it was difficult not to join the organisation. After the *Wende* it is comprised of Germans who are much freer to do as they wish but most do not fall into the original fourteen to twenty-five age range.

The task of the FDJ, before 1989, was to lead young people to a 'socialist consciousness.' The FDJ did not succeed in this. However, via the mechanism of party discipline, it was praised by SED leaders for its achievements regardless of actual performance. Youth could not accept the glorifying words of SED and FDJ leaders, proclaiming the clear superiority of GDR socialism over the Federal Republic, when every day they were confronted with the disparity between these claims and daily life. Furthermore, not only was the FDJ correctly identified by most of its members as being a tool of the SED but it was also too large, too centrally organised and its political role excluded certain groups of young person. This led to much youth displaying only an ostensible commitment to the organisation.

With the collapse of the GDR in late 1989 the FDJ tried to save itself as best it could, suggesting that new youth groups be formed, but within the FDJ orbit. It became clear that such a response was insufficient and so the FDJ begrudgingly accepted the emergence of new groups. This was not enough to save it. In January 1990 the FDJ altered its identity by using lower case letters. Realising that the name *Freie Deutsche Jugend* had become discredited with GDR youth they aligned themselves with the AJL for the forthcoming election and attracted little support. The PDS, once known briefly as the SED-PDS, expresses an agenda for the future. It does not rely chiefly on the argument that life was better for east Germans before unification. FDJ literature of the 1990s, on the other hand, shows an almost fanatical support for the GDR. To describe the process of unification as imperialist or to imply that there is some sort of comparison between west German investment in the new *Länder* and the wartime German invasions of Poland or Czechoslovakia is unrealistic. The demonstrations of late 1989 are ignored. No mention is made of the bankruptcy of the GDR, the lack of serious calls today for a reversal of unification or the flight of many GDR citizens from the country in 1989.

On the positive side, the FDJ does carry out a socially useful role by reminding us of crimes carried out in the German name during World War Two. To this end the FDJ should be applauded in their work, though FDJ literature is strangely quiet about the Holocaust.

The PDS has been able to move away somewhat from an identity which stresses that it is merely the successor to the SED. It is trying to present itself as a party serving eastern Germany. If the PDS has been able to develop from its SED roots it is worth examining why the FDJ has been unable to enjoy similar success. Firstly, the PDS is not the SED. It has changed its name and there may even be some voters who are unaware of its previous title. Whilst it is a socialist party and thus has not totally severed its roots with its SED heritage, it looks to the future and opines on a range of issues that are of interest to German voters now. It is possible to vote for the PDS; it is not for the FDJ as they put up no candidates.

Membership of a party can last a lifetime. Indeed Erich Honecker joined the *Kommunistischer Jugendverband Deutschlands* at the age of fourteen. He then joined the KPD which became the SED and, after expulsion from that party in 1989, rejoined the recently refounded KPD.[18] Most members of a youth organisation lose their connection with it as they become older. Thus in 1989 a fifty year old member of the SED could consider membership of the PDS; it is unlikely that a twenty-five year old member of the FDJ would consider maintaining membership of the organisation after the *Wende*.

Younger east Germans, prior to the Wende, will have experienced the *Thälmann Pioniere* and the FDJ but not necessarily the SED. Thus first or second time voters may have approached the September 1998 elections with a more open mind to the PDS. The FDJ, on the other hand, reminds them of their childhood and hence is seen as something they need not be concerned about any longer.

What will be the future of the FDJ? Many older members feel emotionally connected to the organisation and would resist moves to alter it radically.[19] However, east German dissatisfaction, assuming the CDU/CSU and SPD cannot provide an answer, may manifest itself in the PDS or the extreme right. Should this occur it is unlikely to work to the benefit of the FDJ as it is an organisation which is too tied down with its GDR inheritance.

NOTES

[1] Zentralrat der FDJ, *FDJ Chronik* (Berlin, 1976), pp. 48ff.

[2] Ibid., p. 73.

[3] The Pionierorganisation 'Ernst Thälmann' was the sister organisation of the FDJ. No other youth organisations, apart from the 'Junge Gemeinde', were permitted to exist in the GDR.

[4] Matthias Hoffmann, *Neuprofilierung und Funktionswandel der FDJ nach der Wende* (Oktober 1989 bis März 1990), July 1992, Diplomarbeit at the Free University, Berlin, p. 90.

[5] Thüringisches Staatsarchiv Rudolstadt, Bezirkspartei der SED Gera, Universitätsparteileitung Jena 1019, *Gedanken zur politischen Lage unter den Studenten*, Jena, 24 April 1989, 110/111.

[6] Richard Schmidt, 'Für einen sozialistischen Studentenbund in einer neuen FDJ,' First Secretary of the FDJ Kreisleitung at Humboldt University in: Humboldt Universität, 26 October 1989, p. 2.

[7] *Kurier: Informationsblatt der Evangelischen Studentengemeinden in der DDR*, Berlin, 28 November 1989.

[8] Hoffmann, p. 90.

[9] 'FDJ-Chefin mit 50,000 Mark dabei', *die tageszeitung*, 9 March 1990.

[10] Sekretariat der Unabhängigen Kommission zur Überprüfung des Vermögens der Parteien und Massenorganisationen der DDR beim Ministerium des Innern, Bericht über das Vermögen der Freien Deutschen Jugend, Berlin, 6 May 1996.

[11] 'FDJ ging in die Kehre', *die tageszeitung*, 29 January 1990.

[12] Hoffmann, p. 86.

[13] See Hans Modrow et al, *Unser Zeichen war die Sonne*, Neues Leben (Berlin, 1996).

[14] Interview with Martina Holzinger of the Berlin FDJ, 24 February 1998, Berlin.

[15] Private communication between the author and the FDJ, February 1998.

[16] Taken from 'Aufstehen statt Strammstehen,' FDJ leaflet.

[17] Ernst Hoffmann, Thesen zur Vorbereitung der FDJ-Diskussion im Herbst 1996: Reaktionen der Jugend auf ihre Lage. Internal FDJ document, Berlin, 14 August 1996.

[18] See Erich Honecker, *Moabiter Notizen*, edition ost (Berlin, 1994).

[19] Interview with an FDJ discussion group, led by Martina Holzinger (chair) and Professor Ernst Hoffmann, Berlin, 6 December 1996.

Thorsten Lauterbach

THE GERMANS REUNIFIED – CHALLENGES TO THE LEGAL SYSTEM

In 1989 the world witnessed a unique phenomenon taking place in Germany. The two German states having been separated for decades as a result of post-war negotiations were finally reunified. This paper looks at some of the effects of this process on Germany's legal system which, by definition, provides the framework and the very foundation of the reunified German society. It is argued that the arbitrary and speedy introduction of the Western system in the Five New Länder did not lend itself fully to dealing successfully with the injustices of the old regime and left many citizens disgruntled with the law.

Introduction

In autumn 1989 the world looked curiously, sometimes anxiously, upon Germany where quite a unique phenomenon took place. By peacefully demonstrating in numbers in various cities of the GDR, the people helped significantly to pave the way towards the reunification of the two German states. With some justification, commentators have generally focused on the socio-economic, political and cultural difficulties that have had to be overcome in the process. However, little has been said about the obstacles in 'reconciling' the legacy of two inherently different legal systems. Effectively, as we know, the process demanded that the East abandon its socialist legal system which was based on the outdated doctrine of Marxism-Leninism in favour of that of its Western counterpart. Since the law provides both the framework and the foundation of reunification, the reader's attention will, in the following, be drawn to just a few issues which have constituted tremendous challenges to the legal system of the Federal Republic in general and to the Five New *Länder* (FNL) in particular – namely, how the East German judiciary and the legal profession dealt with the events of 1989/90 and came to terms with their not so distant past, and what was done to remedy the injustices committed by the *ancien régime*.

Adapting to a new ideology - a case of *déjà vu*

First of all, however, I would like to go back in time a little further to the post-WW-II-years, as the *Justiz* – both in the East and West – had already experienced the problem of adapting to a new ideology. Within Nazi Germany the judiciary and the legal profession had played an important part in making the system work by twisting and turning the constitution in the early 1930s. Once Hitler and his accomplices had fully established themselves in power, the judiciary itself had deteriorated into an infamous and keen instrument of the regime which held terror and injustices to be lawful until the end.[1]

Once Germany had unconditionally surrendered to the Allies on 8 May 1945, not only did the terror come to an end, but so did the administration of justice. The Allies started off by imposing strict measures of denazification (*Entnazifizierung*) on all levels of society. However, in what emerged eventually as the Federal Republic of Germany, the denazification of the judiciary quickly degenerated into a rather unconvincing alibi process. It is no secret that members of the profession and the judiciary gradually, but steadily, managed to claw their way back into their former positions and beyond. The vast majority were classed as *Mitläufer* or even as free of any burden at all (*unbelastet*); this significantly increased the numbers of 'clean'[2] lawyers in West Germany. The past was quickly forgotten – and the question 'How was all this possible?' has never really been seriously posed to the judiciary. *Vergangenheitsbewältigung* was left to others, while numberless members of the profession ended up in high places in administration, politics or higher education. The involvement with Hitler's *Volksgerichtshof*, the 'national-socialist instrument of terror' in the words of the Federal Court of Appeal (*Bundesgerichtshof*),[3] often even constituted the very basis of a flourishing career.

In East Germany the political powers undertook a more rigorous attempt at rooting out all those members of the profession who had collaborated with the regime by removing them from judicial office. Naturally, this was being done by the Soviet authorities, who also imprisoned a large number of innocent people in the process. The net result was a chronic lack of lawyers in East Germany. A survey dated from 1958 shows how drastically the numbers had dropped: while in 1937 there were 3,163 lawyers, by 1948 1,158 were left; in 1958 the figure had dropped to a mere 863.[4]

Legal system – East[5] and West[6]

In the Federal Republic the law has been characterised by the idea of a liberal, democratic, parliamentary state – *freiheitlich demokratische Grundordnung* – based on a written constitution, which developed into a social state based on the rule of law (the *Sozialstaat* and *Rechtsstaat* principles). This combines a high degree of individual freedom with a tight net of social security. The law, generally, is to protect the individual from an over-powerful state.

In the former GDR the story was rather different. According to the doctrines of Marx and Lenin, courts of law as conceived by modern Western democracies were dismissed as 'bourgeois' institutions and were subsequently substituted by socialist institutions. They were part of the omnipotent, uniform state, ruled by the will of one party (the SED) and subordinated to that party's principles – democratic centralism, socialist legality and partiality. In order to have complete control the legal profession was organised in *Kollegien*, collective bodies similar to those in agriculture. The judges, too, were subject to cadre politics. Although formally accepted, the independence of the judiciary was undermined by an extensive system of instruction and control by other state organisations, e.g. so-called *Instruktionsbrigaden*. Civil law played only a minor part, similar in practice to any other socialist legal system. Centre stage was occupied by criminal law, since the primary task of the profession and the judiciary was to fight 'reactionary imperialism' and its agents. By definition, the individual and the rights of the individual were completely subordinated to the will of the state, i.e the SED, predominant.[7] Therefore, the administration of justice was not only founded on a different basis, but also on a much smaller dimension: while there were about 1,400 judges and 600 lawyers in the whole of the GDR, in Northrhine-Westphalia alone 4,200 judges and 13,000 lawyers practised. The Ministry of State Security also played an important part in 'political' cases, as it interrogated witnesses, organised the different stages of a case and even designed judgments. However, especially with regard to the final decade of GDR legal history, one may find it rather difficult to identify cases which were *not* political.

Overall, it may be maintained that while in the FRG the judiciary and the profession exist to protect the individual from the state, in the former GDR it was basically the other way round – the state was to be protected from its people. Due to these fundamental ideological differences between the two systems, 'merging' was never on the agenda: the East had to abandon its system and adopt and adapt to the new order of its Western counterpart – the class enemy No.1.

Reunification – impacts on the legal system

After the GDR leadership had uniformly ignored the significant developments outside the GDR in other Soviet satellite states,[8] where the peoples craved for openness and democracy, the demonstrations in Leipzig and elsewhere subjected the legal hierarchy to a state of shock. What followed was a 'half-U-turn' on the spot by the Council of Chairmen of the *Kollegien*; although admitting that mistakes had been made and, *inter alia*, granting the right to free travel, it still clung to communism as the sole source of ideology and wisdom. The Council wrote on 25 October 1989

> The members of the Council are deeply concerned about the state of our country. We concede that we have indulged ourselves by pursuing wrong directions for far too long, but socialism as the only alternative to capitalism cannot be a matter that should now be up for debate. The solution must be more, not less socialism.
>
> In our analysis and proposals for the future we are guided by the principle that security and certainty of the law do not mean just law and order but are a prerequisite if people are to lead a happy life within their country.
>
> We have admitted that concepts like 'socialist democracy' and 'socialist rule of law' have been taken for granted and treated superficially without having life breathed into them. We must achieve a situation where the word 'socialist' together with these concepts is no longer seen as a restriction but as liberating and enriching [...]
>
> In addition to a new law giving the freedom of travel we consider the following legal changes necessary: A new electoral law should enable the voters to choose between different candidates and ensure public control of the vote counting process at all times.
>
> The constitutionality of legislation and any other kind of governmental action should be judged more carefully than has been the case to date. We feel that an institution ought to be created to which the citizens themselves will be able to apply for such scrutiny.
>
> We need a criminal code that clearly distinguishes between what is permitted and what is forbidden and that concentrates on genuinely criminal behaviour that is regarded as such by the majority of the people [...].

> With respect to the events during the demonstrations of October 7, 8
> and 9 1989, we regret the violation of the demonstration laws by the
> demonstrators. [...]On the other hand we cannot accept the
> maltreatment meted out by police officers when breaking up the
> demonstrations or after the arrest of citizens [...].[9]

It took another few months for the die-hards to admit that the tide could not be stemmed
and, subsequently, the ideological ivory tower crumbled.

In September 1990 the GDR Parliament passed the *Rechtsanwaltsgesetz*
(Advocates Act), an Act which amended the law regulating the affairs of the legal
profession, and put the Eastern legal profession on the same ideological basis as its
Western equivalent. What happened to judges and prosecutors directly after reunification,
i.e. an extensive and detailed search through their former careers and *Stasi*-files, was
delayed for the profession until July 1992, when the Screening of Advocates, Notaries
Public and Lay Judges Act was passed. However, most advocates retained their positions,
and by 1994 only 24 of several thousand had been dismissed from office.[10]

Initially there was a debate amongst both politicians and academic commentators
as to whether it was fair to introduce the legal system of the Federal Republic in the FNL;
however, it was also apparent that the representatives of the GDR would not accept a
'second class' law. Since it was obvious that a uniform legal system would provide the
framework for German integration, the law of the West was eventually accepted with a
variety of provisional solutions.

The attempt to integrate former officials into the new federally structured
administration was made as far as practically possible, depending on their personal and
professional suitability. The new court structure was established by 1993: county courts
(*Kreisgerichte*) became small claims courts (*Amtgerichte*), new *Landgerichte* (county
courts) were introduced, and every regional state (*Land*) received a new Regional Court of
Appeal (*Oberlandesgericht*). In accordance with the system of the FRG, separate labour,
administrative, finance and social affairs courts had to be established. To undertake this in
any country within such a short spell of time would have been a huge task; in a state which
was founded on socialist ideology the challenge, arguably, was even greater.

Since it had been a prerequisite for prospective judges or advocates in the former
GDR to be an obedient SED-member who was then delegated to university by the party
and examined on the grounds of cadre political regulations, it would have been simple to
remove them all from office and replace them with officials from the West in order to
make a clean break with the past. Such an extraordinary step, however, would have been
contrary to the smooth transition that was proposed for the reunification process. In order
to retain their position, members of the judiciary had to take an aptitude test, which the
FNL left to special committees (*DDR-Richtergesetz*, July 1990). The criteria differed from
Land to *Land*, but in every single case the final judgment had to indicate whether the
applicant would be led by the new order of values and laws of the Federal Republic and be
accepted by the citizens as a credible representative of a judiciary based on principles of
the *Rechtsstaat*. In the end, more than 50% retained their position.

Coming to terms with injustices of the *ancien régime*
After the disintegration of the SED-regime the task to face was similar to that of the post-
war situation: to remedy the injustices committed by the regime. The criminal

prosecutions have been hampered above all by the principle of legality which is the German understanding of the Latin maxims *nulla poena sine lege* and *nullum crimen sine lege*: no penalty without legislation and no crime without an offence, thus precluding retroactive criminal laws.[11] This principle is given absolute authority in Germany by its inclusion in the *Grundgesetz* Article 103(2)[12] and Paragraph 1 StGB.[13] Such actions would have probably been interpreted, at best, as mere Western arrogance or, at worst, as *Siegerjustiz*,[14] which would not have been politically prudent. Consequently, such crimes may only be punished if they constituted an offence under the law of the Federal Republic and the GDR at the time. With regard to many delicts/torts, e.g. wrongful deprivation of personal liberty, bodily harm, unlawful interception of communications and forgery of election results, this has been possible, as the rules were essentially the same in both states.

However, a heated debate has been going on with regard to whether an accused may rely on GDR law which demanded or justified the respective behaviour, eg. in relation to the order to shoot, torture in prisons, maltreatment or blackmail. The most spectacular cases concern the allegedly illegal crossing of the border (*Republikflucht*), the order to shoot and the GDR *Grenzgesetz* (Border Act) which permitted shooting by border patrols in order to prevent *Republikflucht* by ordinary GDR citizens. Some may be of the opinion that behaviour which was in accordance with GDR law may not be prosecuted and punished; the BGH, however, held that such laws are illegal and unenforceable if they are contrary to the generally recognised human rights in a gross and unbearable manner.[15]

In relation to the many cases of 'perversion of the course of justice' the federal judicial privilege could not be applied since the judges of the former GDR had not been independent. The renunciation of the proceedings against Honecker as the main person responsible for the inhumane injustices of the regime encouraged those who argue that the past should be considered a closed file and that amnesties or pardons should be granted to the alleged offenders. However, these people seem to forget that reconciliation with offenders is misplaced at the beginning and belongs at the very end of a process of change and remorse. The precondition for spiritual renewal is to remember the past, not to forget and repress it.

Concluding remarks: discomfort with the legal system in the FNL
For a considerable time since reunification Germans have shown a genuine discomfort with their legal system; this has turned into a state of exasperation in the East, which seriously questions and undermines the possible development of a legal conscience among the population comparable to the Western equivalent. People are genuinely dissatisfied with many of the outcomes of legal disputes, e.g. with regard to property issues, and complain about the hypertrophy of the law, the flood of Acts, codes and paragraphs, the codification of social life and the lack of intelligibility of the over-complicated legal system. Those who seek shelter and protection within the law are lost in a labyrinth of paragraphs.

Therefore, many are disillusioned and disappointed that, while liberty of the individual may well be protected, the law itself seems to be paralysed and too unwieldy once it has to deal with problems such as increasing criminality, corruption and the adequate punishing of SED-crimes. Latest examples are cases brought by former GDR soldiers who deserted the forces in order to flee to West Germany, thereby committing the offence of *Republikflucht*. The German judges cleared these applicants of the latter offence but not of the former, since desertion still constitutes a criminal offence in today's Germany. The courts refuse to recognise and follow the logical argument that desertion had only been committed to 'leave' the country, thereby usually escaping maltreatment by the GDR system. Consequently, they are still seen as convicted offenders in the reunified Germany, unable to clear their names and records. This may well diminish their chances of entering into employment and leading a 'normal' life. Who is prepared to listen to and believe their explanations for their convictions?

The people in the FNL have been confronted with an over-perfect legal system which regularly appears to be rather helpless to them. Furthermore, many believe that the legal profession only exchanged one ivory tower for another.[16] A historic chance has been missed to simplify a legal system that has lost its direction amongst its procedural shortcomings and which seems to have lost touch with its citizens. This would have contributed considerably to a quicker and more harmonious, less painful integration process than has hitherto been the case.

This becomes even more apparent if one contrasts this state of affairs with the prospective enlargement of the European Union and the integration of a number of Central and Eastern European countries. So-called Europe Agreements, which give Associate EU member status and free access to the EU market for most goods and set out the framework for future relations, have been negotiated with Poland, Hungary, Bulgaria, the Czech and Slovac Republics, Romania, Slovenia and the Baltic States. The overall aim of these agreements is to raise the economic, social, political, democratic and legal standards of applicant states to an EU level over a comparably long period of time, which may simplify their integration upon entry into the Union in the future. Against this practise the integration of the former GDR into a reunified Germany and, subsequently, the European Union resembles a rather hurried and badly-drafted affair.

NOTES

[1] For an excellent and frightening account of the role of the judiciary during the Hitler regime and its adaptation to the new deal in West Germany, see I. Mueller, *Furchtbare Juristen. Die unbewältigte Vergangenheit unserer Justiz* (Munich, 1989).

[2] That is lawyers who had not previously collaborated with the regime.

[3] BGHSt 9, p. 309

[4] See R. Maurach et al., *Der Rechtsanwalt im Ostblock* (Berlin, 1958)

[5] For an enlightening account of the development of the legal profession in East Germany before reunification see: M. Bohlander et al., 'The legal profession in East Germany – past, present and future', *International Journal of the Legal Profession*, 3 (1996), 255-280.

[6] For an excellent introduction to the legal system of the Federal Republic of Germany see: N. Foster, *German Law and Legal System* (London, 1993); C.H. Beck (ed.), *Einführung in das deutsche Recht*, 3rd ed. (Munich, 1990)

[7] This resulted in dubious ethics and methods employed by the legal profession. In order to get to the truth, advocates would even pressurise their clients to give self-incriminating evidence – as demanded by the *Kollegien*.

[8] Members of the legal profession as prominent as Gregor Gysi and Friedrich Wolff were writing articles which adhered to the traditional party-political line as late as December 1988; see *Neue Justiz* (1988), p. 494

[9] Reproduced in and translated by Bohlander et al, op cit, note 6, p. 263.

[10] This is the result of the jurisprudence of both the BGH and the Federal Constitutional Court, who decided that, unless there are gross or extreme instances of misbehaviour, the candidate in question should receive the benefit of the doubt.

[11] See German Criminal Law Code, para. 2 [Temporal effect]:

The punishment and its additional incidents are to be determined in accordance with statute law which applies at the time of the act.

If the punishment provided for is changed during the commission of the act, the statute law to be applied is that which was effective at the end of the act.

If statute law, which applies at the end of the act, is changed before the court's decision, the least severe statute law is to be applied.

A statutory provision which is only to be effective for a determined period is also to be applied to acts which are committed during its validity when it has ceased to be effective. This does not apply insofar as a statutory provision provides otherwise.

[12] Art. 103 [Basic rights of a defendant] [...] (2) An act can only be punished if its criminality was determined by statute before the act was committed.

[13] Criminal Law Code, para. 1 [No punishment without statutory provision] An act can only be punished if the criminality was provided for by statute before the act was committed.

[14] This expression, created in the wake of the Nuremberg trials where German war criminals were tried by Allied judges and prosecutors, implies a form of justice imposed by the victors.

[15] BGH, 4 November 1992, NJW 1993, p.141

[16] Traditionally, the legal profession, as it developed in Western democracies, has led a very cloistered existence, with its professional bodies displaying a rather protectionist attitude towards anything that is new or semi-revolutionary. This, however, may be subject to change due to developments at European level, as the liberal professions may be scrutinised under the competition law provisions of the Treaty of Rome (see Commission decision re The Colegio de Agentes de la Propiedad Industrial (COAPI) (case IV/33.686) [1995] 5 Common Market Law (Antitrust) Reports 468).

SECTION FIVE

WOMEN, ECONOMY AND THE REGIONS

Chris Flockton

INTRODUCTION

The three papers presented in this section cover widely differing topics and yet they share a common theme, which is how much direct intervention from higher-level authorities is needed to moderate the impact of the profound economic restructuring on people's lives, and what kinds of networks at a more local or grass roots level could promote innovation, new productive structures and supporting social structures. In each of the papers, it is clear that the 'creative destruction' of the transformation in the east, and the imposition of the western social market and social security systems, have wrought the profoundest changes and have knocked away valued support mechanisms. In response, those most affected are seeking positively to reassert their identity and values.

Bettina Iganski, in her paper on 'The meaning of women's "second family" for current patterns of discontinuity in rural east Germany', makes clear that the workers' collective on state and co-operative farms in the GDR was a source of emotional support and purpose for many women in farming, literally a 'second home'. These small, task-oriented workers' collectives were of course a politicised institution for the generation of socialist relations, but they were also a fundamental means of labour and social organisation. Socially, the collective provided a local social structure, it governed access to child care, to lifelong learning, to release from household duties. It also organised social events and voluntary work. The dramatic changes in farming wrought by the *Wende* led to the collapse of social structures and all the support mechanisms which had fostered the high work participation of women, so enabling a combination of work and the home. One-third of women employed in farming in Mecklenburg-West Pomerania were aged over 50 years at unification and so early retirement was widely used to effect workforce reductions. To those affected, the collective had not been the 'instrument of paternalist manipulation', since they reported active participation in planning and mutual support.

Vanessa Beck's study of 'The impact of unemployment on women in the new *Bundesländer*', likewise traces the unemployment impact of the profound restructuring and of the loss of social support, working women's support, etc. Her focus is, however, primarily to assess whether, as in earlier western analyses, unemployed women sink over time into a 'learned helplessness model of depression'. Does the loss of material and social support lead to a retreat into fatalism, into acceptance of the male breadwinner model of employment? On the basis of interviews with unemployed women in Saxony-Anhalt, the Land most affected by unemployment, the author found a continuing high work motivation of women, a resilience given the realisation that they may not find better-qualified, full-time work again, and flexible, active coping strategies. They founded self-help groups, created voluntary work and looked actively for alternative occupations.

In the third paper, Corinne Nativel and Hannah Tooze assess the 'Significance of the region in east Germany's economic transition'. The recreation of the *Länder*, abolished in 1952, the regrouping of the GDR *Bezirke* into *Länder*, and the establishment of regions at sub-*Land* level are discussed fully, and the authors demonstrate how the industrial inheritance from socialist planning, now in full decay, has produced sectoral and therefore regional crises, because of the degree of geographical specialisation of activity. The role of the eastern 'region' in counteracting these powerful, externally-imposed forces is, however, somewhat uncertain. The concurrent changes in western regional development policy, the 'sandwiching' of the region between *Land* and local authorities, and the evident difficulty for a region in promoting purely internal, autonomous forces for regeneration, all present difficulties. Specifying an 'ideal regional model', the authors elucidate much that is required, but decisions on the shape, roles and powers of the regions must first be taken.

Bettina Iganski

THE MEANING OF WOMEN'S 'SECOND FAMILY' FOR CURRENT PATTERNS OF DISCONTINUITY IN RURAL EAST GERMANY[1]

The following paper revisits workers' collectives on state and co-operative farms in the GDR. Apart from simply being state developed units of surveillance and monitoring, collectives offered both emotional support and comradeship for a large proportion of women in rural areas. Beyond this, collectives represented social microcosms of local societies, through which many social relations were channelled. The dramatic impact of the Wende *on farming in the former GDR is complemented by the women's loss of community associated with the collective. Further measures are needed to counter this loss and to assist women in rural areas in adapting to the new social, economic and political parameters in a unified Germany.*

'[The collective] really was women's second home. After 'the Wende' they really started to experience this, because they were so used to being with someone from morning till evening. They practically shared happiness and sorrow with their neighbours at work and [...] they felt, or had practically a purpose. They felt satisfied. And the very moment this collapsed, something was missing.' (035)[2]

Introduction

The working collective in the GDR was a small, task-oriented group of workers. Initially, the industrial working class was organised into collectives, but the socialisation of agricultural land into co-operatives created a basis for the establishment of collectives in rural areas. The collective not only embraced the labour process but also extended its activities into the private sphere of the workers and was consequently significant for ideological developments. Few publications describe the purpose and meaning of the collective in the GDR although some authors consider its loss as significant for the socialisation of women (see, for example, Böckmann-Schewe et al., 1995; Luutz, 1993; Panzig, 1995).

Gleserman (1973)[3] states that the collective became a 'fundamental unit of society'. Initially, the collective had been a politicised institution with the aim of developing a mechanism for the generation of social(ist) relationships among industrial workers. This paper, which is based on research carried out in Mecklenburg-West Pomerania, asserts that many women regarded employment as a major component of their lives and look back at their collective as a 'second family'. The experience of widespread and long-term unemployment since unification has caused women to become socially disorientated and isolated. The loss of regular patterns in women's everyday lives, and discrimination and stigmatisation of women in the public sphere, are key factors contributing to women's disorientation and isolation. The research for this paper indicates that the continuity and security experienced in the collective had been an important means of identification for rural women. This suggests that current patterns of discontinuity for women in the New Germany can be attributed at least to some extent to the vanishing of their collectives and the work context, as well as the loss of work itself.

This paper, which forms part of a wider programme of doctoral research, aims to explore the nature of the agricultural working collective and its meaning to women in light of the current transitions in Mecklenburg-West Pomerania in the former GDR. Retracing the functions and meanings of the collective requires consultation of various sources. The evidence presented here is derived from secondary sources and primary data. Data collected for this research consists of correspondence with forty women, ten of whom have written to the author on a regular basis since October 1996; interviews with 55 key-informants and focus groups in six villages in the region of Uecker Randow.

The paper presents key characteristics of the former collectives and outlines some experiences of women in collectives. An interpretation is made of why certain features of the collective were important in the context of women's contemporary experience. Finally, issues raised by this paper will be contrasted with criticism of women's 'emancipation' in the GDR evident in some feminist writing.

Characteristics of the collective

Rural women in the GDR were more likely than men to be employed in group-based and labour-intensive manual work. Their tasks commonly included work in the fields collecting stones, work in the animal sheds raising piglets, or milking cows. Despite the political claim that women were incorporated into 'male-dominated' sectors, men were far more likely to be involved in individualised mechanised labour operating heavy machines or tractors. Consequently in rural areas the collective had a greater meaning for women's every-day lives than for men.

Informed by the theories of Marx, the political leadership believed that the collective 'emotional' atmosphere would enhance the efficiency of the labour force and that this could only be achieved through socialism (Jetzschmann, 1988). The working collective was a fundamental means of labour organisation under socialism. It was critical to the development of a collective 'emotional' atmosphere as the majority of people worked in collectives, and a substantial period of a worker's social life was organised within the collective.

Collective experience began in kindergartens. More than 90% of children attended kindergarten or other childcare facilities 'full-time' (Winkler, 1990), and their social life was dominated by living and learning in their 'mini-collective'. At school-age, 81% of children attended after-school supervision (Nave-Herz, 1990) and their FDJ[4] group (Giessmann, 1990; Völzer, 1996). Since school vacation was several weeks longer than parents' annual leave, children normally attended holiday camps with their school class as well.

The collective consequently provided the context for the socialisation of young people and the development of a socialist personality. For adults especially, the collective provided an important mechanism of socialisation. It additionally served as a platform for social security, co-operation in the labour-process, comradeship, mutual support, comfort, and consequently the overall well-being of its workers.

In addition to the animal and crop production plans, the agricultural co-operative (LPG[5]) provided detailed plans for socio-cultural activities. The end-of-year assembly of the LPG, for instance, was normally closed with a social event. Celebrations were also held on 'International Women's Day' and the 'Day of the Republic'. Further initiatives were taken by some LPG leaders, mayors or groups such as the 'DFD'[6], 'FDJ', or 'Volkssolidarität'[7] to organise celebrations in the collective, seasonal festivities such as summer harvest and Christmas, the 1st of May, 'International Children's Day', excursions and private celebrations such as weddings or special birthdays. All activities were recorded in the 'brigade book' both to commemorate the events and to provide evidence that LPG plans were being fulfilled. The preparation of the programmes for these events was mostly carried out by women in addition to their usual responsibilities. Carrying out such 'socially useful work' was a key aspect of the Marxist ideology (Edwards, 1985; Autorenkollektiv, 1984) and the majority of co-operative farmers were involved in voluntary work (Krambach, 1985). This level of participation was a consequence, in part, of political and social pressure. Those who were exceptionally active or productive in the village or the workplace were both rewarded and encouraged by awards such as 'Hero of Labour', 'Meritorious Activist' or 'Activist of Socialist Labour' (Shaffer, 1981) usually linked with a small financial incentive. Awards could be given to individuals in the collective, such as 'Best Milking Woman', or to the entire collective, such as the 'Collective of Socialist Work' (Autorenkollektiv, 1984).

In order to demonstrate the efficiency of the political strategy for enhancing the labour process described above, research was carried out by the Academy of Social Science. A study conducted in the 1980s showed that 63.9% of those who had worked in the collective for more than five years 'over-fulfilled' their targets as opposed to 11.6% of workers who had worked in the collective for less than three years. The same study provided an indication of the high level of satisfaction with social relationships in the collective (Jetzschmann, 1988). However, as with all figures in the former GDR, these too have to be considered carefully.

The above description implies a high level of state influence on workers through the collectives. Throughout their lives, people were organised into collectives which pursued a political agenda simultaneously to providing a satisfying work environment. This political agenda included formal socialist education in schools as well as extracurricular activities in clubs. Furthermore, both pupils and workers were made to conform to goals which they sought to achieve as a group, rather than as individuals. Respondents explained that individual initiative and independence were rarely accepted and often alleged to be a sign of opposition to peace. However, the present research demonstrates that women adapted to these pressures and found comfort in social structures within the collective.

Women's experience of their 'second family'
The research for this paper indicates a relationship between the strength of women's attachment to their former collectives and their reaction to the discontinuity of collective social organisation arising from unification, which has resulted in women's economic dependency and consequent stigmatisation, disorientation and isolation.

When evaluating the implications of socio-economic transition, or when implementing programmes to assist women in the process of adaptation to such transition, a reflexive perspective can be significant to develop strategies appropriate to those affected. Whilst it must be borne in mind that people's recollections of past events may be coloured by their experience in the present, such recollections have validity because they affect attitudes towards contemporary experience.

As noted above, women spent a considerable amount of their time working and socialising in their collective. Women were integrated into the collective through the implementation of Women's Politics[8]. Commonly, when women respondents in the research recalled their experiences of the collective they talked about the benefits which were part of Women's Politics. Childcare and the alleviation of household duties were dominant themes. The availability of an extensive network of low-cost childcare facilities enabled women to fully participate in the labour market and, indeed, 90% of women were employed (see, for example, Winkler, 1990).

In addition to a shorter working week for mothers with two or more children, a range of other financial and social benefits are fondly remembered by the women. Every month women were given a day off from work for household duties but commonly the time was used for social outings organised through the collective. Furthermore, the availability of central kitchens, and opening hours of local shops which were adapted to women's working shifts, assisted women's organisation of housework. In most villages the majority of schoolchildren and workers had a hot lunch from the canteen.

A provision less frequently mentioned by the respondents, but essential to Women's Politics, was the principle of life-long learning. The vast majority of women in the GDR were either 'Facharbeiter'[9] or educated to university degree level (87% in 1982 compared with 2% in 1960 (Edwards, 1985)). In addition, it was possible to take further training at the age of 45 or 50 years. A combination of a comprehensive school degree, an apprenticeship, several years of work experience and 'voluntary' activities were a precondition for participation in so-called 'women classes' for further qualifications. The various clubs within the LPG also organised seminars on political and women's issues.

The right to work and the right to housing guaranteed women essential social and financial securities. Furthermore, basic medical provisions were made free-of-charge and basic foodstuffs were heavily subsidised. The close proximity of local services was essential to women since only a small proportion of women had a driver's licence. Even though women's earnings were on average lower than men's, their contribution to the household budget was significant. Furthermore, most co-operative farming households had their own private farming plot for which the woman in the household was largely responsible. The earnings from this informal work could amount to the equivalent of six months of income from the LPG. Hence, women had the impression that they not only 'got by', but had more money than they could spend. Women were also, as one respondent suggested, 'used to being economically independent [and to] standing on [their] own two feet' (039).

The consolidation of social bonds had been a key aim behind the establishment of collectives in rural areas. In addition to the measures discussed above, the lack of anonymity of individuals in small villages contributed to continuous exposure to the collective experience. Descriptions of LPG celebrations and happy occasions at work dominated the accounts of the respondents for this research. Women described situations of support when a child was sick, or emphasised the significance of the collective beyond the workplace, for instance, when women were on maternity leave or when they were pensioners. A number of respondents used the term 'family' to describe the feelings of integrity, purpose and reward in the collective. Some respondents described feelings of empowerment through the collective:

> When I got on my bike in the mornings to go to work and meet with the other women, all my sorrows were forgotten. (121)

> We also had monthly discussions in the collective about the progress of work. They were really vigorous sometimes. But we had a say and we contributed to decisions being made. (123)

Discontinuity

Unification created a considerable space for new freedoms and consumer choices. In the initial phase, where 'everything was still possible' (029), the 'new Germans' were promised 'blooming landscapes' by the then-Chancellor Kohl. These promises were rewarded by a high vote for the CDU which included 46% of female voters.[10] But a sharp rise in unemployment, the loss of many social services, and the rising cost of housing and consumption following unification caused discontent among many former GDR citizens.

The most dramatic change was that the right to work no longer existed. Between 1989 and 1995 86% of agricultural employees in Mecklenburg-West Pomerania were made redundant (Krambach et al., 1997) compared with 75% throughout the GDR (Müller, 1996). These figures conceal a significant gender-differential. Many sectors in rural areas in which women were predominantly employed were rationalised, such as the production and storage of produce, and trade and administrative functions. Women represented 93% of the total workforce in these sectors. Specialised professions such as 'milking woman' or 'veterinary engineer' ceased to exist in post-unification agricultural production (020). In addition, approximately one-third of women in farming in the GDR were over 50 years old (Isda, 1991) and unification introduced a wave of pre-retirement and early pensioner schemes for these workers. As a result of all of the economic rationalisation, 75% of jobs that were lost had been occupied by women (Deutscher Bundestag, 1992) and women constituted 60% of all the unemployed (Bläss et al., 1991; Wiebensohn, 1991) in the former GDR.[11] Women in marginal regions, such as Mecklenburg-West Pomerania, experienced greater disadvantage than women in other regions (von Luepke, 1991).

Unemployment has particularly affected women in agricultural villages. Although men and women were similarly affected by the rationalisation of farming, men were twice as likely to be re-employed in other work (Schumann and Jahn, 1991). The 'First Report for Women in Mecklenburg-West Pomerania' (1997) produced by the Equal Opportunities Office for the region shows a rise in male employment between 1993 and 1995, but a fall in employment for women. The report also shows that employment policies reinforce the traditional 'male-bread-winner' model. Women frequently encounter discrimination on the grounds of their age, their marital and family status (DeSoto and Panzig, 1995; Nickel, 1990). Thus, married women are more likely to be unemployed than single women. The disadvantage and marginalisation faced by women in the new *Bundesländer* was articulated by a number of respondents used in this research. For instance, one woman argued that:

> It is the CDU's opinion that it really is very bold of women to demand employment now. It should be left to men. Women should stay in the home with their kids until the situation in the labour market changes. (020)

The loss of employment for women post-unification has been significant not only in terms of the resultant economic insecurity but also because of the loss of the social context of work which was women's central means of identification in the GDR (Böckmann-Schewe et al., 1995). Although some of the positive aspects of collectives are disputed by Herbst et al. (1994), Rueschemeyer's findings (1981, 1983), based on a case study of an academic collective, indicate that the collective was positively experienced as serving its members' needs as well as the needs of the labour process. The collective was not thought of as an 'instrument of paternalistic manipulation' since respondents reported active participation in planning and gained support from within the collective. The research on which this paper is based also produced similar findings. Women respondents have internalised through the collective a strong desire for participation in the workplace and for associated social networks. Consequently, their unemployment has caused them to become immobile and detached from public life (Dölling, 1991; Fink et al., 1993). They experience a sense of uselessness and withdraw to the private sphere 'whether they like it or not' (Rosenberg, 1991) and experience village life in a 'vacuum' (DeSoto and Panzig, 1995). This provides a significant contrast to women's memories of their previous integration into village life and the benefits they enjoyed. Respondents stated that it was made clear to women throughout their lives that they were an essential part of society. Women were proud to have managed their multiple burden of employment, private farming, family life, housework, and voluntary activities. They felt emancipated, not oppressed.

Unification dealt a severe blow to Women's Politics. Most social institutions maintained by the LPGs, such as childcare, canteens, culture centres and local shops, were either privatised or fell under the responsibility of the community. Both private owner and community could usually not afford to keep costly institutions if there was no legal obligation to do so. Women have thus lost what they perceived as benefits of the previous political system. Since farmers today operate under the pressures of EU agricultural policies and the international market, awards and subsidies which were obtained in the GDR are no longer provided. This led to both a decline in the social status of co-operative farmers as well as the loss of a common product for the entire village and hence, the loss of a means of community solidarity. Villages have suffered severely from the abrupt social and economic changes which express themselves in divisions between those who still work and those who are unemployed.

Women have had to re-evaluate their role in the public and the private spheres whilst, at the same time, familiarising themselves with the new 'rules' of the new society. The devaluation of previous values and meanings, and a sense of 'Ostalgia',[12] developed into barriers for many women, inhibiting them from participating in the restructuring process of the New Germany. Furthermore, women began to isolate themselves because, as one respondent concluded, they 'aren't worth anything anymore' (019). The sense of collective achievement is largely lost and replaced by the need for individual fulfilment often based on inaccessible material goods. As a consequence of the restricted influence in decision-making and mobility, women have neither the time, space nor the desire to become involved in activities for the village on a voluntary basis.

Edwards (1985) suggests that women who are more educated and qualified relative to others become more involved in voluntary work. This was also evident in my research. Unemployed women who generally were less qualified than those in work were less likely to engage in voluntary work. Widespread passivity has been a dilemma for policy-makers who direct resources to structural improvements within a 'central-town' system and depend largely on voluntary initiatives to revive social structures.

'Feminist perspectives'
Different theoretical frameworks have been constructed by scholars to account for the impact of political ideologies and social structures on women in the GDR. Several authors working within the feminist tradition have made strong claims that the intention and impact of socialist policies was deceitful. Political measures in favour of women failed to address issues such as women's multiple burdens, the role of men and thus, the true emancipation of women.[13] My research does not dispute such observations, for women's experiences of the difficulties in managing multiple burdens were addressed by respondents. Those who wished to travel to the West or sought promotion at work had to demonstrate their allegiance to the state. But, as stated above, a number of women in this study's findings believed that they were indeed emancipated. Respondents frequently evaluated their GDR experience in comparison to their current situation. Most freedoms today seem to be inaccessible to them. Many women respondents claimed that they had more rights to freedom of speech and democracy in the GDR as a consequence of their participation in the collective. In light of their current feelings of uselessness, they define their previous multiple burdens as proof of their ability to work and, at the same time, cope with other demands and pressures. With regard to the political pressures in the GDR, the majority of women respondents did not know about the full extent of the control they were subjected to, an impression which was confirmed by the key informants in this study. It is only today, since political direction and control has disappeared, that women have become more aware of the fact of how much influence the state had over their lives. A number of women respondents acknowledged that their needs and wants were defined by the state but still they were satisfied with the situation the way it was.

As mentioned above, respondents re-define many past experiences in the light of new ones. They feel insecure about the value of their own previous achievements and either question and deny, or vehemently defend, the previous value system. Either way, women feel estranged from their environment which causes them to isolate themselves. Women thus become increasingly inaccessible to policy-makers. A precondition for a number of integrative development programmes, such as LEADER II or Agenda 21, is a high level of motivation and voluntary initiative which seems almost impossible to introduce in many rural areas. The maintenance of 'soft' skills, such as solidarity, mutual support and motivation can possibly be enhanced through communication. Empowerment may thus begin with the creation of new discussion channels for women which resemble a 'collective' setting (see also Panzig, 1995). Some respondents describe the establishment of some local groups as helping women 'see the light at the end of the tunnel'. (108) At a practical level, the research presented here has also contributed to this process of women's empowerment by offering initial opportunities for discussion.

Conclusion

In contrast to some of the literature discussed above, the research on which this paper is based shows that the collective was significant to women's everyday lives and that its loss through the sudden transition initiated by unification led to insecurities for many women. The GDR regime had suppressed personal initiative for forty years and, at the same time, operated a pressure and reward system which does not exist under contemporary socio-political organisation. Political involvement does not now have an appeal for many women as they believe it is laborious and yields no rewards at the personal level. Younger women in particular are not prepared to help a state which in their eyes does not help them. Graham and Regulska (1997) argue that women can be most effective at the local level, despite existing barriers. In order to relieve women's 'mental trap', both political leaders and local women need to develop realistic structures for public participation which lead to visible outcomes at the local level and thus reward women's initiative for the village. Women need more assistance to develop a vision of their future and to trust opportunities provided by political structures today. Women respondents acknowledged that they have to show an impetus to become involved in local activity. As one respondent stated, 'if [they] aren't strong for [their] own sakes, no one will be and [they] will be forgotten'. But they also believe that someone must be there to 'push' them and offer them encourage-ment.

Mechanisms for developing a sense of local democracy can be provided through local groups or the implementation of participatory planning approaches. Such initiatives can be beneficial for women as they may lead to strengthening women's willingness to explore opportunities, to learn skills useful for the labour market, gain experience in networking, co-operate with political groups, and develop creativity in problem-solving (Kamenista, 1997). Some of the women respondents who were unemployed believed that participation in the labour market will recreate the sense of well-being and personal esteem that they had in the collective in the GDR. However, even women respondents in employment reported that the workplace does not provide the positive experience that they enjoyed in the collective.

NOTES

[1] Many thanks to Mark Cleary and Hans-Wolf Graefe for their comments on this paper.

[2] Numbers refer to respondents in the fieldwork for this paper.

[3] Cited in: Jetzschmann (1988), p. 24

[4] Free German Youth.

[5] *Landwirtschaftliche Produktionsgenossenschaft.*

[6] *Demokratischer Frauenbund Deutschlands* (German Democratic Women's Association).

[7] People's Solidarity.

[8] See, for instance, Dölling, 1991; Einhorn, 1989; Kolinsky, 1996; Marx-Ferree, 1993.

[9] A 'Facharbeiter' is a qualification resulting from an apprenticeship.

[10] In: Sourbut (1997).

[11] Direct unemployment results from redundancies, whereas indirect unemployment includes short-term employment measures such as ABM (work creation schemes), SAM (structural work schemes) and 249h (partly-funded work schemes). In addition, further education, retraining measures and early retirement are included.

[12] This expression was frequently used by respondents in this research to describe nostalgic feelings about the GDR.

[13] See, for example, Dölling, 1991; Einhorn, 1989; Kolinsky, 1996; Marx-Ferree, 1993; Nickel, 1990; Penrose, 1990; Rosenberg, 1991, or Rueschemeyer and Szeleny, 1989.

SOURCES

Autorenkollektiv. *Stadt und Land in der DDR. Entwicklung-Bilanz-Perspektiven* (Berlin (Ost), 1984)

Bläss, P. et al. Hearing 'Lage der Landfrauen in den neuen Bundesländern'. Bonn. In: *Dokumentation AK Feminisierung der Gesellschaft*. PDS/ Linke Liste. (Bonn, 1991)

Böckmann-Schewe, L. et al. '"Es war schon immer so, den goldenen Mittelweg zu finden zwischen Familie und Beruf war eigentlich das Entscheidende." Kontinuitäten und Veränderungen im Leben von Frauen in den neuen Bundesländern'. In: *Berlin Journal für Soziologie*, Heft 2, 1995: 207-222

DeSoto, H.H., Panzig, C. 'Women, Gender and Rural Development'. In: *Tagungsbericht 16. Bis 18. Juni 1994* 'Frauen in der ländlichen Entwicklung'. Landwirtschaftlich-Gärtnerische Fakultät der Humboldtuniversität. (Berlin, 1995)

Deutscher Bundestag. Drucksache 12/3910 vom 03.12.92. 'Antwort der Bundesregierung auf die grosse Anfrage der Abgeordneten Petra Bläss und der Gruppe PDS/ Linke Liste'- Drucksache 12/2360-. 'Perspektiven für Frauen in ländlichen Räumen in den neuen Bundesländern' (Bonn, 1992)

Dölling, I. 'Between Hope and Helplessness: Women in the GDR after the "Turning Point"'. In: *Feminist Review* 39: 3-15, 1991

Edwards, G.E. *GDR Society and Social Institutions* (London, 1985)

Einhorn, B. 'Socialist Emancipation: The Women's Movement in the German Democratic Republic'. In: Kruks, S., Rapp, P., Young, M.B. *Promissory Notes: Women in the Transition to Socialism* (New York, 1989)

Fink, M., Grajewski, R., Siebert, R., Zierold, K. '"Es müsste schon ein Wunder geschehen, wenn man nochmals Arbeit findet." Frauen im ländlichen Raum Ostdeutschlands'. In: *Landbauforschung Völkenrode* 44(1): 13-25, 1993

Giessmann, J. In: G. Burkhardt (ed.) 'Sozialisation im Sozialismus. Lebensbedingungen in der DDR im Umbruch', *Zeitschrift für Sozialforschung und Erziehungssoziologie*. 1. Beiheft, 1990.

Graham, A., Regulska, J. 'Expanding Political Space for Women in Poland. An Analysis of three Communities' Paper presented at the 'Third European Feminist Research Conference.' Coimbra, Portugal. July 8-12, 1997

Herbst, A. et al. *So funktionierte die DDR*. Band 1 (Hamburg, 1994)

Isda Institut für Sozialdatenanalyse e.V. 'Zur Lage der Landfrauen in den neuen Bundesländern'. In: *Dokumentation AK Feminisierung der Gesellschaft*. PDS/ Linke Liste. (Bonn, 1991)

Jetzschmann, H. 'Die Rolle der Arbeitskollektive bei der Entwicklung der sozialen Struktur'. In: Autorenkollektiv unter Leitung von R.Weidig. Sozialstruktur der DDR. (Berlin (Ost), 1988)

Kamenista, L. 'East German Feminists in the new German Democracy: Opportunities, Obstacles and Adaptation'. In: *Women and Politics* 17(3): 41-68, 1997

Kolinsky, E. 'Women in the New Germany'. In: G. Smith, W. Paterson and S. Padgett (eds.)., *Developments in German Politics*. (Basingstoke, 1996)

Krambach, K. *Wie lebt man auf dem Lande?* (Berlin (Ost), 1985)

Krambach, K. et al. 'Wirtschaftliche Entwicklung in den drei Nordbezirken- Agrarwirtschaft, Agrarpolitik und Lebensverhältnisse auf dem Lande'. In: Landtag *Mecklenburg-Vorpommern. Schwerin (ed.)* Leben in der DDR. Leben nach 1989- Aufarbeitung und Versöhnung. (Schwerin, 1997)

Luutz, E. 'Zur sozialen Lage von Landfrauen'. In: J. Ludwig und M. Franzke. *Einspruch. Leipziger Hefte* 9(3): 36-49, 1993

Marx-Ferree, M. "The rise and fall of "Mommy Politics": Feminism and Unification in (east) Germany'. In: *Feminist Studies* 19(1): 89-115, 1993

Müller, K. 'Landwirtschaft in Ostdeutschland: Fünf Jahre nach der deutschen Wiedervereinigung.' In: *Agrarbündnis: Der kritische Agrarbericht* 1996

Nave-Herz, R. 'Die institutionelle Kleinkindbetreuung in den neuen und alten Bundesländern - ein altes und doch weiterhin hochaktuelles Problem für Eltern'. In: *Frauenforschung* 8(4): 45-59, 1990

Nickel, H.M. 'Geschlechtersozialisation in der DDR. Oder: Zur Rekonstruktion des Patriarchats im realen Sozialismus'. In: G. Burkhardt (ed.). *Sozialisation im Sozialismus. Zeitschrift für Sozialforschung und Erziehungssoziologie* (ZSE). 1. Beiheft, 1990

Panzig, C. 'Ostdeutsche Frauen im Transformationsprozess'. In: *Tagungsbericht 16. Bis 18. Juni, 1994* 'Frauen in der ländlichen Entwicklung', Landwirtschaftlich-Gärtnerische Fakultät der Humboldt-Universität zu Berlin, 1995

Penrose, V. 'Vierzig Jahre SED-Frauenpolitik: Ziele, Strategien und Ergebnisse'. In: *Frauenforschung* 8(4): 60-77, 1990

Rosenberg, D.J. 'Shock Therapy: GDR Women in Transition from a Socialist Welfare State to a Market Economy'. In: *Signs. Journal of Women in Culture and Society*, 17(1): 129-151, 1991

Rueschemeyer, M. and Szeleny, S. 'Socialist Transformation and Gender Inequality: Women in the GDR and Hungary'. In: D. Childs, T.A. Baylis and M. Rueschemeyer (eds.)., *East Germany in Comparative Perspective*. (London, 1989)

Rueschemeyer, M. 'Social and Work Relations of Professional Women: an Academic Collective in the GDR'. In: *East Central Europe* 8(1-2): 23-37, 1981

Rueschemeyer, M. 'The Work Collective: Response and Adaptation in the Structure of Work in the German Democratic Republic'. In: *Discursive Anthropology* 7: 155-163, 1983

Schumann, F., Jahn, W. 'Zur Lage der Landwirtschaft in der BRD'. In: *Dokumentation AK Feminisierung der Gesellschaft*. PDS/ Linke Liste. (Bonn, 1991)

Shaffer, H.G. *Women in the two Germanies. A Comparative Study of a Socialist and Non-socialist Society.* (Oxford, 1981)

Sourbut, C.A. 'Constructions of Motherhood: Representations and Realities of Women's Experiences as Mothers in the Former GDR under State Socialism and Capitalism'. Unpublished dissertation. (University of Bath, 1997)

Völzer, K. 'Die Freie Deutsche Jugend (FDJ) - ein Beispiel für den Alltag in der DDR'. Unpublished 'Diplomarbeit'. (Universität Bremen, 1996)

Von Lüpke, K. 'Berufliche Chancengleichheit für Frauen auf dem Lande?' In: *Dokumentation AK Feminisierung der Gesellschaft*. PDS/ Linke Liste. (Bonn, 1991)

Wiebensohn, L. 'Gutachten zur Anhörung 'Die Frau in der Landwirtschaft'' im Ausschuss Frauen und Jugend. In: *Dokumentation AK Feminisierung der Gesellschaft*. PDS/ Linke Liste. (Bonn, 1991)

Vanessa Beck

THE IMPACT OF UNEMPLOYMENT ON WOMEN IN THE NEW *BUNDESLÄNDER*

Following unification and the various implications of social transformation, unemployment has become a major problem for East German women. Here, the responses and coping strategies of unemployed women in Magdeburg, Saxony-Anhalt, are explored. It is suggested that, in contrast to findings from previous research, women have developed highly successful methods to replace functions formerly filled by employment. At an individual level they must thus be classified as highly active and resilient as they do not give up despite the problems they still face at the institutional level.

Introduction

Since the first phase of institutional transformation ended, some kind of normalisation has set in for the former GDR. But this normalisation is a problematic one and especially so for women as they still have to adapt to completely new role models as well as expectations and conditions for their life plans. This is happening within the continuing social transformation, which includes two parallel developments:

1. The whole of German society is moving away from the male breadwinner model and towards an individualised as opposed to family based social security system.

2. Although adaptation to western standards and norms continues, the new *Bundesländer* are maintaining a distinctive identity.

Women's continuous work motivation (e.g. Kolinsky, 1997) is a clear example of the latter and also a good indicator for the extent of the process of social transformation. It will be shown that employment, including its compatibility with the family, was an important part of East German women's lives. Although preconditions to carry on these patterns of life no longer exist, there are strong indications that these changes are not merely accepted. The decline in marriages, the so-called birth-strike (Liebscher *et al.*, 1995, 73) and the increase in divorces, even from the high GDR rates, have prompted women to find alternatives that will maintain their independence and enable a continuation of life plans. The founding of a family which now occurs much later in life than during GDR times, as well as the continuously high figures of single mothers, indicate that the male breadwinner model – still the basis on which, for example, unemployment benefits are calculated – is rejected.

Within these developments unemployment has been a major issue and especially so in Saxony-Anhalt, the *Land* with the highest unemployment rates in the unified Germany. In July 1998 the average rate was 21.1%, which divides into 18.3% for men and 24.2% for women. This signifies that after the first big waves of unemployment in 1993/4, which hit women much harder than men, the figures are now levelling out. The pressure on women is still greater, though, not only because they are still more affected but also due to expectations for them to withdraw from the labour market. In January 1998 the West German Peschel Institute published a study on unemployment in Saxony-Anhalt which stated women would halve the problem by withdrawing from the labour market. It is expected that they become part of the 'silent reserve' and remain content with the role of housewife and mother because the double burden of additional employment is too great a pressure to bear. The reaction to the study was an outcry by women and the suggestions were similarly rejected by speakers from all political parties, including Gerlinde Kuppe, at the time the SPD's minister for employment and social affairs.[1]

The question this paper addresses is how women whose life plans and self-perception are based on employment cope with unemployment. How do they react to this entirely new experience? It will be argued that the traditional results of studies on unemployment do not serve as satisfactory explanations for East German women's reaction to unemployment. The distinctive feature seems to be that, despite disadvantages at an institutional level, there is more individual potential. On the basis of the specific situation in the new *Bundesländer* some selected empirical results from interviews will be compared with the traditional findings of studies of unemployment. It will thus be shown that these women are very flexible and active in their coping strategies and cannot be seen as helpless, not in the feminist sense nor in the sense of the learned helplessness model of depression (Miller / Seligmann, 1975, 235).

It should be noted that some of the results introduced here could hold for men but this was not examined in the context of this study. It is assumed that men react differently due to a different attitude to work. The male breadwinner model still prevails in attitudes, even in the new *Bundesländer*, as stereotype gender roles, albeit in a weaker form, did also exist in the GDR (Ostner, 1997). The findings presented here are based on in-depth interviews with 22 unemployed women conducted in Magdeburg in April 1998. This is a very small sample and therefore not entirely representative, but was considered sufficient as the focus was on the individual level of how women cope with and react to unemployment.

Contact with the participants was made via official help structures such as the equal opportunities office and various women's projects. Due to this it must be assumed that the sample is part of the more active group of unemployed as they were in contact with these institutions. Considering that Magdeburg and Saxony-Anhalt in general has a large network of these structures and a reasonable participation rate within them, the interviewed individuals cannot necessarily be seen as untypical. The interviews were one-to-one, oral and taped, to be consequently transcribed for analysis. Each woman was met once and interviewed for an average of 1½ hours. The interviews were semi-structured as all of them covered the same issue areas[2] but the individual questions varied in the course of the different interviews.

Profile of the women interviewed

A total of 22 women were interviewed. All of them considered themselves as officially unemployed although some of them were currently on an ABM[3] scheme. All of the women had been in ABM or FuU[4] at least once. Most interviewees were part of the older cohorts as they were mainly between 40 and 50 years of age. In contacting unemployed women several problems were encountered to find interviewees from different age groups. It was striking that older women – and the threshold for this has now been reduced as far down as 40/45 – were much more likely to agree to an interview whereas most young women rejected even informal chats. Although several reasons for this have been suggested there is as yet no conclusive evidence for the different reactions between age groups.

Qualifications varied and do not seem to play a vital role as the sample included both highly qualified engineers and academics as well as factory floor workers. Only one woman stated 'unemployed' as her current occupation so that, in general, a strong identification with the respective occupation and qualification can be detected.

Often the problem is that the women are overqualified for the jobs that would be available. It is striking that out of the total of 22 interviewees, 8 had more than one qualification or were not working in the area they had originally trained for. These dual or even triple qualifications had all been achieved during GDR times. Added to the involvement in work creation schemes and in further education and retraining, this would result in a high occupational flexibility.

Family status and existence of children strongly reflected the age of the sample as the majority (13) were married. Despite their age many women still lived in what might be called 'alternative' family situations, such as unmarried partnerships and as single parents, indicating that life patterns have been maintained from GDR times.

Most of the interviewees must be classified as long-term unemployed, i.e. they have been out of work for longer than one year. Although the average was a length of over four years, it should be noted that these are periods stated by the women themselves, who do not consider ABM or FuU as an end or even an interruption to their unemployment. Official figures from the employment office would probably vary considerably.

The importance of the second labour market

Specific problems have arisen due to the active intervention by and for women. Nearly all women interviewed were, or are, involved in ABM or FuU but due to this feel their hopes and abilities are being played with. The employment offices introduced many of these schemes in the first years of unification with the aim of providing the developing market economy with the qualifications required, but only relatively few participants could be re-integrated into the labour market. Moreover, these measures are limited to one or a maximum of two years and can therefore result in ultimate *Bastelbiographien* as the women can merely plan ahead for one year at a time.

The measures are officially designed to aid causes that promote public interest, increase the chances of creating new full-term jobs and benefit the difficult cases, which include women, of the long-term unemployed. This is proving to be unrealistic. Although the proportion of women in some of the schemes is higher than that of men, consequential improvements of conditions for women on the first labour market have not been found. Most women see the measures as a means of improving their unemployment benefits and prefer them to being entirely unoccupied. ABMs may have a temporary beneficial effect, although long-term implications are unpredictable. Eichler (1997) comes to the conclusion that, despite active labour market measures having a beneficial effect on unemployment statistics and, in part, on individuals, they can also lead to a deterioration of human capital and result in a decline of chances on the first labour market.

Although it is illegal to do voluntary work for more than 14 hours per week, some women take the risk and by this demonstrate how important a meaningful occupation is to them.

Previous research on unemployment

The above distinguishes unemployment in the new *Bundesländer* from the typical experience of unemployment given in traditional works and is schematically presented in Figure 1.

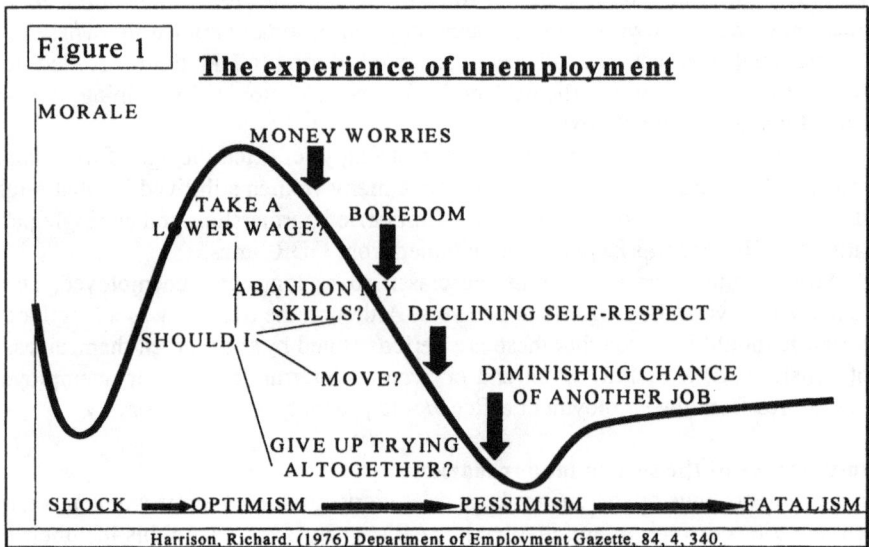

Figure 1 The experience of unemployment

Harrison, Richard. (1976) Department of Employment Gazette, 84, 4, 340.

Within this traditional research Heinemann *et al* (1983) have conducted one of the very few studies looking explicitly at the impact of unemployment on women. They found them, in general, to be less affected than men as they have the role of the mother and housewife to fall back on. As in most traditional research, the male breadwinner model is thus assumed as a basis. It is interesting to see, though, that some of Heinemann's findings indicate that a removal of this basis would result in a reversal of the study's outcomes. As GDR society was not based on this model, East German women's responses would be expected to reflect 'normal male' workers' reactions.

Although the findings of traditional research can, in part, be extended to women in the new *Bundesländer*, the labour market conditions as well as their background socialisation and resulting expectations make their position distinct. The main difference is that East German women seem to adapt at a different, individual level, depicted in Figure 2.

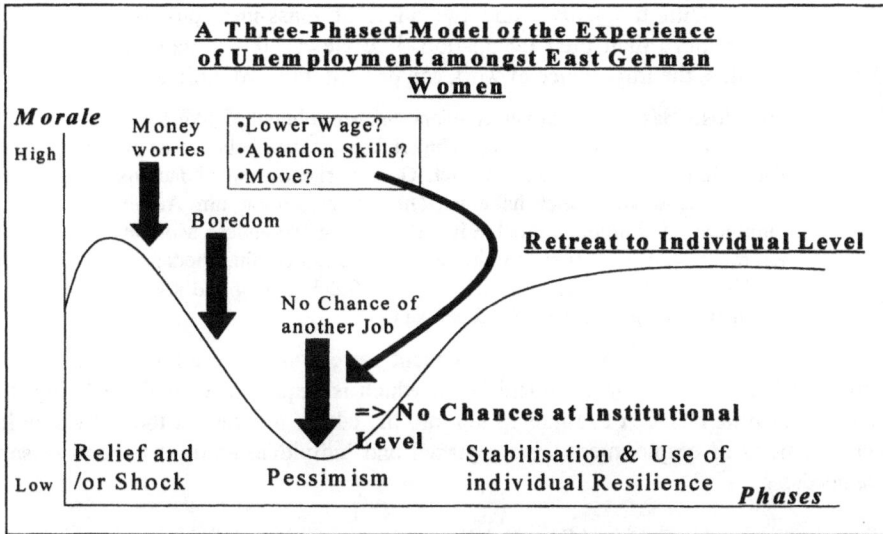

A Three-Phased-Model of the Experience of Unemployment amongst East German Women

Morale — High / Low

Money worries
•Lower Wage?
•Abandon Skills?
•Move?

Boredom

Retreat to Individual Level

No Chance of another Job

=>No Chances at Institutional Level

Relief and /or Shock

Pessimism

Stabilisation & Use of individual Resilience

Phases

Although this is a broadly generalised picture, it does give indications of the overall results that were found in the interviews. The first two phases show similarities to the results of traditional studies but they are then followed by a stabilisation as women 'retreat' to the individual level. The term 'retreat' is used here to suggest that East German women do not rely on official structures for a solution, which could, according to previous research, lead to fatalism. These women know support of this kind to be unlikely and therefore become active themselves by relying on their own resources.

The interview results

A. The meaning and importance of work

As expected from the widely documented work motivation of East German women the responses reflected the centrality work had in the GDR as well as the complete novelty unemployment was to GDR citizens. All women stated to miss social contacts as well as being needed and challenged.

> 015: Nee, da bin ich ja isoliert. Und so wenn ich zur Arbeit gehe, habe ich 'n Umfeld, habe ich Menschen, habe ich Kontakte. Das ham'se doch so nicht.

This cannot be surprising when considering that the work place was also a social institution in the GDR, which often provided social networks, health and child care facilities.[5] These are functions of employment that housework is obviously unable to replace. When asked directly nearly all interviewees stated that housework does not have the same value as employment. The former was considered as a necessity to be accomplished on the side, whereas employment was portrayed as being a value in itself and thus being fulfilling.

The importance of work is thus also linked to the position women hold in society. Both of these can only be maintained if there are possibilities to combine employment with the family. With the *Wende* and the onset of mass-unemployment, the women therefore lost far more than their occupation. Interviewee 004's statement shows how, following from this, the importance of work can be split into two main areas.

> 004: Also, das sind zwei verschiedene Sachen; einmal, denke ich, muß ich mir Arbeit suchen, weil ich, wenn ich keine Arbeit habe, so ist meine Einstellung zu der Sache, laufe ich Gefahr irgendwann obdachlos zu werden. Und von daher habe ich 'nen Zwang mich um Arbeit zu kümmern. Und arbeiten möchte ich, und das ist 'ne andere Motivation, ich möchte auch arbeiten, damit ich unter Menschen bin, wieder, damit ich Kontakte habe, und damit ich mich ein Stück geistig und körperlich und manuell ein bißchen befriedigen kann.

This division of functions of employment corresponds to the levels of reactions to be outlined below. At the institutional level, which is important to make a living, these women stand little chance of re-integration into the labour market. At the individual level social functions of employment were replaced and individual solutions found to satisfy these needs.

B. Entering unemployment and first reactions to it

The first reaction to unemployment was often a mixture of shock and relief. The latter was due to the double burden, bad work conditions and/or stress. Many women at first looked forward to having time for themselves but this soon turned into boredom. The social component of employment was clearly lacking. Moreover, the hopes and expectations of the first phase of unemployment soon died down and were then followed by a depressed phase. In the Warsaw Study on unemployment Zawadzki and Lazarsfeld (1935) suggest individual responses develop from initial anger over various stages of adaptation and restricted optimism to apathy and fatalism. Excluding the final, fatalistic outcome, a similar development was detectable in the interviewees as they soon realised that they had few, if any, chances of re-integration into the labour market. Although nearly all women continued looking for employment they were at the same time aware of their position at the institutional level.

C. Current feelings towards unemployment – individual and general

After the initial shock or relief of becoming unemployed, most of the interviewed women went through a depressed phase but then recovered and became active again. The following quotation is a typical example of individual women's coping strategies.

> 013: Ich hab' wirklich 'n halbes Jahr gebraucht, um zu begreifen, daß ich arbeitslos bin, und erst konnte ich das überhaupt nicht fassen, ich hab zu Hause nichts mehr machen können, ich hatte Mühe meine Wohnung überhaupt wieder in Ordnung zu bringen, oder einzukaufen. Es hat mich nichts mehr interessiert und da hab ich gedacht, nee, so kanns nicht bleiben. Ich ändere damit nichts an der Tatsache, es bleibt so. Und da habe ich mich dann wieder aufgerappelt und hab gesagt, 'Nee, irgendwas, irgendwie muß es weitergehen.'

Not only is the development in responses clearly visible here, but so too is a specific coping strategy. Most women had accepted the fact that the general situation would not be changed and had consequently found individual solutions.

Although many women were struggling to cope with unemployment they were also determined not to give up and accept their fate. As Interviewee 002 states, they even found, to some extent, pleasure in finding alternative ways to get by.

> 002: Ich denke auch, wenn man aufgibt, dann hat man verloren. Also, ich füge mich nicht dem Schicksal, das bringt mir dann irgendwo auch Spaß.

These responses suggest resilience rather than fatalism and could, in addition, indicate an old enforced flexibility of women who always had to and always did cope somehow. During GDR times women were fully integrated into the work force and, in addition, usually fully responsible for the household as well as children. Quite apart from this dual burden political participation was necessary if a career was to be pursued, and shortages in daily necessities, or even the lack of technology, made the role of a housewife more time-consuming and difficult. This indicates the capabilities of these women. The profile of the women interviewed here shows that they also found time to gain further qualifications. This was often done at night or virtually whilst caring for children.

East German women thus use their past experiences from GDR times to cope with the present problems induced by unemployment. Before looking at what the coping strategies actually consisted of, it is necessary to consider the financial implications of unemployment as these were often found to be the basis from which responses can be explained.

D. Financial implications

The financial situation of an unemployed individual is usually a determining factor regarding their responses. In the interviews it was found that hardship depends strongly on whether a family exists, whether the husband is still in work and how good, i.e. how well paid, the last job was. Statements regarding the financial situation of the unemployed were very controversial. One single mother stated she was doing fine due to the benefits she received for her children but most thought single parents were worst off. This must be seen as individual differences in expectations and demands in addition to the importance of the last wage as the basis for calculating the benefits. No clear-cut structure could therefore be established for differences in the financial situation.

The most important result from the questions about the women's financial situation is that all wanted to regain employment regardless of the level of pay, although the issue was of course more pressing for those who find it hard to cope on what they currently have. For those who are slightly better off the financial independence from others, especially a partner or husband, becomes more important. This reflects the changing position women hold in society.

Employment and a wage-packet of their own made women more independent in that they, for example, found it easier to divorce a husband they did not depend on. In many cases this independence was now, at the least, threatened. The decline in marriages and increase in divorces mentioned earlier thus show East German women's determination to continue their life plans despite the harshness of circumstances. They also give indications of the coping strategies, as a single woman's unemployment benefits, for example, could not be calculated on the basis of a husband's wage. Independence is thus a key factor in coping, although it will be shown in the following that 'mental' independence is even more important than financial independence.

E. Physical and emotional well-being

Although most interviewees felt the impact of unemployment strongly and admitted to having 'bad patches', only very few thought this had implications for their health. The depressions mentioned earlier were thus considered as a phase and, although they would return temporarily, were not considered a solution or permanent response. Throughout the interviews illness was often mentioned but was usually never specified or made into an issue. Ill health and especially psychosomatic problems do not seem to be as widely accepted by these women as in the west. In this context answers to the questions about where help or compassion was looked for are very interesting. If women sought help at all it was usually within the family but even there some did not want to be a burden on others. It seems that problems, depressions or fears are seen as individual problems that are either nobody else's business or that nobody else can help with anyway.

> 006: Ja, Hilfe? Ich hatte immer das Gefühl, wenn ich mir allein nicht
> helfe, denn können andere das auch nicht.

As here, there were some cases where there almost seemed to be a certain pride in coping alone. It should be noted, though, that the family is, in most cases, part of the individual level and, consequentially, part of the coping strategies. The most common tactics within these strategies were activity as well as social contacts, which helped overcome the loss of employment with all the beneficial side effects it had during GDR times. It was thus very important to all women to maintain or even expand their social contacts. This was due to an awareness of the dangers, such as inactivity, isolation and withdrawal from society that can result from unemployment as they had usually experienced them during their depressive phases. They therefore consciously attempted to counteract them.

F. The family and social contacts

Partly due to these individualised coping strategies social contacts become very important. The circles of friends have usually changed very little in size although contact with former colleagues is often reduced and replaced by other activities. The women interviewed were found to be very active and inventive in finding replacements to satisfy the needs formerly covered by employment. As already mentioned some do voluntary work, they also 'invent' ABM schemes,[6] they look for alternative occupations (such as women's groups, evening school, sport clubs) or do part-time work (e.g. for the husband's job, cleaning, etc.). Many of these activities are not necessarily found via official help structures such as the employment offices and social contacts are, in addition, providers of information and a way to find loopholes in the bureaucracy that is both new and problematic. These social contacts and activities can therefore be seen as a continuation of the informal networks that were so important in the GDR.

It is important to acknowledge that all these 'solutions' are individual ones. The little official help offered by employment offices is not used or rather is not considered as help; on the contrary, it is often thought to be stigmatising and insulting, as the following quotation suggests.

> 005: Sagen wir mal so, wenn ich hin [zum Arbeitsamt] mußte, dann war
> der Tag für mich immer – dann war ich moralisch irgendwie am Ende
> […] und habe irgendwie gedacht, naja, was willste denn noch werden.
> Biste denn nun überhaupt nichts mehr wert.

Due to these sentiments towards the official help structures, the family and social contacts become all the more important. Within both these spheres structures of daily life were strong and disciplined. The loss of a time-structure, found to be typical of the unemployed, could therefore not be detected and this was independent of the existence of children who are often considered to give mothers a vital link to reality.

G. Outlook on the future

The generally positive outlook of most of the women interviewed was reflected by their thoughts on the future. The majority of women (7) were optimistic or had mixed feelings towards the future (6). This was to a large extent due to the fact that they had come to terms with and accepted the changes in their individual lives. A recurrent theme in many of the responses was an acknowledgement that patterns of life established before the *Wende* could not be continued as the GDR's security and the possibility to plan ahead for a whole life no longer exist. This has now been replaced by a high degree of flexibility as employment and life plans are only made from one year to the next.

H. Learned helplessness

Due to all these developments one could have speculated that women had learned to be helpless. Traditional gender patterns did exist in the GDR, not only in the separation of the workforce but also, and much more obviously, in the division of household and family chores. In addition, the state promoted the helplessness of the population by implementing a paternalistic approach, especially in social policies. As Interviewee 009 states:

> Wir waren sehr unselbständig, sehr, sehr unselbständig. Wir durften ja
> gar nicht denken und auf einmal müssen wir jetzt anfangen zu denken.

Finally, the whole of the transformation process could have turned out to be an enforcement of western norms and values. This, in turn, could have provoked a response of learned helplessness and of depression (see for example Freese *et al.*, 1996).

Yet East German women are not helpless. Firstly, not in the feminist sense of learned helplessness as they have maintained their self-respect gained through their lives in a socialist society. Whether due to this or due to the general move away from the male breadwinner model, East German women are insisting on 'emancipated' ways of life and partnerships.

As for the learned helplessness model of depression, this is the phenomenon that people learn passivity if they have repeatedly experienced their responses to their environment to be ineffective. This renders, for example, the unemployed unable to ameliorate their situation, if they have adapted themselves to a narrower scope. Again, this is not the case for women in the new *Bundesländer*. They have found individual solutions to make the situation bearable for themselves. Although these 'solutions' do not necessarily involve employment, most of them entail work at a personal level that will substitute at least some of the functions formerly satisfied by employment. The most important of these functions is a sense of being needed and social contacts. Financial security is, of course, also important but is less so, if the women feel they are not in danger of falling through the social net.

This twin-track strategy adopted during GDR times of always having to, but also having been able to cope on the institutional level on the one hand, and their flexibility and determination on a personal level on the other hand could prove to be very effective.

Conclusion

Although there is a lot of pressure on East German women to withdraw from the labour market, which in part amounts to structural disadvantage and discrimination, women are nevertheless not giving up. Many advantages they had in the GDR have been reversed, whereas the gendered structure of the GDR's labour market has been reinforced. These conditions have had a slight impact on work motivation as most women are determined to continue their occupational career and combine it with the family. With their distinctive response to unemployment East German women are proving to be more resilient than may have been expected. As a consequence of this the traditional results of research on unemployment need to be reconsidered. East German women are not willing to withdraw from the labour market and go back to the household and mother role as the latter to them is an addition to full employment, which can be either managed on the side, with short disruptions, or temporary part-time employment. Neither the household nor family duties can therefore replace the functions of employment but many women have found alternative means to achieve this.

Parallel to continuing their search for employment the interviewed women 'retreated' to the individual level in that they find individual solutions to the problems unemployment can encompass. In doing so East German women prove to be highly resilient against the social pressures that are attempting to restrict women to the role of the housewife and mother. The flexibility and activity demonstrated may not only be the future essentials for inclusion in the labour market, but may also improve women's position in the society of unified Germany.

NOTES

[1] Magdeburger Volksstimme, 21/1/1998, 1.

[2] These were: Background Information, Summary of Developments before and after the Wende, Being made Redundant, Feelings at the Current Stage of Unemployment, Financial Implications, Personal and Emotional Implications, Family and Social Contacts, Flexibility and Activity, and Outlook on the Future.

[3] ABM = Arbeitsbeschaffungsmassnahme; work replacement scheme.

[4] FuU = *Fortbildung und Umschulung*; further education and retraining.

[5] See Bettina Iganski's contribution in this volume for more on the importance of work for women in the GDR.

[6] For example, a project in Magdeburg which operates in schools to help teenagers find a job they would be interested in and for which it is still worth while training for. The initiative for this ABM was a response to the perceived inability of the employment office to aid young people in their life choices.

SOURCES

Martin Eichler, Arbeitsbeschaffungsmaßnahmen (ABM) in Sachsen-Anhalt: Vorläufige Ergebnisse einer Untersuchung der Beschäftigungschancen von Teilnehmern im ersten Arbeitsmarkt, *Forschungs-beiträge zum Arbeitsmarkt in Sachsen-Anhalt (Gelbe Reihe)*, 10, 1997, pp. 25-56

Michael Freese, Wolfgang Kring, Andrea Soose and Jeannette Zempel, Personal Initiative at Work: Differences between East and West Germany, *Academy of Management Journal*, 39 (1), 1996, pp. 37-63

Richard Harrison, The demoralising experience of prolonged unemployment, *Department of Employment Gazette*, 84, 1976, pp. 339-348

Klaus Heinemann, Peter Röhrig and Rolf Stadie, *Arbeitslose Frauen - Zwischen Erwerbstätigkeit und Hausfrauenrolle, Eine empirische Untersuchung* (Weinheim and Basel, 1983)

Eva Kolinsky, Recasting Biographies: Women and the Family, in Eva Kolinsky (ed.), *Social Transformation and the Family in Post-Communist Germany* (Basingstoke, 1997), pp. 118-140

Reinhard Liebscher, Sonja Menning and Enno Nowossadeck, Bevölkerungsentwicklung und Bevölkerungsstrukturen, in Gunnar Winkler / Sozial-wissenschaftliches Forschungszentrum Berlin-Brandenburg e. V. / Hans-Böckler-Stiftung (eds), *Sozialreport 1995* (Berlin, 1995), pp. 48-80

William R. Miller and Martin, E.P. Seligman, Depression and learned helplessness in man, *Journal of Abnormal Psychology*, 84-3, 1975, pp. 228-238

Ilona Ostner, Gender, Family and the Welfare State – Germany before and after Unification, in Eva Kolinsky (ed.) *Social Transformation and the Family in Post-Communist Germany* (Basingstoke, 1997), pp. 82-96

Bohan Zawadzki and Paul Lazarsfeld, The psychological consequences of unemployment, *Journal of Social Psychology*, 6, 1935, pp. 224-251

Corinne Nativel and Hannah Tooze

THE SIGNIFICANCE OF THE REGION IN EAST GERMANY'S ECONOMIC TRANSITION

With reference to an ideal-type of the pro-active region derived from current west European policy trends and academic consideration of regional development, this paper questions the contribution of regionally focused policy and regional units to the restructuring of East Germany's economy. The re-formation of the Eastern Länder, distribution of regional subsidies, regionalisation of structural policy and active labour market policy are considered as key issues for East Germany's regions. The paper concludes that, without considerable refinement and more careful implementation, regional policy predicated on the ideal-type may lead to increased divergence in East Germany's economic development.

Introduction: understanding the east German region

The simultaneous collapse of political, social and economic systems that has struck East Germany in the process of transition has led to the adoption of numerous strategies for the successful mastering of this change. An emphasis on regional structures and strategies has been prominent among these policy responses. This has taken the form both of constitutional reform, creating the new federal states in eastern Germany, and of specific policy initiatives for the regional level. This paper sets out the tensions that have arisen from some of the expectations that have been attached to the region in the context of East Germany's economic transition. These are considered as not simply symptomatic of the depth of East Germany's problems, but of a more general discrepancy between theory and practice in thinking about regions, which becomes particularly critical in a context of such severe and sudden economic restructuring.

During a period of over 40 years of central planning, the East German regions were shaped according to the socialist division of labour within the German Democratic Republic and within the broader framework of the Comecon. Regions were assigned specific productive functions within the economic system, a logic which resulted in high levels of vertical and horizontal concentration. The absence of a diversified sectoral structure led to the establishment of monostructures at the regional level: as a result, whole regional economies became dependent on single employers (e.g. the *EKO Stahl* conglomerate in Eisenhüttenstadt, which employed some 40 percent of all the metalworkers in the GDR). For many regions the current structural crisis is thus largely a sectoral crisis, reflecting their domination by declining branches such as the coal-mining, chemical and heavy industries.[1]

The sheer magnitude of the East German regions' economic backwardness clearly necessitates investment in modern infrastructure, equipment and human capital to boost their competitiveness and enable them to export their products on world markets.

However, the socialist heritage is more complex than a simple emphasis on sectoral dominance. Selective labour migration, with the typical higher exit mobility of younger, more highly trained workers from depressed areas, has further undermined the competitiveness of many East German regions. Yet for much of the population migration is neither feasible nor desired as the regions are also the place for identity formation. They thus incorporate an important socio-cultural dimension. This suggests that regional redevelopment concepts also need to integrate some element of continuity for the indigenous population.

Furthermore, the transition also involves the double challenge of restructuring the whole of the East German territory - with overall deficits in infrastructure and human capital – and overcoming emerging regional disparities. Indeed, whilst on the one hand the new Länder are in danger of becoming a new *Mezzogiorno*, permanently dependent on Western fiscal transfers, the disparities in regional GDP and unemployment rates already indicate an unevenness of economic opportunities.[2]

The transformation of the East German economy consists primarily in the necessity of 'catching up' through an economic upswing that will reveal the 'blooming landscapes'. The *Aufschwung* may be seen in terms of a Schumpeterian creative destruction and of modernisation processes.[3] Even where industries are modernised and maintained, the reduction in the level of employment post-restructuring implies the need for further interventionist policies to secure employment bases. The central question remains how the positive dynamics for development can be generated.

Regional debates have usually revolved around the problem of uneven development and the risk of polarisation.[4] Both traditional regional policies and new growth theories, which are based on neo-classical assumptions, have paid close attention to regional disparities. More recently a policy trend has developed that considers that positive outcomes may be achieved by the empowerment of regions to give them the responsibility to generate their own economic development. Here the region loses its purely spatial and passive dimension as the site of production or *Standort* and becomes an expressive and instrumental form. It becomes an agency, an actor in its own right. Since this entity incorporates a myriad of sub-actors, no particular group or policy instrument can be singled out. Furthermore, regional policy provides an interface between economic agents and central government. In the new regionalism the design of strategies to attract private capital is believed to be best left to the expertise of local organisations which can compile information more accurately and rapidly than central government. National government policies have often been criticised for their absence of targeting or local knowledge[5] and against this background, regionalism may thus be seen as a way to reduce uncertainty and increase efficiency. The effects of the regional strategy, though, only become apparent in the medium-term.

The growing significance of the region is demonstrated by the following 'ideal-type'. In this schematic outline, the region is presented as a multi-faceted construct which assumes various overlapping roles.[6]

Regional Policy: An 'ideal-type'

The Region as **innovator**: ability to promote infrastructural investment and to target future-oriented growth, using creative ideas.

The Region as **local expert**: ability to react more quickly than national agents, because of the proximity and prior knowledge of existing structures and available instruments which enable rapid access to information.

The Region as **efficient manager**: ability to maximise scarce resources, to promote both 'hard' and 'soft' locational factors, attracting inward investment.

The Region as **co-ordinator**: ability to create networks, mediating various local interests (internal/horizontal mediation) and providing an interface between the other regions as well as the federal and supra-national organisations (external/vertical mediation).

The Region as **protector** of the socio-cultural fabric: ability to unveil its indigenous strengths and to create a strong feeling of local identity and 'belonging' amongst its citizens, while defending the regional identity at super regional levels through lobbying.

The Region as **centraliser** of development concepts: encouraging synergy effects between measures and instruments applicable to the Region (*Verzahnung der Strukturpolitik*).

The resulting thesis: the Region is the motor in the dynamics of **competitiveness, creativity** and **growth**, while simultaneously reinforcing social cohesion and political stability. The Region is the perfect actor to achieve sustained, positive development by **blending change and continuity.**

Source: Nativel and Tooze, 1999

This trust in the pro-active capabilities of regions to tackle structural decline has emerged in West Germany since the early 1980s under the heading *Regionalisierung der Strukturpolitik* (regionalisation of structural policies). A similar line of reasoning prevails in European policy-making. However, it remains unclear whether the unprecedented need for structural adjustment in the East will also respond well to such policy initiatives. Furthermore, regional policy in East Germany is torn between the objectives of development and redistribution.[7] Will this act as a driving force for a major re-conceptualisation of regional policy? The responses to the East German regional problems thus extend the perspectives of change to the national level.[8] The concrete problems in the implementation of regional policy, which will be raised next, point to the need to reassess existing federal structures to take account of the dynamics of industrial change in a unified but diversified German territory.

Actual east German experiences

With unification East Germany was placed under the dual pressures of introducing West German structures in all spheres of the economy and society, while simultaneously implementing individual policies to cope with the difficulties of economic restructuring. In so doing it has taken over traditional German policies that were evolved for the more gradually changing and politically stable West German environment. Further complicating this development, unification has occurred at a time of policy innovation in the West. It is therefore necessary to consider the problems both of introducing the traditional structures and policies, and attempts at more innovative policy evolution that challenge some of the traditional roles.

The most immediate spatially oriented problem in joining the Federal Republic was the definition of the *Länder*. Although the ambiguity about what a region consists of means that it is not adequate simply to define German regions as corresponding to the *Länder* borders, the *Länder* are an important influence on regional identity and policies for the sub-national level. Furthermore, the debates around the formation of the new *Länder* illustrate some of the difficulties in reconciling regions of historic development and identity with regions that function as economically coherent units or with political and administrative territorial boundaries. The territory of the former GDR had an existing *Länder* structure until their dissolution in 1952 and the recreation of the *Länder* in 1990 has corresponded to these previously existing units with minor readjustments to the borderlines. These are deemed to fit the criteria set out for the *Länder* formation in article 29 paragraph 1 of the *Grundgesetz* in terms of their 'landsmannschaftlichen Verbundenheit, die geschichtlichen und kulturellen Zusammenhänge der wirtschaftlichen Zweckmäßigkeit sowie die Erfordernisse der Raumordnung und der Landesplanung.'[9]

While reassuming the historical boundaries was clearly the least politically controversial option, it dodged issues of economic efficiency. As in many policy areas it also meant that an opportunity for reform in Western Germany in tandem with change in the East, here of its *Länder* structure, was not taken. Furthermore, the *Länder* also acted as a continuation of the *Bezirke* of the GDR period. These were grouped to form the new *Länder,* which accounts for the slight divergence of the new *Länder* boundaries from those of pre-1952. The *Länder* formation has thus achieved a compromise between the administrative structures of the GDR period and the historic *Länder* boundaries.[10]

The *Länder* have had some successes in promoting positive economic development, their external political profile and social identity. The significant resonance among the population and enjoyment of their loyalty is, for example, demonstrated by the failure of the referendum on unifying Berlin and Brandenburg and the rising turn-out in *Länder* elections. In the increasingly competitive environment that seems to be the most clear indication of an evolving Europe of the regions, the *Länder* are engaged in place-marketing campaigns and are promoting themselves at EU-level. Within the Federal Republic there is clear evidence of the influence of regional politicians such as Kurt Biedenkopf (Minister President of Saxony) in asserting regional interests even in conflict with their central party priorities. At a lower level there are some cases of positive regionalised thinking such as the cross-border planning in the Halle-Leipzig region, or the developing Euro-region across the Polish border centred on Frankfurt a. d. Oder.

However, there are also clear disadvantages to the decision not to carry out a more radical reform. The area known as *Mitteldeutschland*, the highly industrialised region based around the triangle Halle-Leipzig-Chemnitz reaching into the edges of Thuringia but above all split between Saxony and Saxony-Anhalt, is considered the most striking example of the failure of the *Länder* formation to correspond to the actual regional economic structures of post-GDR East Germany. The administrative divisions to which this economic region is subjected are a clear disadvantage for policy making and undermine the identity and coherence that are meant to be the contribution of the 'region' to positive economic development.[11]

The main tool of German regional policy, the community initiative *Gemeinschaftsaufgabe 'Verbesserung der regionalen Wirtschaftsstruktur'* (GRW) of 1968, requires the co-ordination of federal, *Länder* and local spending to promote the regeneration of disadvantaged areas,[12] while the *Länder Finanzausgleich* promotes financial transfers from prosperous to disadvantaged regions. However, more recent regionalisation initiatives require the sub-*Länder* regions to take the initiative in deciding on subsidy allocation and developing and promoting economic development strategies themselves. This has come to influence the GRW but has also been implemented by the *Länder* to co-ordinate other policy areas with a spatial impact.[13]

The German understanding of regions as existing at the sub-*Land* level reflects the belief that it is at this level that a more coherent identity for policy-making exists, in particular in the economic sphere. Since the late 1980s in West Germany there has been a trend towards the regionalisation of structural and *Länder* economic policy in line with the perceived potential for regional effectiveness suggested in the ideal-type. In the context of reduced public funding and the perceived need for active policies to respond to the pressures of restructuring, this has involved the creation of 'regional' alliances between key public and private sector actors, for example the *Zukunftsinitiative Nordrhein-Westfalen* (1989) policy. Despite some variations between *Länder*, these groups are generally expected to carry out an assessment of the region's strengths and weaknesses and generate strategic aims for its future economic development. Through a prioritised list of projects, these proposals feed back into the *Länder* subsidy decision-making processes. The aim of the regional conferences is also to create local networks, exploit indigenous potential and develop regional strategic thinking in order to increase competitiveness and innovative potential.

A major criticism of the activities of these structures in East Germany has been their focus on accessing external funding. The lack of any co-financing model reduces the potential for such alliances to make difficult choices about the allocation of limited resources. There is no motivation to restrict the number of projects added to the list and to make necessarily controversial choices between preferred projects. The deficiency of historically rooted structures either in terms of established firms and private sector interest representation groups or of an experienced local public sector, both in administrative and political terms, further weakens the capacity for regional thinking and alliance.

There are also tensions created by local authority individualism. Local authorities may appeal to the *Land* level bypassing the regional panels and thus undermining their significance as decision-making and strategy-evolving bodies. The capacity for achieving concerted thinking varies between different areas of spending. Where clear criteria are set externally on limits and targets, such as in education, it has been far easier to reach regional consensus. The necessity to share primary schools between different local authorities in a single catchment area, for instance, has tended to lead to successful co-operation, whereas such footloose facilities as leisure pools have been the subject of strong controversy.[14]

Local government structure has exacerbated many problems. The lowest level, the *Gemeinden*, have a constitutional mandate to regulate matters pertaining to their communities. In the enthusiastic wave of local government reconstitution in 1990, these units were often created on a far too small basis, frequently covering populations as small as 200-500.[15] They view regionalisation initiatives as an impingement on and threat to their powers and independence.[16] Precisely in light of the extreme weakness of local government under the so-called 'democratic centralism' of the GDR period, local authority prerogatives are now vehemently defended. Thus the change to the decentralising federalism of the Federal Republic may have become a barrier to further change and reform. Despite the relatively recent foundation of the *Kreise* and *Gemeinden* they have already become deeply rooted, resisting administrative reform to create units on a scale that would correspond to more meaningful regions for strategic policy making.

The problem of such particularism is exacerbated by the failure of higher levels of government to set out clear guidelines on funding distribution. The *GRW* covers the whole of East Germany and the prioritisation of subsidy distribution, while clearly not being uniform across the whole area, does not follow explicit selectivity criteria other than a vague requirement to generate so-called regional development concepts, resulting in the so called *Giesskannenprinzip*. Thus local authorities may perceive each other as direct competitors and there is little incentive to take on a wider regionally-based thinking. The regionalisation initiatives are frequently interpreted by the *Land* as empowering the lower levels to define priorities in the necessary shift away from the commitment to blanket subsidies. However, the failure to create explicit bidding systems with clear criteria has resulted in confusion about the relation of regional strategies to the formal decision-making processes of the *Länder*, which undermines the potential of such bodies to assert themselves over individual local authority interests.

Difficulties also exist in the relations with other groups in German society. The intention generally exists to include non-public sector actors actively in regionalisation processes in order to maximise the regional expertise and potential that are drawn into the process. The highly formalised and legalised nature of most spheres of German economic and institutional relations has continued despite some limited reforms to achieve greater flexibility or rapidity in public sector decision-making in the face of the depth of East German problems (e.g. the *Vorhaben und Erschließungspläne* now permitted in land use planning). In general, procedures have not been adapted to the new, more flexible, structures that are the usual aim of regionalised policy initiatives. This undermines the ability of the latter to establish effective communicative networks, as the lack of integration into these formal procedures undermines the motivation of actors to become involved in the new structures and invest significant time, effort or financial resources in their functioning. This criticism was voiced by the *Industrie und Handelskammer* in Saxony-Anhalt[17] for instance, who preferred their usual channels of influence directly to the *Land* ministries over the intangibility of the new regional structures. It appears East Germany already suffers from many of the rigidities that are typical of West Germany, while at a local or regional level the actors in the East do not have the rooted experience and self-confidence to branch out beyond their narrowly defined roles. In some cases they are even less flexible than their West German counterparts.

For many key investment decisions substantial levels of public subsidy have been decisive. The chemical industry of *Mitteldeutschland* is such a case. Although it has been retained as the *Chemie Standort Mitteldeutschland*, and privatisation in the form of acquisition by the American corporation Dow Chemicals has been achieved, this only occurred after massive public sector investment. A pipeline has been constructed to Rostock to give sea-port access. This public sector funded venture was, however, a federal project with intervention at the highest level. Helmut Kohl visited the East German plants four times, eventually opening the pipeline.[18] However, this example also demonstrates the regional role in exploiting such investment to maximise their potential for the region more generally. Research networking with local universities is being promoted, planning decisions have included the promotion of small business and technology parks for local small firm suppliers of the corporate plants and to promote spin-offs. Major investment by an international corporation in one of Germany's key industrial sectors is exploited for place-marketing purposes to promote further investment.

In terms of awakening the interest of external investors, a clear advantage has been achieved by the regions' well-known urban centres and their *Hinterland* in particular around the Berlin conurbation, sites along major transport routes, particularly *Autobahnen* and locations that have been promoted with high public sector investment or developed as new technology parks. Uneven development in East Germany as elsewhere is not reduced by the formation of regional alliances and strategies, rather these become a further factor in differentiating what individual regions have to offer.

Despite these tensions in relation to the region, difficulties in defining it and in achieving the convergence of fragmented local authorities into units for concerted thinking, there are a broad range of policies that are regionally effective and where regional actors function. Particularly in the context of competition for inward investment, more policy areas are co-opted into the aim of making the region more competitive. Central among these are policies affecting the labour market, the importance of which has grown as modern industries are increasingly discerning in the skills base they prefer. The Active Labour Market Policy (ALMP) introduced in Eastern Germany established Employment and Training Companies (ETCs) as a result of a dialogue between the *Treuhand*, the *Länder*, the federal employment office, local employers and the trade unions. Their primary task was to avoid the disintegration of local identities by providing substitute employment for workers facing the prospect of redundancy. Moreover, ETCs were also explicitly created to act as structural agents, bundling a number of policy areas, more precisely active labour market policy and investment in the field of infrastructural and environmental regeneration.[19]

ETCs have been strongly criticised for creating displacement effects because of competition with similar jobs in the local economy. However, many are still operating today and have managed to set up smaller commercial units which act on a competitive basis, fostering process and product innovation.[20] They have been successful in maintaining and creating new 'real' jobs. ETCs have undoubtedly encouraged innovative structures of governance by fostering a dialogue between labour market policy agents and regional planners. However, these measures were initially implemented through necessity more than by design. They represent a temporary and partial strategy which can be regarded as successful because of the particular structural requirements and problems faced by regions after unification. It may be imprudent to propose that this experimental model of regional policy could be transposed elsewhere. Instead, the experience with integrative structural policies in the new *Länder* indicates that the regional approach remains fragmented, context-specific, and open-ended. The concept of regional economic policy is consequently still in the process of being defined.

Conclusions

Although regions can play an important part in promoting economic development and providing the focus for political and social identity, they should not be regarded as the cure-all for the problems of restructuring and the economic and social costs it may present. The difficulty with the prevalent ideal-type (presented at the beginning of this paper) is that it appears to provide such a universal solution, while avoiding a strong relation to specific local conditions. There is a further danger that it will come to mean all things to all people and be expected to reconcile competing and basically divergent ends.

The nebulous thinking about the role of regions is demonstrated by the lack of a universal definition of what a region is. The EU might regard the whole of East Germany or at the very least individual *Länder* as a region, whereas the *Länder* themselves see regions as areas within their boundaries. Although the formation of the *Länder* and of policies for the regional level can tap into sub-national historical identities that are particularly strong in Germany because of its pre-20th century fragmented past, the role described in the ideal-type is essentially a new one for the sub-national level, particularly in terms of the increased participation in economic policy making. In the East German context the ability of local actors to live up to such expectations is patchy. The structurally disadvantaged regions suffer doubly. Not only do they have negative locational factors but the weakness of regional actors in many cases makes them unable to become successfully engaged in proactive regional policy. This further prejudices their chances of positive economic development, particularly in a political context that is placing increasing weight on such regionalised strategies.

Policy areas like ALMP clearly do benefit the region and demonstrate the importance of locality in the restructuring process. However, here the region is the object on which the policy acts and which passively receives benefits. Unlike the ideal-type, which considers the region as an independent agent that can act to benefit the economy although it defies definition itself. It is this proactive version of the region that is more dubious in its applicability to the East German context, with the severity of the externally imposed restructuring challenge that it faces. The fundamental problems of the East German economy, that are caused by its position as a part of the larger integrated German economy, must be solved at the national level where they are induced.

Despite these limitations, there is scope for a positive, regionally based contribution to economic development. However, no effective, universally applicable model for regions as political units or as the generators of, or focus for, policy has yet been developed. For the East German context we would suggest that the following points need to be clarified before the region can come into its own:

> A definition of the size of geographical unit and the criteria for determining it must be forthcoming.

> A clarification must be achieved as to whether these 'regions' are to become the basis for a redrawing of *Länder* boundaries and if this is not the case what the relation to these primary federal units and to the local authorities is to be.

> Pro-active policies from the regions must be supported by higher levels as for many East German regions 'pulling themselves up by their own boot straps' is not an option.

> A more flexible model may be to accept that different policy areas may have differing regions suited to them and to accept a plurality of overlapping regions within the *Länder*.

A consensus also needs to be reached on the debate of whether the role of regional policy is to promote growth poles, and thus further strengthen already leading areas, or whether it is to encourage redistribution to the least favoured areas. Effectively this is a decision between neo-liberal or social-democratic growth models.

The East German experience, with regard to regions, is of relevance to the EU as a whole. The political motivation of the project 'Europe of the Regions,' as an attempt to promote post-national identities and loyalties, should not be ignored. However, the ability of localities to approximate to the regional ideal-type suggested above is uneven. It acts as a further area of inequality and divergence, rather than the key to promoting more coherent, convergent and even development. Even within Germany this becomes evident in comparing the lobbying capacity, level of popular and historical identity and even extent of regional economic circulation of, for instance, Bavaria and Saxony-Anhalt. The introduction of inadequately defined or incoherent, regionally based policy as the major policy for the promotion of economic development, while ignoring these differences, will be exploited by the most able regions, further increasing divergence in development. Extreme divergences in economic conditions in turn undermine overall economic efficiency and social coherence.

NOTES

[1] Heimpold G. and Junkernheinrich M., Regionale Wirtschaftspolitik in den neuen Bundesländern - Bestandsaufnahme, Probleme, Perspektiven in Wegner M. (ed.), *Wirtschaft im Systemschock* (Berlin 1994), 149-169.

[2] Locke R. and Trigilia C., *Mirror Images? Political Strategies for Economic Development in Eastern Germany and Southern Italy*, paper presented at the Workshop 'A tale of two Regions', Minda de Gunzburg Center for European Studies, Harvard University, 20-21 March 1998.

[3] See for example Müller K., Joseph Alois Schumpeters ökonomische Lehre und die gegenwärtige Systemtransformation, *Deutschland Archiv*, Heft 5 1991, 495-502 and Zapf W., *Modernisierung, Wohlfahrtsentwicklung und Transformation* (Berlin, 1994).

[4] See Gunnar Myrdal's concept of equalising 'spread effects' being overcome by 'backwash effects' that heighten discrepancies or Alfred Hirshman's model of 'polarization' versus 'trickle down effects' with the latter dominating, in Myrdal G., *Economic Theory and Underdeveloped Regions*, London 1957, Hirshman A., *The Strategy of Economic Development* (New Haven, 1958).

[5] Particularly in association with the dual pressures of globalisation and the increased heterogeneity of regional development in the post-Fordist epoch see for example Jessop B., Post-Fordism and the State, in Amin A. (ed), *Post-Fordism. A Reader* (Oxford, 1994).

[6] Here we have purposefully 'personified' the region so as to express its pro-active role more vividly.

[7] About the conflict between '*Aufbaupolitik*' and '*Ausgleichpolitik*', see Junkernheinrich M. and Skopp R., Wirtschaftliche Konvergenz und räumliche Wachstumspole, in R. Pohl (ed.), *Herausforderung Ostdeutschland* (Berlin, 1994).

[8] A discussion of the implications for the supra-national level goes beyond the scope of this paper.

[9] In the English version of the *Grundgesetz* this is translated as 'regional, historical and cultural ties, economic expediency and the requirement of regional policy and planning.'

[10] Rutz W., Die Wiedererrichtung der östlichen Bundesländer, in *Raumforschung und Raumordnung* 1991 49/5, 279-286.

[11] Points raised in interview with Dr. Raschpichler, Landratsamt Bitterfeld 6.3.98.

[12] Although the GRW does promote subsidiarity and has recently adopted the principle of regional development concepts these are still voluntaristic and exemplary, and do not provide uniform coverage.

[13] For a detailed examination of the GRW, see Tetsch, A. *Die Bund-Länder-Gemeinschaftsaufgabe 'Verbesserung der regionalen Wirtschaftsstruktur' Ein Leitfaden zur regionalen Wirtschaftsförderung in Deutschland* (Bonn, 1995).

[14] Points raised in interview with Herr Stier, Ministerium für Wirtschaft, Technologie und Europaangelegenheiten Sachsen-Anhalt 20.2.1998.

[15] Rutz W., 249.

[16] See Kregel B. [Director of the Sachsen-Anhalt Local Government Association], Chance oder Gefahr? Regionale Entwicklungskonzepte – Folgen für die kommunale Selbstverwaltung, in *Die Neue Verwaltung* 1/1996, 20-22.

[17] Industrie und Handelskammer Halle-Dessau statement on regionalisation 1997.

[18] Interview with Dr. C. Mühlhaus of the BSL Olefinenverbund Schkopau Bhuna Werk 18.02.1998.

[19] The German expression is ABS Gesellschaften or *Gesellschaften für Arbeitsförderung, Beschäftigung und Strukturentwicklung*. Such experiments had already been undertaken on a smaller scale in West Germany with the so-called BQG (*Beschäftigungs -und Qualifizierungsgesellschaften*).

[20] In 1997, approximately 400 ETCs were operating in the new *Bundesländer*. The operating costs of the commercial units, also known as 'Profi Centres', are fully independent of the ETC. The opponents of the maintenance of such companies have argued that they are incompatible with *Ordnungspolitik* (order policy), a principle according to which obstacles to competition should be removed.

LIST OF CONTRIBUTORS

Diana Alberghini, PhD candidate at the University of Bath.

Peter Barker, teaches German Studies at the University of Reading.

Vanessa Beck, PhD candidate at the Institute for German Studies, Birmingham.

Simon Bevan, PhD candidate at the University of Bath.

Stephen Brown, PhD candidate at Reading University.

David Clarke, PhD candidate at the University of Wales, Swansea.

Paul Cooke, completed a PhD at the University of Birmingham. Lecturer in German Studies at the University of Wales, Aberystwyth.

Chris Flockton, Professor of European Economic Studies at the University of Surrey.

Jonathan Grix, completed a PhD at the Institute for German Studies, University of Birmingham, where he is now a Lecturer in German Studies.

Jennie Hawksley, PhD candidate at the Institute for German Studies, University of Birmingham.

Daniel Hough, PhD candidate at the Institute for German Studies, University of Birmingham.

Bettina Iganski, PhD candidate, University of Portsmouth.

Astrid Ihle, PhD candidate at the Courtauld Institute of Art, London and now working at Galerie EIGEN+ART in Berlin.

Martin Kane, Reader in Modern German Studies, University of Kent at Canterbury.

Thorsten Lauterbach, Lecturer in Law at the University of Paisley.

Corinne Nativel, PhD candidate at the Institute for German Studies, University of Birmingham.

Michael Ploetz, PhD candidate, King's College, London.

Julian Rhys, PhD candidate, University of Sheffield.

Gordon Charles Ross, PhD candidate, Aberdeen University, currently lecturing at Jena University.

Brendan de Silva, PhD candidate, St Antony's College, Oxford.

Hannah Tooze, completed a PhD at the Institute for German Studies, University of Birmingham. Analyst in the Government and Public Sector Department of the PA Consulting Group.

Ian Wallace, Professor of German at the University of Bath.

Wilfried van der Will, Professor of Modern German Studies at the University of Birmingham.

GERMANY AND EASTERN EUROPE: CULTURAL IDENTITIES AND CULTURAL DIFFERENCES

Ed. by Keith Bullivant, Geoffrey Giles and Walter Pape

Amsterdam/Atlanta, GA 1999. VI,366 pp.
(Yearbook for European Studies/Annuaire d'Études Europeennes 13)
ISBN: 90-420-0688-9   Bound Hfl. 175,-/US-$ 97.-
ISBN: 90-420-0678-1   Paper Hfl. 55,-/US-$ 30.50

The opening up, and subsequent tearing down, of the Berlin Wall in 1989 effectively ended a historically unique period for Europe that had drastically changed its face over a period of fifty years and redefined, in all sorts of ways, what was meant by East and West. For Germany in particular this radical change meant much more than unification of the divided country, although initially this process seemed to consume all of the country's energies and emotions. While the period of the Cold War saw the emergence of a Federal Republic distinctly Western in orientation, the coming down of the Iron Curtain meant that Germany's relationship with its traditional neighbours to the East and the South-East, which had been essentially frozen or redefined in different ways for the two German states by the Cold War, had to be rediscovered. This volume, which brings together scholars in German Studies from the United States, Germany and other European countries, examines the history of the relationship between Germany and Eastern Europe and the opportunities presented by the changes of the 1990's, drawing particular attention to the interaction between the willingness of German and its Eastern neighbours to work for political and economic integration, on the one hand, and the cultural and social problems that stem from old prejudices and unresolved disputes left over from the Second World War, on the other.

----------------------------   *Editions Rodopi B.V.*

USA/Canada: 2015 South Park Place, Atlanta, GA 30339, Tel. (770) 933-0027, *Call toll-free* (U.S.only) 1-800-225-3998, Fax (770) 933-9644

All Other Countries: Tijnmuiden 7, 1046 AK Amsterdam, The Netherlands. Tel. + + 31 (0)20 6114821, Fax + + 31 (0)20 4472979
          orders-queries@rodopi.nl — http://www.rodopi.nl

INSTITUTIONAL VIOLENCE

Ed. by Deane Curtin and Robert Litke

Amsterdam/Atlanta, GA 1999. XVII,413 pp.
(Value Inquiry Book Series 88)
ISBN: 90-420-0508-4   Bound Hfl. 200,-/US-$ 110.-
ISBN: 90-420-0498-3   Paper Hfl. 65,-/US-$ 36.-

Violence can be physical and psychological. It can characterize personal actions, forms of group activity, and abiding social and political policy. This book includes all of these aspects within its focus on institutional forms of violence. Institution is also a broad category, ranging from formal arrangements such as the military, the criminal code, the death penalty and prison system, to more amorphous but systemic situations indicated by parenting, poverty, sexism, work, and racism. Violence is as complex as the human beings who resort to it; its institutional forms pervade our relational lives. We are all participants in it as victims and perpetrators. The chapters in this book were written in the hope that violence can be explicated, even if not fully understood, and that such clarification can help us in devising less violent forms of living, even if it does not lead to its total abolition. The studies bring new aspects of violence to light and offer a number of suggestions for its remedy.

Editions Rodopi B.V.

USA/Canada: 2015 South Park Place, Atlanta, GA 30339, Tel. (770) 933-0027, *Call toll-free* (U.S.only) 1-800-225-3998, Fax (770) 933-9644

All Other Countries: Tijnmuiden 7, 1046 AK Amsterdam, The Netherlands. Tel. ++ 31 (0)20 6114821, Fax ++ 31 (0)20 4472979
orders-queries@rodopi.nl — http://www.rodopi.nl

ANNE FUCHS

A Space of Anxiety
Dislocation and Abjection
in Modern German-Jewish Literature

Amsterdam/Atlanta, GA 1999. VII,200 pp.
(Amsterdamer Publikationen zur Sprache und Literatur 138)
ISBN: 90-420-0797-4   Hfl. 70,-/US-$ 38.50

A Space of Anxiety engages with a body of German-Jewish literature that, from the beginning of the century onwards, explores notions of identity and kinship in the context of migration, exile and persecution. The study offers an engaging analysis of how Freud, Kafka, Roth, Drach and Hilsenrath employ, to varying degrees, the travel paradigm to question those borders and boundaries that define the space between the self and the other. *A Space of Anxiety* argues that from Freud to Hilsenrath, German-Jewish literature emerges from an ambivalent space of enunciation which challenges the great narrative of an historical identity authenticated by an "originary" past. Inspired by postcolonial and psychoanalytic theories, the author shows that modern German-Jewish writers inhabit a "Third Space" which poses an alternative to an understanding of culture as a homogeneous tradition based on (national) unity.
By endeavouring to explore this "third space" in examples of modern German-Jewish literature, the volume also aims to contribute to recent efforts to rewriting literary history. In retracing the inherent ambivalence in how German-Jewish literature situates itself in cultural discourse, this study focuses on how this literature subverts received notions of identity and racial boundaries. The study is of interest to students of German literature, German-Jewish literature and Cultural Studies.

Editions Rodopi B.V.

USA/Canada: 2015 South Park Place, Atlanta, GA 30339, Tel. (770) 933-0027, *Call toll-free* (U.S.only) 1-800-225-3998, Fax (770) 933-9644

All Other Countries: Tijnmuiden 7, 1046 AK Amsterdam, The Netherlands. Tel. + + 31 (0)20 6114821, Fax + + 31 (0)20 4472979
E-mail: orders-queries@rodopi.nl —— http://www.rodopi.nl

THE GRUPPE 47 FIFTY YEARS ON A RE-APPRAISAL OF ITS LITERARY AND POLITICAL SIGNIFICANCE

Ed. by Stuart Parkes and John J. White

Amsterdam/Atlanta, GA 1999. 296 pp.
(German Monitor 45)
ISBN: 90-420-0687-0   Hfl. 150,-/US-$ 83.-
ISBN: 90-420-0677-3   Hfl. 50,-/US-$ 27.50

Fifty years after its inception the Gruppe 47 remains a controversial part of the intellectual history of Germany. Particularly in the light of new material that has become available in recent years, this volume takes stock of both the overall significance of the Group and of the roles of individual writers within it. It contains general essays on the beginnings of the Group and the short-lived periodical *Der Ruf*, the situation of the Group in the 1950s and 1960s, its image as seen by others as well as its self-image and an overall assessment of the Group in literary-sociological terms. Among authors dealt with in detail in relation to the Group are Ilse Aichinger, Alfred Andersch, Ingeborg Bachmann, Johannes Bobrowski, Heinrich Böll, Hubert Fichte, Peter Rühmkorf and Martin Walser. This volume will be of interest to all those with an interest in German literature. It breaks away from traditionally held views of the Group to present an incisive re-appraisal of the one of the most significant phenomena of German post-war cultural development.

Editions Rodopi B.V.

USA/Canada: 2015 South Park Place, Atlanta, GA 30339, Tel. (770) 933-0027, *Call toll-free* (U.S.only) 1-800-225-3998, Fax (770) 933-9644

All Other Countries: Tijnmuiden 7, 1046 AK Amsterdam, The Netherlands. Tel. ++ 31 (0)20 6114821, Fax ++ 31 (0)20 4472979

E-mail: orders-queries@rodopi.nl — http://www.rodopi.nl

NATION BUILDING AND WRITING LITERARY HISTORY

Ed. by Menno Spiering

Amsterdam/Atlanta, GA 1999. XV,220 pp.
(Yearbook of European Studies/Annuaire d'Etudes Europeennes 12)
ISBN: 90-420-0627-7   Hfl. 110,-/US-$ 61.-

Contents: Authors in this volume. Introduction.
Annelies van HEES: N.M. Petersen and the Case of Denmark.
Egil TÖRNQVIST: Henrik Schück as Historiographer of Swedish Literature. Klaus F. GILLE: *Germanistik* und Nation in the 19th Century. George VIS: Literary Historiography in the Northern and Southern Netherlands between 1800 and 1830. D. van der HORST: Jan Frans Willems: A Literary History for a new Nation. Joep LEERSSEN: A la recherche d'une littérature perdue: Literary History, Irish Identity and Douglas Hyde. Ton HOENSELAARS: A Taste of George Saintsbury: *A Short History of English Literature* (1898). Menno SPIERING: The Englishness of English Literature and Literary History: The Lectures of Sir Arthur Quiller-Couch. Ruud MEIJER: Travailler Pour La Patrie: Gustave Lanson, The Founder of French Academic Literary History I. Manet van MONTFRANS: Travailler Pour La Patrie: Gustave Lanson, The Founder of Academic Literary History in France II. Lily COENEN: M. Menendez Pelayo: Literary History in the Context of a Religious Question. Fernando VENÂNCIO: 'Quick Fleeting Sketches': Literary History in Portugal in the 19th Century. Lucas BRUYNING: From Tiraboschi to Francesco De Sanctis: Italian Literary History as a Legitimation of National Unity. Dina ARISTODEMO: National Values and Literary Form in De Sanctis' *History of Italian Literature*.

Editions Rodopi B.V.

USA/Canada: 2015 South Park Place, Atlanta, GA 30339, Tel. (770) 933-0027, *Call toll-free* (U.S.only) 1-800-225-3998, Fax (770) 933-9644

All Other Countries: Tijnmuiden 7, 1046 AK Amsterdam, The Netherlands. Tel. + + 31 (0)20 6114821, Fax + + 31 (0)20 4472979 *E-mail:* orders-queries@rodopi.nl — http://www.rodopi.nl

AGNES C. MUELLER

Lyrik "made in USA" Vermittlung und Rezeption in der Bundesrepublik

Amsterdam/Atlanta, GA 1999. X,249 pp.
(Internationale Forschungen zur Allgemeinen und Vergleichenden Literaturwissenschaft 36)
ISBN: 90-420-0487-8   Hfl. 90,-/US-$ 50.-

Diese Untersuchung analysiert erstmals umfassend die westdeutsche Vermittlung und Rezeption amerikanischer Gegenwartslyrik seit dem Zweiten Weltkrieg. Entgegen herkömmlichen Auffassungen konnte eine breite und erfolgreiche Rezeption der US-Lyrik erst in den später 60er Jahren, zeitgleich mit den Studentenunruhen und der westdeutschen Entdeckung der *beat generation*, stattfinden. Während amerikanische Prosa, sowie Film und Massenkultur in den frühen Jahren nach Kriegsende eine intensive Aufnahme in den westdeutschen Kanon erfuhren, blieben die immerhin bereits um 1950 begonnenen ernsthaften und gezielten Versuche einer Vermittlung zeitgenössischer US-Lyrik noch weitgehend unbeachtet.

Editions Rodopi B.V.

USA/Canada: 2015 South Park Place, Atlanta, GA 30339, Tel. (770) 933-0027, *Call toll-free* (U.S.only) 1-800-225-3998, Fax (770) 933-9644

All Other Countries: Tijnmuiden 7, 1046 AK Amsterdam, The Netherlands. Tel. ++ 31 (0)20 6114821, Fax ++ 31 (0)20 4472979 *E-mail:* orders-queries@rodopi.nl —— http://www.rodopi.nl

CAROLINE JOAN ("KAY") S. PICART

Thomas Mann and Friedrich Nietzsche
Eroticism, Death, Music, and Laughter

Amsterdam/Atlanta, GA 1999. XXII,151 pp.
(Value Inquiry Book Series 85)
ISBN: 90-420-0557-2   Hfl. 55,-/US-$ 30.50

Traditional interpretations of Thomas Mann's relation to
Nietzsche's writings plot out a simple relation of earlier
adulation and later rejection. The book argues that Mann's
disavowal of Nietzsche's influence was, in the words of T.J.
Reed, a "necessary political act" when the repudiation of
Nietzsche's more hysterical doctrines required such a response.
Using a genealogical method, the book traces how Mann labors
ambivalently under the shadow of Nietzsche's writings on his
own political artistry through a detailed analysis of Mann's
Death in Venice, Dr. Faustus, the *Joseph* tetralogy, and
Confessions of Felix Krull, Confidence Man. Using the
recurring Nietzschean themes of eroticism, death, music, and
laughter as a guide, it arrives at a rough picture of how Mann
both takes up and discontinues Nietzsche's poetic heritage. The
book derives the vision of the interrelationships binding these
four leitmotiv elements from Dürer's magic square as depicted
in *Melancholia I.* The link with Dürer is far from arbitrary
because Mann directly aligned Nietzschean insight with
Dürer's world of passion, sympathy with suffering, the
macabre stench of rotting flesh, and Faustian melancholy.

Editions Rodopi B.V.

USA/Canada: 2015 South Park Place, Atlanta, GA 30339, Tel. (770)
933-0027, *Call toll-free* (U.S.only) 1-800-225-3998, Fax (770) 933-9644

All Other Countries: Tijnmuiden 7, 1046 AK Amsterdam, The
Netherlands. Tel. + + 31 (0)20 6114821, Fax + + 31 (0)20 4472979
E-mail: orders-queries@rodopi.nl — http://www.rodopi.nl

VON GOETHE WAR DIE REDE ...

Hrsg. von Jattie Enklaar und Hans Ester

Amsterdam/Atlanta, GA 1999. 212 pp.
(Duitse Kroniek 49)
ISBN: 90-420-0597-1   Hfl. 65,-/US-$ 36.-

Der 1749 geborene Goethe war ein rastlos tätiger und kreativer Mensch. Als großer Deutscher und Europäer reicht seine Bedeutung weit über das 18. Jahrhundert hinaus; sein Werk ist wesentlicher Bestandteil der Geschichte Deutschlands und Europas und durch die Auseinandersetzung mit seinem Werk ist er bis zum heutigen Tag lebendig geblieben. Die hier gesammelten Beiträge eint ihr unverhohlenes Interesse an Goethes Werk, mehr noch die Faszination, die an exemplarischen Texten dargestellt, zeigt, wie modern und zugleich überzeitlich Goethe in seinen literarisch ästhetischen, weltanschaulichen und politischen Ansichten wirkt. Das hier Vorgelegte provoziert, indem es Eingegrenztes überschreitet und die heutigen Leser dazu anregt, die Goethesche Tiefe mit neuen Augen zu entdecken.

Editions Rodopi B.V.

USA/Canada: 2015 South Park Place, Atlanta, GA 30339, Tel. (770) 933-0027, *Call toll-free* (U.S.only) 1-800-225-3998, Fax (770) 933-9644

All Other Countries: Tijnmuiden 7, 1046 AK Amsterdam, The Netherlands. Tel. ++ 31 (0)20 6114821, Fax ++ 31 (0)20 4472979
E-mail: orders-queries@rodopi.nl —— http://www.rodopi.nl

WORD AND MUSIC STUDIES
DEFINING THE FIELD

Proceedings of the First International Conference
on Word and Music Studies at Graz, 1997

Ed. by Walter Bernhart, Steven Paul Scher and Werner Wolf

Amsterdam/Atlanta, GA 1999. 352 pp.
(Word and Music Studies 1)
ISBN: 90-420-0587-4   Bound Hfl. 160,-/US-$ 88.50
ISBN: 90-420-0577-7   Paper Hfl. 55,-/US-$ 30.50

The nineteen interdisciplinary essays assembled in WORD AND
MUSIC STUDIES 1 were first presented in 1997 at the founding
conference of the International Association for Word and Music
Studies (WMA) in Graz, Austria. Diverse in subject matter,
theoretical orientation, critical approach, and interpretive strategy,
they share a keen scholarly interest in contemporary word-music
reflection. Registering the impact of cultural studies on word-music
relations, as manifested in the 'new musicology' and other
'historicist' approaches, the volume aims to assess the entire field of
word and music studies, to define its subject, objectives, and
methodology and to describe the field's state of the art.
Within the broader context of generic, structural, performative, and
ideological considerations concerning the manifold interrelations
between literature and music, contributors explore wide-ranging
topics, such as the vexing question of terminology (e.g. 'word and
music', 'melopoetics', 'interart', 'intermedial', 'transmedial');
inquiry into the meaning, narrative potential, and verbalization of
music; analysis of texted music (the Lied and opera) and
instrumental music; and discussion of individual issues (e.g.
'ekphrasis', 'musicalization of fiction', 'word music', and 'verbal
music') and interart loanwords (e.g. 'narrativity', 'counterpoint', and
'leitmotif').

Editions Rodopi B.V.

USA/Canada: 2015 South Park Place, Atlanta, GA 30339, Tel. (770)
933-0027, *Call toll-free* (U.S.only) 1-800-225-3998, Fax (770) 933-9644

All Other Countries: Tijnmuiden 7, 1046 AK Amsterdam, The
Netherlands. Tel. + + 31 (0)20 6114821, Fax + + 31 (0)20 4472979
E-mail: orders-queries@rodopi.nl — http://www.rodopi.nl

CENTRE STAGE: CONTEMPORARY DRAMA IN AUSTRIA

Ed. by Frank Finlay and Ralf Jeutter

Amsterdam/Atlanta, GA 1999. VII,240 pp.
(Amsterdamer Publikationen zur Sprache und Literatur 137)
ISBN: 90-420-0525-4   Hfl. 80,-/US-$ 44.-

In this volume, scholars and theatre practioners from Austria, Britain and Germany explore the current state of Austrian drama in studies of the themes, forms and concerns of some of the most important contemporary playwrights. Many of the contributions address works which have not previously been the subject of scholarly analysis. The writers discussed include: Wolfgang Bauer, Thomas Bernhard, Elias Canetti, Peter Handke, Fritz Hochwälder, Elfriede Jelinek, Jakov Lind, Felix Mitterer, Hermann Nitsch, Gerhard Roth, Werner Schwab, Marlene Steeruwitz, Peter Turrini, and the film-maker, Wim Wenders.

This collection, which includes photographs and an essay on the problems of translating, will be of particular interest to teachers, students and translators of German-language drama, as well as to a wider theatre-going public.

Editions Rodopi B.V.

USA/Canada: 2015 South Park Place, Atlanta, GA 30339, Tel. (770) 933-0027, *Call toll-free* (U.S.only) 1-800-225-3998, Fax (770) 933-9644

All Other Countries: Tijnmuiden 7, 1046 AK Amsterdam, The Netherlands. Tel. ++ 31 (0)20 6114821, Fax ++ 31 (0)20 4472979 *E-mail:* orders-queries@rodopi.nl —— http://www.rodopi.nl

WERNER WOLF

The Musicalization of Fiction
A Study in the Theory and History
of Intermediality

Amsterdam/Atlanta, GA 1999. XI,272 pp.
(Internationale Forschungen zur Allgemeinen und
Vergleichenden Literaturwissenschaft 35)
ISBN: 90-420-0457-6   Hfl. 90,-/US-$ 49.50

This volume is a pioneering study in the theory and history of the imitation of music in fiction and constitutes an important contribution to current intermediality research.

Starting with a comparison of basic similarities and differences between literature and music, the study goes on to provide outlines of a general theory of intermediality and its fundamental forms, in which a more specialized theory of the musicalization of (narrative) literature based on contemporary narratology and a typology of the forms of musico-literary intermediality are embedded. It also addresses the question of how to recognize a musicalized fiction when reading one and why Sterne's *Tristram Shandy*, contrary to what has been previously said, is not to be regarded as a musicalized fiction.

In its historical part, the study explores forms and functions of experiments with the musicalization of fiction in English literature. After a survey of the major preconditions for musicalization - the increasing appreciation of music in 18th and 19th-century aesthetics and its main causes - exemplary fictional texts from romanticism to postmodernism are analyzed. Authors interpreted are De Quincey, Joyce, Woolf, A. Huxley, Beckett, Burgess and Josipovici. Whilst the limitations of a transposition of music into fiction remain apparent, experiments in this field yield valuable insights into mainly a-mimetic and formalist aesthetic tendencies in the development of more recent fiction as a whole and also show to what extent traditional conceptions of music continue to influence the use of this medium in literature.

The volume is of relevance for students and scholars of English, comparative and general literature as well as for readers who take an interest in intermediality or interart research.

Editions Rodopi B.V.

USA/Canada: 2015 South Park Place, Atlanta, GA 30339, Tel. (770) 933-0027, *Call toll-free* (U.S.only) 1-800-225-3998, Fax (770) 933-9644

All Other Countries: Tijnmuiden 7, 1046 AK Amsterdam, The Netherlands. Tel. ++ 31 (0)20 6114821, Fax ++ 31 (0)20 4472979
    E-mail: orders-queries@rodopi.nl —— http://www.rodopi.nl

TEXT AND VISUALITY:WORD & IMAGE INTERACTIONS III

Ed. by Martin Heusser, Michèle Hannoosh, Leo Hoek,
Charlotte Schoell-Glass and David Scott

Amsterdam/Atlanta, GA 1999. 321 pp.
(Textxet 22)
ISBN: 90-420-0736-2   Bound Hfl. 160,-/US-$ 88.50
ISBN: 90-420-0726-5   Paper Hfl. 50,-/US-$ 27.50

Editions Rodopi B.V.

USA/Canada: 2015 South Park Place, Atlanta, GA 30339, Tel. (770)
933-0027, *Call toll-free* (U.S.only) 1-800-225-3998, Fax (770) 933-9644

All Other Countries: Tijnmuiden 7, 1046 AK Amsterdam, The Netherlands.
Tel. ++ 31 (0)20 6114821, Fax ++ 31 (0)20 4472979
orders-queries@rodopi.nl — http://www.rodopi.nl

MARGINAL VOICES
MARGINAL FORMS
Diaries in European Literature and History

Ed. by Rachel Langford and William West

Amsterdam/Atlanta, GA 1999. 211 pp.
(Internationale Forschungen zur Allgemeinen und Vergleichenden Literaturwissenschaft 34)
ISBN: 90-420-0437-1   Hfl. 70,-/US-$ 38.50

Diaristic writing has often been relegated to the fringes of literary studies as a marginal cultural activity. This volume seeks to challenge that marginality by exploring some of the wide-ranging forms of literary practice encompassed by diaristic writing in Europe from the Renaissance to the present day. The volume deals with questions of the value and status of the diary, of the functioning of the diary in society and history, and of the reception and interpretation of the multifarious forms of first-person daily writing. The volume investigates diaries across national borders and linguistic boundaries, so as to make the hitherto marginal place of the private journal a site of fruitful interdisciplinary encounters. Australian, British, Catalonian, French, German and Italian critics examine diaries dating from the sixteenth to the twentieth century, within the context of the literature, history and literary history of Catalonia, England, France, Germany and Italy. A prime concern of the essays in this collection is to highlight the cultural, generic and historical diversity of the diary, while emphasising the points of convergence between different texts and differing critical approaches to the texts. The volume will be of interest to students and teachers of European and comparative literature.

Editions Rodopi B.V.
USA/Canada: 2015 South Park Place, Atlanta, GA 30339, Tel. (770) 933-0027, *Call toll-free* (U.S.only) 1-800-225-3998, Fax (770) 933-9644

All Other Countries: Tijnmuiden 7, 1046 AK Amsterdam, The Netherlands. Tel. + + 31 (0)20 6114821, Fax + + 31 (0)20 4472979
E-mail: orders-queries@rodopi.nl —— http://www.rodopi.nl

SUBJECTIVITY

Ed. by Willem van Reijen and Willem G. Weststeijn

Amsterdam/Atlanta, GA 1999. VI,330 pp.
(Avant Garde Critical Studies 12)
ISBN: 90-420-0738-9   Bound Hfl. 140,-/US-$ 77.50
ISBN: 90-420-0728-1   Paper Hfl. 50,-/US-$ 27.50

Contents: Introduction
Mario MORONI: Dynamics of Subjectivity in the Historical Avant-Garde
Hubert van den BERG: Dadaist Subjectivity and the Politics of Indifference. On Some Contrasts and Correspondences between Dada in Zürich and Berlin
Christine van BOHEEMEN: Subjectivity in a Post-Colonial Symbolic. The Anxiety of Joyce
Annelies SCHULTE NORDHOLT: Proust and Subjectivity
Matthijs ENGELBERTS: A Glimpse of the Self. Defence of Subjectivity in Beckett and his Later Theatre
Willem G. WESTSTEIJN: The Subject in Modern Russian Poetry
Manfred FRANK: Self-Awareness and Self-Knowledge. Mental Familiarity and Epistemic Self-Ascription
Willem van REIJEN: Tested to the Breaking Point: Postmodernity in Modernity
Boris GROYS: The Russian Novel as a Serial Murder or The Poetics of Bureaucracy
Albrecht von MASSOW: Subjectivity as a Basic Presupposition of Modernity in Music
Patricia PISTERS: New Subjectivity in Cinema. The Vertigo of Strange Days
Saskia KERSENBOOM: It Takes Three to Epistemology

-------------------------------   *Editions Rodopi B.V.*
USA/Canada: 2015 South Park Place, Atlanta, GA 30339, Tel. (770) 933-0027, *Call toll-free* (U.S.only) 1-800-225-3998, Fax (770) 933-9644

All Other Countries: Tijnmuiden 7, 1046 AK Amsterdam, The Netherlands.
Tel. ++ 31 (0)20 6114821, Fax ++ 31 (0)20 4472979
          orders-queries@rodopi.nl —— http://www.rodopi.nl

www.ingramcontent.com/pod-product-compliance
Lightning Source LLC
Chambersburg PA
CBHW020352270326
41926CB00007B/403